上海市人民政府 国际智库咨询
发展研究中心系列报告 系列报告

SHANGHAI 2050

VISION AND CHALLENGE

2050年的上海
发展愿景与挑战

2015上海国际智库咨询研究报告

Consultation Report of
Shanghai International Think Tank, 2015

肖 林 主编　Chief Editor Xiao Lin

格致出版社　上海人民出版社

主　编　　　Chief Editor
肖　林　　　Xiao Lin

副主编　　　Subeditor
周国平　　　Zhou Guoping
周师迅　　　Zhou Shixun

编　辑　　　Editing Team
（按姓氏拼音排列）　(in alphabetical order)
高　瑛　　　Gao Ying
潘春来　　　Pan Chunlai
谭　旻　　　Tan Min
吴苏贵　　　Wu Sugui
姚　治　　　Yao Zhi
张明海　　　Zhang Minghai
朱惠涵　　　Zhu Huihan

上海市人民政府常务副市长屠光绍致辞

Closing remark by Tu Guangshao, Executive Deputy Mayor of the Shanghai Municipal People's Government

上海市人民政府发展研究中心主任、党组书记肖林致辞

Opening address by Xiao Lin, Director General of the SDRC

论坛现场
Conference Site

论坛现场
Conference Site

上海市委研究室副主任邢邦志发言

Speech by Xing Bangzhi, Deputy Director General of the Research Office of Shanghai Committee of C.P.C

麦肯锡全球合伙人、全球研究院中国区负责人陈有钢作主旨演讲

Keynote speech by Chen Yougang, Partner of McKinsey & Company, Head of MGI Greater China

埃森哲大中华区能源业董事总经理钱蔚作主旨演讲

Keynote speech by Qian Wei, Managing Director of Resource Service, Accenture, Greater China

中国社科院学部委员、国际研究学部主任张蕴岭作主旨演讲

Keynote speech by Zhang Yunling, Director of International Studies, CASS

普华永道亚太区零售消费品税务主管合伙人汪颖作主旨演讲

Keynote speech by Jane Wang, PwC Leading Partner of Retail Consumption Duty for Asia Pacific

野村综研中国董事长叶华作主旨演讲

Keynote speech by Ye Hua, Chairman of Nomura Research Institute Shanghai

高风咨询董事长谢祖墀作主旨演讲

Keynote speech by Edward Tse, Founder and CEO of Gao Feng Advisory Company

中国欧盟商会上海总经理琼安娜作主旨演讲

Keynote speech by Ioana Kraft, General Manager, Shanghai Chapter, European Union Chamber of Commerce in China

强生中国主席吴人伟作主旨演讲

Keynote speech by Jesse Wu, Chairman of Johnson & Johnson China

哈佛中心上海执行董事王颐作主旨演讲

Keynote speech by Wang Yi, Executive Director at Harvard Center Shanghai

德勤管理咨询合伙人张小平作主旨演讲

Keynote speech by Zhang Xiaoping, Partner of Deloitte Consulting

北京大学全球治理研究中心副主任范德尚作主旨演讲

Keynote speech by Fan Deshang, Deputy Director and General Secretary of the Center for Global Governance Studies at Peking University

日本贸易振兴机构上海所所长小栗道明作主旨演讲

Keynote speech by Michiaki Oguri, President of Japan External Trade Organization in Shanghai

美中贸易全国委员会上海首席代表彭捷宁作主旨演讲

Keynote speech by Jacob Parker，Director & Chief Representative of Shanghai office, US−China Business Council

上海美国商会代表泰科电子亚洲区政府事务高级总监来咏歌作主旨演讲

Keynote speech by Reggie Lai, Senior Director of Government Affairs Asia, TE Connectivity

上海发展研究基金会副会长兼秘书长乔依德作主旨演讲

Keynote speech by Qiao Yide, Vice Chairman & Secretary General of Shanghai Development Research Foundation

麦肯锡公司全球资深董事合伙人李广宇作总结发言

Summary statement by Li Guangyu, Senior Partner of McKinsey & Company

嘉宾合影
Group Photo of Guests

PREFACE

序

　　改革开放以来，上海经过几次发展战略大讨论，形成了上海发展战略和功能定位的共识，对上海经济社会发展产生了重大及深远的影响。当前，上海已经步入继往开来、谋划新的发展战略的重要时期。一方面，上海在 20 世纪 90 年代提出的"到 2020 年基本建成国际经济、金融、贸易、航运中心和社会主义现代化国际大都市"的目标，再有一个五年即可基本实现；另一方面，国家提出了到中华人民共和国成立 100 周年实现中华民族伟大复兴"中国梦"的宏伟目标，要求上海按照"两个百年"的战略目标进一步谋划，实现城市的新跨越、新发展。因此，在新的历史方位中，立足城市发展积淀和特殊基因，顺应城市发展潮流和理念，科学谋划未来 30 年的发展方向和战略，明确上海在实现中华民族伟大复兴"中国梦"中的历史使命，具有十分重大的意义。

　　展望未来，全球城市发展将伴随科技进步进入一个不断变革、颠覆传统的时代，发展理念和愿景创新已成为全球城市制定发展战略的重要内容。比如，纽约在《2030 年的纽约规划》中，更加强调"韧性城市"和"公平公正"；伦敦在《2030 年的大伦敦规划》中，更加强调生活质量和品质；巴黎在《2030 年的大巴黎规划》中，更加强调确保其 21 世纪的全球吸引力。因此，上海谋划未来 30 年的发展战略规划，必须在城市发展理念和愿景上进行创新。

　　为配合"面向未来 30 年的上海"发展战略研究，探讨城市发展理念及愿景，明确上海未来面临的瓶颈与挑战，2015 年 12 月 18 日，由上海市人民政府发展研究中心主办，上海国际智库交流中心、上海发展研究基金会和麦肯锡公司联合承办，举行了"2015 年上海国际智库峰会"。作为"面向未来 30 年的上海"发展战略研究系列论坛之一，本次峰会以"2050 年的上海：发展愿景与挑战"为主题，吸引了来自麦肯锡、埃森哲、普华永道、德勤、IBM、野村综研、哈佛上海中心、强生中国、高风咨询、美中贸易全国委员会、上海美国商会、欧盟上海商会、日本贸易振兴机构、泰科电子等 17 家国际智库的专家参与。上海市常务副市长屠光绍、上海市政府秘书长李逸平莅临会议，屠光绍常务副市长作了热情洋溢的致辞。与会嘉宾围绕 2050 年上海发展的愿景、面临的瓶颈与挑战以及实现这些愿景的思路和对策建议进行了广泛深入的研讨。活动被中央电视台等多家主流媒体广泛宣传报道。

呈现在读者眼前的这本《2050 年的上海：发展愿景与挑战》，便是这次上海国际智库峰会的全景展现，详实记录了与会专家对未来 30 年上海发展愿景与挑战的"畅想"，为上海城市发展战略研究留下了宝贵的历史资料。希望本书能够对关注全球城市发展的人们有所裨益，并启发我们以前瞻性和战略性的发展眼光，在更广阔的视野探索研究上海未来建设全球城市的实践，为全球城市理论发展做出贡献。

是为序。

肖林　博士

上海市人民政府发展研究中心主任、党组书记

Since the reform and opening-up began, Shanghai has made a consensus concerning Shanghai's development strategies and functions after several strategic discussions, which exerted a significant and profound impact on economic and social development of Shanghai. Currently, Shanghai has been embracing the future, drafting for a new important round of development. On the one hand, Shanghai is just 5 years away from the goal proposed in the 1990's, that is, "basically build Shanghai into an international economic, financial, trade and shipping center and socialist modern international metropolis by 2020", and on the other hand, China has initiated the grand objective of achieving the great rejuvenation of the Chinese nation by the 100th anniversary of the founding of People's Republic of China, Shanghai is planning for a new-round development and leapfrog in line with China's new strategic goal of "two hundred years". Thus, in the new historical orientation, standing firm on the urban development heritage and specific genes, conforming to the trend of urban development, we are poised to scientifically planning for development and strategic direction for the next 30 years, and clarify the historic mission of Shanghai in achieving the great rejuvenation and the "Chinese Dream" of the Chinese nation.

Looking ahead, global urban development will enter into an era of constant change and disruption accompanied by scientific and technological progress; innovation on development philosophy and vision has become an important part of making global urban development strategies. For example, in *New York Plan 2030*, more emphasis are placed on *Reliance City* and *Fair and Justice*; London attaches more importance to quality of life in *Smart London Plan 2030 — Greater London Authority*, Paris' Master Plan *Greater Paris Region 2030* gives more priority to ensure its global appeal in the 21st century. Therefore, while planning for the future in 30 years, Shanghai must innovates in its urban development philosophy and visions.

To complement the "Shanghai in the next 30 years" development strategy research, and to examine the philosophy and vision of urban development, clarify bottlenecks and challenges facing the future of Shanghai, on December 18th, 2015, sponsored by Development Research Centre of Shanghai Municipal People's Government, and jointly organized by Shanghai International Think Tank Exchanges Center, Shanghai Development Research Foundation and McKinsey & Company, this "2015 Shanghai international Think Tank Summit" is themed "Shanghai 2050: Vision and Challenge", as a part of the series of Strategic Research Forum "Shanghai in the next 30 years". The summit has attracted participants from McKinsey, Accenture, PricewaterhouseCoopers, Deloitte, IBM, Nomura Research Institute, Johnson & Johnson (China), the US-China Business Council, the American Chamber of Commerce Shanghai, European Chamber Shanghai Chapter, the Japan External Trade organization (JETRO), TE Connectivity and other 17 international experts of international think tanks. Tu Guangshao, Executive Deputy Mayor, and Li Yiping, Secretary-General of Shanghai Municipal People's Government, attended the meeting. Executive Deputy Mayor Mr. Tu delivered a passionate closing remark. Guests exchange in depth the vision of Shanghai's development in 2050, bottlenecks and challenges as well as ideas and solutions to achieve these proposals, and this event is broadly covered by CCTV and many other mainstream media.

Presented in front of you is the *Shanghai 2050: Vision and Challenge*, a panorama show of this Shanghai International Think Tank Summit. This book has a detailed record on the "imaginations" of the guests on the vision and challenge for Shanghai in 2050. This is inevitably valuable historical data, hoping to benefit people who focus on global urban development and its research, inspire us to study the practice of building Shanghai into a global city with a broader view and make contribution to the theoretical studies on the global cities development with a forward-looking and strategic vision.

Dr. Xiao Lin

Director of the SDRC

CONTENTS

目　录

1　**开幕致辞** / 肖林

7　**主旨演讲**

9　面向未来 30 年的上海：如何激活与世界城市地位匹配的创新力 / 陈有钢

13　打造循环经济优势 / 钱蔚

23　预测未来：世界大势与战略选择 / 张蕴岭

26　2050 年的上海——全球领先的创新城市 / 汪颖

30　2050 年的上海——具有全球影响力的文化与思想策源传播"中心" / 叶华

34　2050 年的上海——第一个全球性的 21 世纪城市 / 谢祖墀

36　2050 年的上海——从经济金融中心到人才中心 / 琼安娜

40　2050 年的上海——全球最健康的城市 / 吴人伟

44　面向未来的上海和塑造未来的教育 / 王颐

47　2050 年的上海——最智慧的城市 / 张小平

49　科技变革、社会变迁与城市治理 / 范德尚

54　2050 年的上海——一个日本经济从业者的视点与期待 / 小栗道明

58　积极行动亦实现上海 2050 年辉煌 / 彭捷宁

61　创新型工程师在上海 2050 年发展愿景中的角色扮演 / 来咏歌

65　2050 年全球货币格局以及上海国际中心地位 / 乔依德

143　**互动讨论**

157　**总结发言** / 李广宇

169 **闭幕致辞** / 屠光绍

179 **峰会综述**

191 **附件**
193 未来纽约城市发展愿景与挑战
200 大伦敦未来发展愿景与挑战
203 2030 年"巴黎大区"发展愿景与挑战
206 2030 年东京城市发展愿景与挑战
210 未来 50 年新加坡发展愿景与挑战

249 **附录**
251 2015 年上海国际智库峰会办会、参会方简介

273 **后记**

1   OPENING ADDRESS / Xiao Lin

7   KEYNOTE SPEECHES

68 Towards Shanghai in Future 30 years: How to Invigorate the Innovation Capability Well Matched with the

    Status of a Global City / Chen Yougang

74 Creating the Circular Economy Advantage / Qian Wei

87 Predicting the Future: the Global Trends and Strategic Options / Zhang Yunling

91 Shanghai in 2050: A World-Leading Innovation Hub / Jane Wang

96 Shanghai in 2050: A "Center" of Culture and Ideas with Global Influence / Ye Hua

101 Shanghai in 2050: The First Global City of 21st Century / Edward Tse

103 Shanghai in 2050: From Economic and Financial Center to Talent Center / Ioana Kraft

109 Shanghai in 2050: The World's Healthiest City / Jesse Wu

115 Future Shanghai and Shaping the Future Education / Wang Yi

118 Shanghai in 2050: The Smartest City / Zhang Xiaoping

121 Scientific Revolution, Social Change and City Governance / Fan Deshang

127 Shanghai in 2050: The Viewpoint and Expectation of a Japanese Businessman / Michiaki Oguri

132 Actions to Ensure Shanghai is as Successful in 2050 as It Is Today / Jacob Parker

135 Role of Innovative Engineers in Shanghai's Vision of 2050 / Reggie Lai

139 Global Currency Landscape and Shanghai as an International Center in 2050 / Qiao Yide

143 COMMENTS & DISCUSSIONS

157 SUMMARY STATEMENT / Li Guangyu

169 CLOSING REMARK / Tu Guangshao

179 **CONFERENCE REVIEW**

191 **ATTACHMENTS**

216 New York City's Future Development: Vision and Challenges

226 The Great London's Future Development: Vision and Challenges

230 The Metropolis of the Great Paris in 2030: Vision and Challenges

234 Tokyo in 2030: Vision and Challenges

239 Singapore's Future 50 Years: Vision and Challenges

249 **APPENDIX**

260 Introduction to Summit Organizers and Think Tanks

273 **POSTSCRIPT**

OPENING ADDRESS

开幕致辞

肖　林　Xiao Lin

上海市人民政府发展研究中心主任、党组书记

Director General of the SDRC

改革开放以来，上海邀请国内外的专家、学者，开展了几次发展战略的大讨论。这些发展战略的研究成果，明确了上海发展的战略目标和功能定位，对上海改革开放和经济社会转型发展，都产生了重要而深远的影响。

当前，国际、国内形势处在一个关键的转折点上，世界经济重心向东亚转移。上海经济社会发展，也进入了一个新的阶段。

按照既定目标，到 2020 年，上海要基本建成国际经济、金融、贸易、航运中心和社会主义现代化国际大都市，建设形成具有全球影响力的科技创新中心的基本框架。这些目标，业已临近，再有一个 5 年，都可实现。国家提出了到中华人民共和国成立 100 年实现中华民族伟大复兴中国梦的宏伟目标，上海也需按照我国"两个 100 年"目标，进一步实现城市未来发展的新跨越。

为此，上海市委、市政府决定，由上海市人民政府发展研究中心牵头，组织国内外专家学者，开展"面向未来 30 年的上海发展"战略研究。新一轮战略研究，要求研究者从全球视野、国家战略高度出发，立足城市发展积淀、特殊基因，把握城市发展规律，科学分析和预测 2020 年以后未来 30 年上海发展趋势、前景以及面临的机遇挑战，引领上海城市发展向更高目标迈进。

这项"未来 30 年上海发展战略"研究，已经开展了近两年的时间。我们广泛吸收国内外专家意见，动员了全国近 80 个课题组和研究团队，其中包括中央部委的近 10 个研究团队；同时，委托世界银行和国务院发展研究中心开展平行研究，将分别形成国际版和国内版两个总报告。

上海经济社会已经进入一个新的发展阶段。在外部经济环境错综复杂的情况下，上海经济仍然保持了稳中求进的基本态势，创新转型和结构性改革积极效应正在显现。2015 年，上海经济增长速度预计达到 7% 左右。2016 年将是新的"十三五"规划的开局之年，将为未来的发展奠定重要基础。推动未来上海的发展和全球城市建设，必须具有长远的眼光、汇聚全球智慧。上海将按照党的十八届五中全会提出的"创新、协调、绿色、开放、共享"五大发展理念，科学分析国际国内发展大趋势，把握大机遇，应对大挑战，明确上海未来发展的大格局。我们衷心期待国际智库的各位与会代表，围绕峰会主题，充分研究、讨论、交流观点，凝聚共识，为上海未来发展提供你们的真知灼见，不断拓宽"面向未来 30 年的上海"发展战略课题研究的全球视野和战略思维。

Since the initiation of the reform and opening up drive, Shanghai invites domestic and foreign experts and scholars to carry out great debates on development strategies. The research results of development strategies have clarified strategic objectives and function positioning of Shanghai's development, and have had a significant and far-reaching influence on Shanghai's reform and opening up as well as economic and social transformation and development.

Currently, international and domestic situation are at a critical turning point in which the world's economic center of gravity shifts towards East Asia. Shanghai's economic and social development also has entered a new stage.

In accordance with established goals, by 2020, Shanghai will become an international economic, financial, trade and shipping center and socialist international metropolis, and will basically come into shape the basic framework as a sci-tech innovation center with global influence. We are approaching these objectives, and we are confident that within another five years, such goals can be realized. China has set up a grand goal of achieving the great rejuvenation of the Chinese nation by the 100 anniversary since the founding of People's Republic of China, Shanghai also need to achieve a new leap forward into the future in accordance with China's "goals for the two centuries".

Therefore, Shanghai Committee of C.P.C and Shanghai Municipal People's Government made the decision that under the leadership of the Development Research Center of Shanghai Municipal People's Government, experts and scholars at home and abroad shall carry out strategic researches that is oriented to "the development of Shanghai for the next 30 years". In the new round of strategic research, the task group is required to base their research on Shanghai's development legacy and special DNA, starting from global vision and national perspective, to conduct a scientific analysis and forecast on the development trends, prospects, challenges and opportunities to be faced in the next 30 years to guide Shanghai to march toward higher goals.

The research on "Shanghai Development Strategy for the Next 30 Years" has been carrying out for nearly two years. We extensively solicit suggestions from domestic and foreign expertise and mobilize nearly 80 task groups and research teams home and abroad. Among them, there are nearly 10 research teams from central government and ministries, meanwhile, we are also entrusting the World Bank, the Development Research Center of the State Council to conduct parallel studies. So, Chinese version and international version reports will be published respectively.

Shanghai's economic and social development has entered a new stage. In the intricacies of the external economic environment, Shanghai's economy maintains a steady growth; results of innovative transformation and structural reforms are showing. It is expected that Shanghai's annual economic growth rate will reach around 7% in 2015. The year 2016 marks the first year of "the Thirteenth Five Year Plan (2016—2020)", and to promote the future development of Shanghai so as to build Shanghai into a global city, we must put things into perspective and pool global wisdom. Shanghai will follow the five development mindset, that is "innovation, coordination, green, openness and sharing" proposed by the Fifth Plenary Session of the 18th Central Committee of the Chinese Communist Party, conducting scientific analysis on the international and domestic development trend, seize opportunities and meet challenges to understand the big picture of future development of Shanghai. We sincerely expect that attendees from international think tanks to study, discuss, exchange views around the theme of the summit, providing your insights to the future development of Shanghai so that our global vision and strategic thinking of strategy research on "Shanghai in the next 30 years" will be broadened.

KEYNOTE SPEECHES

主旨演讲

面向未来 30 年的上海：如何激活与世界城市地位匹配的创新力

陈有钢

麦肯锡全球合伙人、全球研究院中国区负责人

综观全球世界级大城市，除了超强的经济实力外，无一不具有非凡的创新能力，而上海要在未来 30 年成为下一个新的世界级大城市，激活世界级的创新能力是一项必须完成的任务。

从纽约、伦敦这两大公认的国际经济中心的发展不难发现，一个国际经济中心必然是一个创新中心，拥有良好的创新环境、多样的创新活动及丰富的创新成果。纽约凭借硅巷（Silicon Alley）的成功，崛起为美国东海岸的科技重镇，被誉为"美国新科技之都"。通过减税计划、公私合营和完善配套设施，纽约在都市中心打造了一个无边界的高科技园区。硅巷目前拥有超过 500 家初创企业，创造科技就业岗位全美第二，成为风险资本竞相投资的热土（从 2007 到 2011 年，硅巷风投交易量暴涨 32%，2012 年第三季度激增至 44%，投资总金额上升到 2.18 亿美元），成为 2008 年金融危机之后纽约经济增长的主要引擎，被誉为继硅谷之后美国发展最快的信息技术中心地带。早在 20 世纪 90 年代，伦敦利用其自身的人才资源和大都会的优势，率先提出"创意之都"的口号。通过平台搭建、金融支持等途径建立优质健康的创新环境，扶持和推动了这些高附加值的、可持续的文化创意产业的发展。伦敦现已是全球三大广告产业中心之一、全球三大最繁忙的电影制作中心之一和国际设计之都，文化创意产业也已成为仅次于金融的第二大支柱产业。

在亚洲，与上海同等级的城市作为竞争者也在创新方面取得了骄人的成就。新加坡将创新视为推动经济转型的引擎，将智力资本看作新加坡发展的关键。政府大力增加科技研究与开发资金的投入，扩大科技人员队伍，发展高新技术产业，兴建科技园，吸引跨国公司从事技术开发等。通过政府的合理规划和有效的执行力，新加坡已成为国际科研中心以及亚洲

创新中心。

由此可见，创新能力与经济地位是相辅相成的关系。如何激活城市的创新力，正是建设世界城市的核心命题。

而上海在城市创新力上的现状却并不乐观，在很多方面落后于北京与深圳，面临创新转化效率低，创新氛围和企业家精神缺乏和创新基础环境欠缺的瓶颈。

对比国内其他一线城市，上海在很多创新活动方面落后于北京和深圳。例如，2011年上海的专利申请数仅为1439项，相当于北京的55%，深圳的18%，东京的12%；在创新投资方面，北京的投资案例2倍于上海，规模超过2.5倍。究其原因，主要有以下几方面：

一是创新转化的效率低。上海历年来在科研上的投入并不少，2010年每百万人中研发人员数量是日本的2.5倍，研发投入占GDP比例已经2倍于英国，但在创新成果转化和高科技产业比例上仍落后于国际先进城市。前端科研投入诚然能催生技术的创新发展，但科创中心的本质更在于创新链与价值链的融合，在于如何实现成果的价值转化。

二是创新氛围和企业家精神缺乏。上海在全球城市企业家精神排名中仅列第21位。在全国民企五百强中，上海只有19家，落后于长三角地区的邻居省份（浙江省123家，江苏省98家）。国有企业和外资企业依然是上海经济的主要贡献者，民营企业活跃度严重不足，市场缺乏活力。

三是创新的基础环境有待提高。上海在创新资源的开放、创新生态的营造和软环境方面都有所欠缺。在信息数字化时代大背景下，上海市政府在数据收集和整合方面已起步，但在数据公开和鼓励公众使用方面仍有较大提升空间。创新主体之间缺乏联动，各类型企业、企业与科研机构及创新企业与资本之间还缺乏有效联动的平台。与此同时，环境问题与空气污染对人才和投资吸引造成负面的影响，上海的国际化和开放程度与世界城市仍有很大差距。

要探索上海的创新优势，需要深刻理解不同的创新原型，找准上海的功能定位，利用工商之都"工商并举"的传统优势，在工程技术型创新与客户中心型创新上做文章。

创新并不简单地等同于"发明"。观察成功实现商业化的所有创新类别，我们看到创新可以归纳为四大原型：（1）通过基础性研究成果的商业化来开发新产品的科学研究型创新；（2）通过整合供应商与合作伙伴的技术来设计开发新产品的工程技术型创新；（3）通过产品和业务创新来解决客户问题的客户中心型创新；(4) 通过生产环节的优化来降低成本、缩短生产时间、提升质量的效率驱动型创新。

上海作为工商之都，应利用"工商并举"的传统优势，着力打造创意汇聚、应用加速和价值创造为主要功能的创新转化平台，而不必刻意追求催生原生性的基础创意和发明。依托已有的工业基础，如汽车、飞机等制造业，上海可进一步鼓励创新者通过设计平台、整合经销商网络技术，进行产品开发，在工程技术型创新继续前行。另一方面，上海服务业的高度发达，拥有规模巨大、充满活力的消费市场，新产品与服务快速商业化的潜力不容低估。上海应引导创新者通过客户互动了解市场需求、偏好和服务不足的细分市场，据此开发新的产品和商业模式，在客户中心型创新上不断实践。

面向未来的 30 年，我们有信心看到上海成为全球创新领导的城市。为了实现这一目标，上海政府应从以下四个方面入手，充分激活市场创新力，提升城市软实力。

第一，支持创业者，让市场发挥作用。

政府最重要的任务之一是营造有利于创业者生存发展的环境。上海市政府应推行创业加速器和创业孵化器等支持项目，并拨款设立创业投资引导基金。早期融资对创业者固然重要，但政府作为投资者，应注意避免过于偏向赢家（或输家），避免排挤私营部门融资。新加坡政府选择与独立的创业投资机构合作，避免了政府的直接投资，从而解决了这些问题。

政府还应简化办事流程鼓励创新。例如，中国的药物审批流程比美国长 7—8 年，这也是中国企业几乎只生产仿制药的原因之一。为了切实给企业提供便利，上海政府可以与业界代表进行磋商，共同提出减少官僚障碍的构想。

上海政府在目前由国企主导的行业持续推行改革，有助于扩大市场竞争和创新：由于垄断国内市场和领导任期制，许多国有企业缺乏以长期眼光开展创新的动力。一个可行方法是引入国际竞争，让国企像民企一样学习在竞争中成长。例如，华为就是在与国际对手的竞争中、与全球客户的合作中提高了自身的创新能力。

第二，成为高要求的创新客户。

在政府是主要采购客户的领域，成为高标准严要求的客户，不断提高技术标准，支持竞争，从而推动创新进步。例如，英国政府为寻求应对医院传染方式而组织的竞标，产生了减少经由通风系统传播的肺炎病例方法，解决了这一重症监护病房的常见问题。

第三，使用衡量创新实效的指标。

上海市政府用研发投资和专利申请数量等容易量化的指标衡量创新效益，设定目标。然而，这些指标的出色表现并未完全转化为高质量的创新成果。为了切实鼓励创新，政策制定者需要对研发支出等传统指标以外的衡量方法予以考虑。

第四，培育强大的地区创新集群。

同一地理区位上的产业集群有助于创业者、研究机构和投资者形成合作，进而推动创新。强大的产业集群是创新成果的摇篮。上海在国际贸易中举足轻重，毗邻长江三角洲制造业群，利用这些优势建设生命科学和工程行业中心。

与此同时，上海市政府可以通过鼓励跨产业集群的合作来强化创新。例如，北京开发出的数据分析软件也许会被用在深圳生产的健康监测品牌产品上，而该品牌产品可能又会被上海的生命科学企业用于移动式临床试验，加快新药研发转化过程。

为了提升创新产业集群的全球竞争力，上海政府应花大力气解决顶尖人才，尤其是科研、工程创新人才最为关心的生活质量问题。目前，上海的空气质量、住房条件、交通等各项生活质量"软指标"得分较纽约等世界级城市依然有一定差距，这是上海政府应当着力解决的目标。

打造循环经济优势

钱 蔚

埃森哲大中华区能源业董事总经理

在上海"十三五"规划中，提出了未来几年要守住几条底线，当中有一条，就是守住上海的生态底线。过去30多年中国经济发展取得了很大成就，但其发展模式很大程度上是"取得—制造—废弃"资源的线性增长方式。但这种模式也带来很多负面影响，比如空气和水体的污染、可利用土地面积越来越少，等等，这都会影响到上海的城市竞争力。对于像上海这样自然资源稀缺的城市，以往那种依靠"取得—制造—废弃"资源的线性增长方式即将失效，要实现可持续发展，构建循环经济模式将成为必然选择。循环经济能利用突破性技术和商业模式，在增长不受限的情况下创造价值。

长期以来，世界各个经济体的增长模式都是基于开发及使用丰富和廉价的自然资源。这种方式本无可厚非，因为依靠自然资源就能支持企业成功。但是随着资源的日益减少，这种建立在"取得—制造—废弃"原则之上的发展方式正在接近临界点，许多不可再生资源的供应已日趋枯竭，而可再生资源也入不敷出。

如果我们不采取措施来应对这一状况，到2050年，不可再生资源（如生物质能、化石能源以及多种金属）总需求预计将达1300亿吨，超出了地球总供给能力的五倍。即使是相对乐观的预期下，2050年不可再生资源的需求量仍将达到800亿吨，能源缺口仍在400亿吨左右（见图1）。如此大规模的资源匮乏很可能给经济造成毁灭性的影响。

未来之路在哪里？答案是循环经济。

1. 循环经济：既往模式的终结

循环经济是一种全新的发展模式，能够实现增长与稀缺资源使用的脱

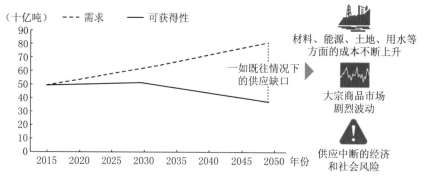

情境分析时只考虑了各种有限的资源贮藏，因此与总体材料消耗水平有所不同。最值得注意的是，其中未涉及工程用矿物量（如砂子和砾石），因为它们基本不具备稀缺性。

图1　资源供给与需求的不平衡状况（2015—2050年）

钩，促进企业加强创新，帮助客户和用户"以更少资源，获得更多价值"。突破性技术以及创新的商业模式是循环经济发展的基础，而创新的商业模式来源于耐久、再生、升级、翻新、功能共享和非物质化等这些循环经济的基本理念。

在循环经济下，企业的关注点不是提高产量，也不是压缩成本，而会从根本出发，集中精力重新思考自身产品和服务，进而全面审视自身业务，直至确定新的客户价值主张。企业采用一种"面向未来"的运作模式，为将来的资源匮乏时代做好准备。

电钻的使用模式可以作为理解循环经济的一个典型例子。每次人们使用电钻通常不到20分钟，使用者往往只需要在墙上钻一个洞，然而市场上的电钻品种琳琅满目，很多还配有高端功能，比如吸尘功能。反之，如果我们能采取另一种方式，大部分使用者不用购买电钻，只是在有需求时才便捷地取用它，那么将能够节省大量金钱和时间；同时，该产品也可以得到优化，比如使用寿命更长、组件可再利用、再循环，等等。这一模式也可以应用到其他商品上，从自己动手组装工具，到卡车、建筑设备、打印机等。

企业若要转向循环业务模式，各个方面都需要随之调整，在生产和销售的同时还要兼顾使用和归还过程。厂家将不再刻意设计那些容易损耗或不考虑环境影响的产品，因此，在循环经济模式下，顾客需求同企业激励因素将重新匹配。

许多企业已开始按照循环经济原则，通过投资与回收可再生能源等多种努力，形成能源和材料的闭环利用。一批具有开拓精神的创新企业在实现循环经济的过程中，不仅显著提升了资源的供应和使用效率，而且还进一步优化了自身的业务模式，开始从客户的角度来看待资源需求。埃森哲通过研究已找到 100 多家真正具有颠覆能力的企业,它们采用循环经济的思维和新技术进行转型,对现有行业格局构成了冲击。我们将这些企业所获得的竞争优势定义为"循环优势"。循环优势来源于资源效率和客户价值的同步创新,并且全面体现在企业战略、技术和运营当中。

耐克公司的 Flyknit™ 技术就是循环经济应用的实例。通过该技术,耐克公司只需几根纤维线就能打造一款鞋面。结果,不但大大减少了生产过程中的浪费(高达 80%),而且鞋款更轻、贴合度更佳,从而有助于提高运动员成绩。

我们的研究显示,企业要想在循环经济中取得成功,先要明白三个关键事项:第一,可供企业使用的五种循环商业模式的出现;第二,构建这些商业模式需要五项新的企业能力;第三,十类数字技术和工程技术将为变革提供支持。

2. 五种循环商业模式

毫无疑问,无论从长短期来看,循环经济都蕴含着巨大商业价值。试想,哪家企业不希望摆脱对稀缺资源的依赖,变废为宝,创造新的收入来源及价值呢?但是知易行难。事实上,如今大部分企业的内在组织架构和运营模式都并不适合发展循环经济,因为它们的战略、结构以及运营都深深扎根于线性增长模式,这是它们的 DNA。因此,企业如果想拥有循环优势,首先要摒弃线性思维的束缚。循环经济模式背后的理念不是"降低危害"而是"带来更加积极的影响"。埃森哲分析了 120 多项采用创新方式提高资源生产率的企业案例,总结出五种基本的商业模式(见图 2)。

这些商业模式各自都有鲜明的特征,可以单独或组合使用,能帮助企业大幅提升资源使用效率;同时还能强化差异化经营和客户价值、降低服务和拥有成本、创造新的收入并降低风险。

(1)模式一:循环供应。

这一模式以提供完全可再生、可回收,或可生物降解的资源投入为基础,支持各种周而复始的生产和消费系统。通过该模式,企业摆脱了线性资源消耗,并逐步放弃使用稀缺资源;同时还能减少浪费、提高资源利用效率。

这一模式特别适用于那些依赖稀缺资源或对环境有重大影响的企业。皇家帝斯曼公司(Royal DSM)从一家原生材料供应商,转型为重新

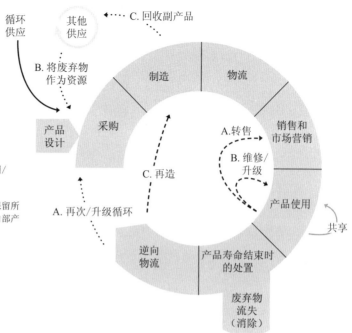

图例：

循环供应：提供可再生能源、以生物为基础或完全可回收的生产材料，以取代单生命周期的材料

资源回收：从废弃产品或副产品中回收有用的资源/能源

延长产品生命周期：通过维修、升级和转售，延长产品和零部件的工作生命周期

共享平台：通过各种可能的共享式利用/使用/拥有方法，提高产品的利用率

产品即服务：提供产品的使用权，但保留所有权，从而使循环式资源生产在企业内部产生收益

*可应用于价值链任何部分的产品流当中

图 2　五种循环商业模式

利用各种材料并提供新型生态友好型原料的企业。例如，该公司开发出一种纤维素生物乙醇，它是作物混合发酵生产糖类的副产品。与化石燃料相比，这种生物化学产品在减少废气和二氧化碳净排放量方面有着很大的潜力。利用这种以往一直被认为价值非常低的原料，纤维素生物乙醇已经为皇家帝斯曼创造了新的收入来源，并且公司预计它最终有望带来超过 7 万个相关工作岗位。

（2）模式二：资源回收。

资源回收是通过创新的回收和升级改造服务，变废为宝。该模式的解决方案从产业共生、完整的闭环式回收，一直延伸至"从摇篮到摇篮®"的设计，从而将废弃产品加工成全新的商品。

这种模式能够帮助企业消除物料流失，最大限度地提高产品的经济价值，非常适合那些产生大量副产品，或是可以将生产废料进行回收和再加工的企业。

在食品行业，这一模式帮助美国食品杂货连锁企业克罗格公司（Kroger）将食物废料转化成为可再生能源。公司旗下的 Food 4 Less 超市的康普顿配送中心每天都会产生 150 吨食品垃圾——处理它们曾经是企业的一项沉重负担，不但侵蚀收入，而且还要支付处置费用并会造成环境污染。但现在，这些原本的"垃圾"已被用于提供廉价、清洁的能源，其规模足够支撑一片占地 49 英亩的园区运转。

克罗格公司依托一套"厌氧消化"系统，将食物垃圾变成沼气，满足园区微型涡轮发电机和锅炉所需的能源，几乎替代了先前使用的天然气。截至目前，这项举措的回报已达到初始投资的 18%。

（3）模式三：延长产品生命周期。

通过延长产品的生命周期能够扩大企业资产的生命周期。通过对产品的维修、升级、再加工或再营销，废弃材料中蕴藏的价值将不再被白白丢弃，而是可以继续使用甚至优化。而且，得益于产品使用范围的扩展，新的收入也会源源不断地被创造出来。采用这种模式，企业会尽可能长时间地确保产品的经济实用性，而且也会以更有针对性的方式进行产品升级。

这种模式适用于以下企业：大多数资本密集型的 B2B 企业（如工业设备企业）；专注于二手市场或是发布新产品版本时小改小革的 B2C 企业。

谷歌正在解决手机过时的挑战：当移动设备无法继续满足使用者需求时，是一扔了之还是变废为宝？谷歌推出了一个名为"Project Ara"的项目，目的是重新设计智能手机结构，将其分解成可以根据用户要求进行组装和定制的可更换模块。利用模块置换功能，使用者可以很容易地借助基本技巧和工具对手机加以改造；并且当手机损坏时，仅需更换有故障的部分就能轻松且低成本地将其修复。通过最大限度地提高手机的使用寿命，谷歌减少了制造新手机所需的原生资源，同时尽量减少电子废弃物规模。这项设计原则还能够得到其他举措的辅助——例如通过一个在线交易市场，使用者可以在此交易各种手机模块，在扩展组件生命周期的同时，重新发掘其剩余价值。

（4）模式四：共享平台。

无论是个人还是组织，共享平台业务模式都可以促进产品用户之间的协作。它们通过共享方式，在能力过剩和能力欠缺之间寻找平衡，从而提高生产率并创造用户价值。这种模式将有助于最大限度地提高资产利用率，使产品和资产利用率或拥有率很低的企业受益匪浅。

这一模式目前适用于那些自己无需制造任何产品、专门研究如何增加产品利用率的企业，它们给传统制造商带来了相当大的压力。

驾车共享公司 Lyft 已利用共享平台商业模式，在出行市场中开辟出一片崭新的天地。Lyft 的各位联合创始人意识到，城市中的轿车运力远远没有得到充分利用，他们估计其中 80% 的座位都被空置。该公司依托移动应用，帮助那些需要搭车去某处的人，向众多拥有汽车的人士提出申请，从而填补这些闲置的座位。搭载和乘车费将通过应用支付（通常比同里程的出租车费低 20% 至 30%），其中 Lyft 会留出 20% 作为自身收入。这一商业模式很快引起消费者的共鸣，还获得了投资人的热捧：公司于 2014 年 4 月宣布，其最新一轮融资规模高达 2.5 亿美元。这种共享租车模式不仅在美国开花结果，而且很快发展到世界其他地方。

（5）模式五：产品即服务。

产品即服务商业模式为人们提供了一种与以往"买入并拥有"方式截然不同的新选择。用户可以通过租赁或按次付费的方式，获得产品的使用权。这种商业模式使厂家将着眼点从数量转向性能。在这一商业模式中，产品寿命的延长、可重复使用及共享性不再被视为蚕食利润的风险，而是成为增加收入和降低成本的驱动力。

这种模式适合于那些产品运作成本占比很高以及较客户而言拥有产品维护管理技能优势的企业。

循环商业模式正在颠覆诸多行业。我们的研究发现，在过去 10 年间这一模式有了爆发式增长。以 Airbnb 为例。该公司帮助用户通过一个网站租用其他成员的房间或整座住宅。这家成立于 2008 年的企业在短短几年中，就已超越洲际酒店和希尔顿全球酒店集团，成为美国国内最大的酒店运营商（提供超过 65 万间客房），并且预订量和收入每年都以数倍的速度在增长。

一开始，初创企业是循环商业模式的主力军；如今，越来越多的大型跨国公司也开始青睐这种模式。H&M 在所有的店面中回收服装，由此形成封闭式纺织品循环；宝马和思科公司则通过翻新和再销售，延长旧产品的使用寿命；飞利浦将"照明作为一种服务"，提供给城市和市政当局；亚马逊把教科书转变成为一种服务；而戴姆勒公司的 car2go 项目（汽车共享服务）在 2014 年已拥有了 60 多万名客户，收入接近 1 亿美元；沃尔玛正通过在店内开展以旧换新计划，积极打入规模达 20 亿美元的二手视频游戏市场。

由此引发的另一个变化是：一些新的生态系统正以创新企业为核心逐步形成，这其中既有初创企业，也包括成立已久的老牌公司。饮料生产商嘉士伯集团及其部分全球供应商也在联手行动，开发下一代包装技术，在优化回收和再利用的同时，保持或改善产品质量与价值。通过"嘉士伯循环经济社区"，这种合作已正式宣告建立，其目标是吸纳 15 家合作伙伴，并且到 2016 年至少有三种产品获得"从摇篮到摇篮 ®"认证。在埃森哲于

2014 年世界经济论坛上举办的活动中，嘉士伯集团 CEO 韦耀国（Jorgen Buhl Rasmussen）表示："我已看到了其中的商业价值，它不但符合消费者的利益，更能够令地球和人类社会获益良多。"

3. 十大颠覆性技术助力循环商业模式

循环商业模式若是放在四五年前还很难全面实现，而今由于一些前沿技术的成熟令循环模式成为现实。其中，最关键的一系列数字技术是社交技术、移动技术、数据分析、云技术，以及"机器对机器"技术。通过研究，我们发现循环经济领先企业普遍采用的 10 种颠覆性技术（见图 3）。这些技术分为三大类：数字化（信息技术）、工程学（物理技术），以及两者的综合应用。

数字技术能够让用户、机器和管理系统间实现实时信息交换。这类技术本质上都是以客户为中心，通过提供信息和连接，使得企业可以在销售活动结束之后，继续保持与客户的联系和互动。比如电信企业沃达丰和 Verizon，通过移动设备的内置功能和数据分析，为客户自动提供二手手机

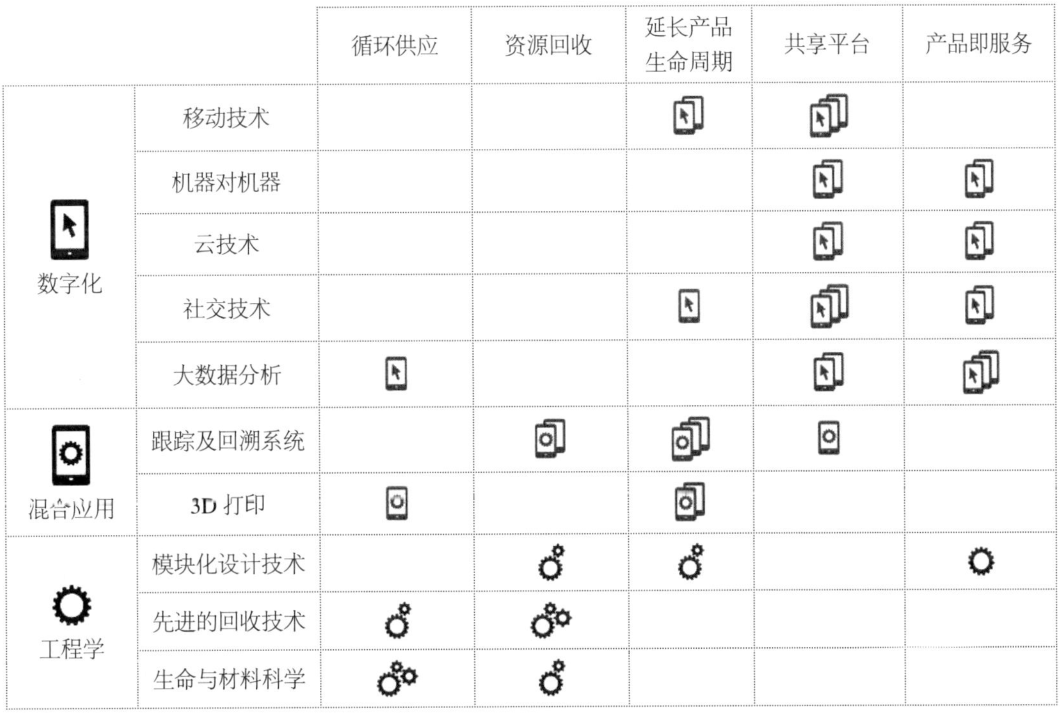

		循环供应	资源回收	延长产品生命周期	共享平台	产品即服务
数字化	移动技术			▪	▪▪	
	机器对机器				▪	▪
	云技术				▪	▪
	社交技术			▪	▪▪	▪
	大数据分析	▪			▪▪	▪▪
混合应用	跟踪及回溯系统		▪	▪▪	▪	
	3D 打印	▪		▪		
工程学	模块化设计技术		▪	▪		▪
	先进的回收技术	▪	▪▪			
	生命与材料科学	▪▪	▪			

注：基于 120 余项案例研究和 50 多次访谈。在表格各框中的图标数量代表其相对重要性。

图 3　领先企业采用的 10 种颠覆性技术

报价，同时帮助他们将手机退回到附近的店面以获得即时返款。

这些连接大大增强了远程可见性和对资产的控制力，因此对于产品即服务、共享平台和延长产品生命周期等商业模式都格外重要。通过转变企业和消费者与实体及数字资产互动的方式，数字技术可以重塑企业价值链，从而令业务增长摆脱资源束缚。

工程学技术包括先进的回收方法、模块化设计，以及生命和材料科学等。它们能帮助企业利用再生资源来生产新的产品，同时开展收集、回收工作，进而处理各类产品和材料，并采取具有成本效益的方法搜集使用过的资产，将它们投入再生产过程。对于已建立了循环供应和资源回收模式的企业而言，上述技术尤为重要。

混合型技术则兼具了数字化和工程学两方面的要素，它可以有效控制资产和物资流动。它将帮助企业以数字化的方式明确材料和商品的来源、位置、状态和使用情况，并且在同一时间，支持以各种方法对它们进行信息收集、处理和再加工。例如，3D 打印允许本地生产机构下载数字化设计方案，再于本地生产出实体物品，而这正是中国企业江苏聚能硅业有限公司的做法。该公司借助 3D 打印技术，使用再生材料在不到一天的时间中就能打印一幢房屋，而其单位成本甚至低于 5000 美元。

4. 领军者必备五种能力

随着各种新技术的崛起，企业在采用循环业务模式时必须掌握一系列新的能力。通过我们的研究，对企业最高决策者而言，以下五种技能对于企业成功实施循环业务模式格外重要。

一是重定企业规划和战略。过去，企业提高收入的着眼点一般放在如何最大限度地提高产量和销售利润率，而未来应该转向如何生产出具备可持续性的产品和实现服务循环。这样做不仅需要企业专注于核心业务，而且还应该积极融入协作性的循环经济网络，充分调动供应商、制造商、零售商、服务提供商和客户等各方力量。至关重要的是，要让整条价值链清楚价值在哪？价值是如何产生的？然后围绕这一核心组织活动。

二是重塑创新和产品开发。企业的关注焦点由为一次性使用而设计，转变为需要考虑众多产品生命周期和用户，同时努力改善材料对环境的影响。调整产品来创造收入的挑战不仅来自销售节点上，也体现在整个使用过程中；同时，如何进行低成本的回收和后续处理都是关键的设计难题。

站在软件端来看，企业往往需要建立成熟的产品生命周期管理能力，扩大对自身系统的定义，将其范围延伸至维修、服务和回收等活动中。

三是重思产品材料再利用及对环境的影响。在采购和制造环节，企业必须确保生产的高效率、在过程中没有资源被丢弃，以及能够保持并显著扩大来自回收链的采购量。后者往往意味着，企业不会再从少数几家供应商处大规模地采购，而是向众多不同门类的商家进行小批量购买。这就要求实现生产的灵活性，从而可以利用不同质量和来源的材料生产有价值的产品，而不是将其填埋或焚烧。

四是重造营销和销售工作。企业要站在客户角度，明确销售和市场营销工作聚焦于创造需求，达到既满足客户需求又取得收入的目的。不过，其方式不再是销售产品和服务，而是推动客户来使用它们。企业还需要开拓新的方法来吸引并激励客户妥善使用和处置自身产品。与之类似，售后服务部门不仅应当继续保持服务水平、销售备件，并管理好渠道合作伙伴，而且还必须更加积极地参与到产品生命周期的管理当中，最大限度地保留其剩余价值。总之，在循环经济中，销售和市场营销工作的实质就是深化对产品使用阶段的理解、反馈客户偏好，从而使产品和服务能够适应循环使用的特征。

五是重审处置和收集工作。在流程的末端，企业需要将循环完整地串联起来，而完成这一步骤的是逆向物流和回收链，或者通俗地叫作处置和收集。降低物流和废弃物管理成本，利用良好的回报计划留住客户，并严格遵从政府法规，将继续成为此项职能工作的主要关注点。但也必须经过有效设计，方可以市场机会为导向，主动从市场中进行回收或回购，并支持本地化的再利用。因此，企业所需关键能力包括质量控制，以及确定最佳回收和再加工链。

企业构建循环优势，可以开启全新业务方式，从根本上提高资源生产率、加强差异化、降低成本和风险、创造强劲的新收入来源，并且改进客户价值主张。那么，企业怎样着手启动这项工作？解答以下五组关键问题可以帮助 CEO 和高管们明确，在构建循环优势过程中所需应对的挑战：

（1）机遇——在现有价值链中，应用循环经济模式的机会在哪里，如何重塑企业未来发展方向？

（2）价值——什么是我们提供给客户的核心价值，循环商业模式怎样帮助我们重新思考这种价值？

（3）能力——如何改进自身经营模式和能力，以支持循环经济商业模式和客户主张？

（4）技术——自然科学、工程学和数字技术中，有哪些对业务有实质性影响的技术趋势，它们是否会颠覆现有的价值链？

（5）时机——如何选择时机，以及为构建循环经济模式设定什么速度和目标？

虽然迈向循环经济的旅途并不平坦，但是已经有越来越多的企业通过应用循环经济原理而赢得了竞争优势，它们通过创新，在提高资源使用效率的同时也给客户创造了价值，在企业内部，也在重塑战略、运营和技术。面对日益严峻的资源短缺问题，不论是决策者还是客户都热切希望企业能生产出更具可持续性的产品，对于企业而言，这是开启循环经济模式、打造企业循环优势的最佳时机。

尽管企业是推动循环经济转型的关键，但政府扮演的角色同样不容小觑。政府需要创建适宜的政策环境，扶植各种循环商业模式发展。这些政策包括：税收基础由劳动力转向资源，制定各行业具体的回收目标，使企业在整个产品生命周期中负起责任，为再生资源的利用提供税费优惠，以及建立废弃物国际标准。

预测未来：世界大势与战略选择

张蕴岭

中国社会科学院学部委员、国际研究学部主任

 预测上海 2050，首先要预测中国，预测世界，预测亚洲和亚太，也就是说把上海放在中国、世界、亚洲、亚太的大局来进行认识。当然，预测未来 30 多年的大趋势很难，有很多的变数，但一些大的趋势性的发展还是可以预测的。

 首先看 2050 年的世界综合经济力对比趋势。根据美国情报委员会所做的一个 2050 年大趋势，中国经济总量会大大超过美国，美国之后是印度，世界三大经济排序是中、美、印，三大经济体，两个在亚洲，三个都在亚洲太平洋地区，这个预测，可能会影响人们对未来的许多新思考。

 从未来世界发展看，变化最大，影响最大的是中国。说到 2050 年，我们马上就会想到中国的"两步走"目标：第一步是 2020 年，全面建成小康社会；第二步是 2050 年，建成发达国家。成为发达国家，不仅仅是经济总量的提升，更重要的是社会和政治的成熟。作为发达国家，中国将成为一个有保障的、共同富裕的社会；应该建立起一个成熟的政治制度和国家治理体系。中国走自己的路，建设有中国特色的社会主义，这对世界是一个贡献，为世界提供一个不同于现行发达资本主义制度的一种模式。中国要做"新型大国"、不走传统大国道路的重要体现，就是让以和谐与合作的"东方思想"参与国家治理与世界事务，在构建新的国际关系与秩序中找到一个最好的结合点，既体现对现有体系的基本继承，又能推动其调整与改革。

 从全球角度来看，2050 年的世界究竟是什么样的呢？悲观者认为，人类会进入一个新的战乱的时代、冲突的时代、大国争夺的时代；乐观者认为，人类将进入一个和平发展的时代，共赢的时代、共生的时代。全球化导致了相互依赖，大家是命运相连的共同体，习近平主席提出要建设地区和世界的命运共同体。推动命运共同体建设有中国传统思想理念的基础，

中国古人就有追求天下太平的美好理念。所谓命运共同体，就是大家和平友好相处，一起考虑生存发展的环境，一起协商合作。如果按这样的理想，这样的理念来努力，或许就能避免战争，让人类进入新的文明时代，这是最好的结果。

我们也要看到，世界正处在大变革时期。这个大变革，有多重含义。一个是世界上国家力量对比转变，大国实力对比发生重大调整。从整体看，二战以后到今天，世界最大的变化，是发展中国家群体崛起，它们如今已经占了世界经济总量的半壁江山，用购买力平价（PPP）计算占的比例更大。从现在到2050年期间，未来发展潜力最大的应该是发展中经济体，中国、印度、印度尼西亚、巴西，等等，将改变发达国家主导世界经济的局面。另一个是发展方式的转变，对大多数发展中国家来说，目前还不能进入后工业化，发展中国家需要有新的发展理念，走可持续的发展道路。在今后的发展中，全球问题越来越突出，其中，影响最大的可能是气候变化。巴黎气候大会达成阻止全球变暖的共识。从这次会达成的协议可以看得很清楚，面对共同的命运挑战，最大转变就是大家都把承担责任放在首位。气候、资源、市场、规则等，以"责任"为前提的这样一种全球治理，恐怕是影响未来世界发展的一个大趋势。同时，由新的技术引领的新产业革命正在深入、扩散，信息化、智能化、新能源、太空等，这将会产生两个效果：一是创造经济发展的新动力，让世界经济进入新的发展期；二是改变经济增长的结构，节能、环保、高效率的经济部门获得快速增长。这些都会影响极大地影响未来世界的发展。

在这个转变过程中，中国作为实现民族复兴的大国，可以发挥很大的作用，有大的作为。前不久我访问伊朗，有一位神学院的教授提出，"伊朗重视的不仅仅是中国的经济，更重视的是其为世界提供了另一种不同的选择"。这个说法很有意义。目前，世界好像只有一种被认可的西方民主体制是好的，它成了一个坐标，不同于它的就是不好的。中国实行不同于西方的政治体制，如果发展成功，就可以提供另外一种不同的成功模式，供世界选择。这个变化很大，意义很深远，关键是中国自己要做好，让和谐哲学，亲、诚、惠、容的精神和公平、正义、文明的原则成为新的普世价值观。

在我看来，预测2050年，最值得重视的是那些我们难以看得清的大变数。世界未来最大的变数到底是什么？最重要的就是不确定性。不确定性表现在各个方面，有经济的、政治的、全球的，也有地区的。在任何未来的规划中，要把变数，即不确定性的因素作为非常重要的影响变量考虑进去。也就是说，面临这样一个世界大转变，不确定性增加的局面，我们要做几个不同的方案。

显然，我们规划上海的未来，要有几个维度：中国大趋势、世界大趋势、新的竞争大趋势，还有就是未知领域的可能趋势。从经济发展的角度来分析，今后几年还会处于结构性的调整期，因此，上海要走在结构转型的前头，成为带头兵，实现脱胎换骨。从竞争力来分析，上海要形成在高度开放形势下的新的竞争优势，做领先部门的竞争优胜者。

作为一个面向未来的城市，上海总体思路上要向创新型、智慧型、宜居型的方向努力，打造上海的新吸引力。创新型是上海未来发展的动力，开放创新，成为创新思想与技术的源头地；智慧型是上海打造领先优势的关键，充分利用信息化、网络化、高技术构建高效率的城市管理和运行体系；宜居型是上海未来的吸引力所在，一个城市的未来吸引力主要是体现在能为居住着提供宜居（绿色、方便、多样、丰富）的综合环境。

未来的上海，究竟是一个什么样的概念？我认为应该是"大规模城市—小结构城区—多维度空间"。说到未来的上海，到底是像纽约、伦敦，还是东京？上海就是上海，要有自己的特色与形象。总体看，要实现由生产型城市到服务型城市的转变，由制造中心到创新中心的转变。未来上海的定位应分三步考虑：2020（国家全面小康）、2030（国家总体经济实力第一）、2050（建成发达国家），在这"三步走"的进程中，上海要走在前面。

2050 年的上海——全球领先的创新城市

汪 颖

普华永道亚太区零售消费品税务主管合伙人

当今全球化和信息化加快发展，各国日益成为交融的命运共同体，同时也面临着更加纷繁复杂的全球性挑战。上海正在贯彻中央政府实施国家创新驱动战略，力争在 2030 年前建成具有全球影响力的科技创新中心。而面对上海市政府"面向未来 30 年的上海"的研究，站在今天的我们，憧憬 2050 年的上海，她将是一个全球领先的创新城市。

据联合国发布的人口报告，在 20 世纪 50 年代，全世界只有不到 30% 的人口居住在城市。目前，这一比例已上升到 50%，到 2030 年，联合国预测，将有 49 亿人成为城市居民。而到 2050 年，全世界的城市人口将增加约 72%。来自农村地区的大规模人口迁移，将是城市人口增长的主要驱动因素。在发达经济体城市和发展中经济体的老城市当中，随着人口的增长，基础设施方面面临的压力，都将达到甚至超过极限水平。与此同时，在新兴经济体当中，新兴城市将迅速崛起，并要求在智能型基础设施方面进行大规模投资，以适应爆炸式增长。我们预计这将对上海产生以下诸多影响：

（1）许多分析人士认为，随着特大城市在扩张广度和数量方面的增长，由于它们的规模庞大，其力量不亚于一个中小型国家。

（2）在城市基础设施方面，将必须兴建更多大型项目（如机场、港口等），以支持新的贸易流动，并且满足教育、医疗、保障、就业等方面的需求。

（3）城市人口的高度集中，信息获取和社交媒体的发展速度增加。

由此，我们的建议是：

（1）日渐高度密集的中心城区已不能再简单扩张，城区建设逐渐从劳动密集型转向智慧密集型，从工业经济转向服务经济。

（2）按照长三角城市群分工协作和上海建设世界级城市的要求，构建互动融合的城乡建设格局，更高层次地打造长三角世界级城市群。

（3）坚持对城市历史风貌进行保护，使"海纳百川"的上海城市文化特色得以延续，提升城市品位，塑造城市精神。

（4）政府如何管理一个庞大的城市，如何保证政务的公开透明、及时有效，如何与市民互动，使上海既经典又创新。

我国经济发展进入新常态，依靠要素驱动和资源消耗支撑的发展方式难以为继，我们必须全面增强自主创新能力，努力打造代表中国参与全球经济科技合作与竞争的科技创新中心，在新一轮全球科技竞争中赢得战略主动。我们觉得，上海已发展到没有创新就不能前进的阶段，我们必须依靠以科技创新为核心的全面创新，重构城市发展动力、激发全社会创新创造活力。

在我们看来，完成这个愿景会涉及诸多成功因素，尤其在三个领域内的卓然进展将对实现全球领先的创新城市这个使命至关重要——它们分别是：优化的产业格局、智慧的投资策略和有效的人才延揽。

1. 产业格局

上海业已成为世界经济中心，其支柱企业成员包括国有企业（SOEs）、民营企业（POEs）和跨国企业（MNCs）。而建立一个能够更优化地连结三种不同性质企业集群间纽带的社区将对上海的创新生态构成极佳推动。企业间的互为授粉——尤其是创新企业在建立之初，若能获得来自成熟企业的业务专长、流程效率和关系网络，将使它拥有明显的发展优势。

要成为全球领先的创新城市，我们必须开拓国际视野，借鉴先进经验。在这方面，纽约市提供了一个范例。华尔街大公司和纽约市当局建立了伙伴关系，出高级管理人员来给创业者提供教练支持，乃至分享客户体系。上海拥有大量来自世界各地的顶尖管理人才，因此像纽约一样建立一个"上海伙伴计划"是可行的，借此在商业领袖与创业企业家、创新公司之间形成纽带，鼓励前者将专长与洞见传授给下一代创新者，将产生不可估量的价值。

同时值得指出的是，国有企业为上海 GDP 贡献了半壁江山，它们引领创新的影响力不容低估。上海的主政者也将在优化未来的产业格局中扮演重要角色，因为一个有助于国企、民企和外企三个支柱企业社群都能获得优化的运营效率的产业环境是所有企业希冀看到的。而且真正的创新成果需要十年或更长的时间显现，因此建立一套有利于绩效和创新相协同的评估体系尤为重要。当这样的绩效评估体系建立起来，无论是机构层面，还是员工个人层面，都会形成趋向于向创新作贡献的行为与绩效标杆。

除了优化企业间的纽带，上海还将从众多创新支持机构（如孵化器）中获得收益。尽管建立更多数量的孵化器依然有其必要性，但更为重要的是，应加紧提升上海的宣介与推广，使其吸引到全球最顶尖的孵化器入驻。成熟企业的内部创新孵化也将造就大量机遇：鼓励"企业内创新"会催生众多小型团队致力于创新事业。因此，对于"在哪里孵化、如何孵化"等需持一种灵活开放态度。

综上，未来当上海在国企、民企、外企和初创公司四者之间形成共生共荣、连结紧密的产业格局和生态圈之时，她也将在建立具有国际影响力创新中心的进程中取得独特竞争优势。

2. 投资策略

初始建立的企业无疑需要资金支持，而上海拥有极佳的风险投资（VC）和私募股权（PE）资本的供给，当务之急则是需要有一个优化的市场发现和投资的机制存在。而所谓"创新"，其涵盖的要义是多维度的——可包括技术、产品和服务、流程以及管理创新诸多方面。无论初创公司或成熟企业都有创新发生的土壤。但上海风投资金往往面临很多"快速退出"的机会和诱惑，因此它们致力于支持"突破性创新"的决心和动力不如其他一些世界经济中心强烈。

上海需要引进风险投资专才来运作早期投资，使具有潜力的创新项目释放最大能效。培育能够发现"下一个引爆点"式的创新（尤其是能进行产业化的技术创新）的专才是重要任务。这本身需要时间，同时机遇和风险也是并存的。企业需要认识到对通向创新之路上的失败应该得到宽容。

上海的发展不必受限于城市地理边界。出于运营成本考虑而投资到周边卫星城市的企业在成长到一定规模之后依然有可能落户上海，这将使上海最终获益。同样，区域间的互荣连结也将助于推动垂直产业领域的枢纽中心诞生，例如生物医药、物流、金融等领域。

3. 人才储备

人才对创新的重要性毋庸讳言。如今上海已拥有很好的大学和研究实验室——很多领域内的专长达到国际水准。而若要打造国际级经济中心，上海需要更大规模的人才库。依托技术发展的支持，上海完全可以开拓创新式的延揽五湖四海乃至全球各地人才的举措，包括建立和拓展虚拟人才库等。

上海政府已经出台一系列户籍改革使八方人才更容易落户本地，同时在城市空间设计上的优化也将利于吸引新来者。例如，发展更多公共休闲活动区域、文化设施，建设安全城区、高质量的学校和教育设施等，都会吸引更多投资者及其全家在此安居。另外，创新和创业（"双创"）往往相互关联：上海市政府在推动双创中鼓励高校研究人员创业、大学生在其中兼职实习等。上述多维度的举措不仅有利于培育和发展人才，也有助吸引更多来自其他城市或国家的"新上海人"入驻。

使命与愿景都已建立，上海将从长远而前瞻的视角矢志不渝地构建四个中心，并迎接个中挑战（包括市场和技术发展、法规法制等）。需特别指出的是，上海所面临的机遇也是独特的：在国企、民企和跨国企业三鼎之支持体系中打通任督二脉、共生互荣地支持初创公司以及创新企业；并且，抱着"创新不问出处"（在成熟企业内同样孵化创新）、建立市场发现和投资创新的机制、提升人才规模，等等，所有都将助推上海完成建设具有国际影响力创新中心的伟大宏图与使命。

韩正书记提出了上海在实现创新中心的过程中分两步走的规划，即2020年前形成科创中心基本框架体系，2030年形成科技创新中心城市的核心功能，到了2050年上海成为世界领先的创新城市。营造一个良好的创业和投资环境，吸引全球多元化人才入驻本市是上海在迈向建设领先创新城市这一美好愿景的重中之重。在此过程中，机遇和困难必将并存，我们憧憬未来也不惧怕挑战．上海必须坚持以人为本，科技创新，走城市可持续发展之路。让我们共同祝愿上海成为创新发展的领头羊，续写城市发展新篇章。

2050 年的上海——具有全球影响力的文化与思想策源传播"中心"

叶 华

野村综研（上海）咨询有限公司董事长

本届峰会的主题是上海 2050 年愿景，题目非常有意义，同时极具挑战性。我们无法精准预测 35 年后的上海，因此需要大胆畅想。

我所畅想的 2050 年的上海，应该是具有全球影响力的文化与思想的策源传播"中心"。但是，我不知道今后文化和思想的策源与传播是否具有中心性，能不能形成中心，该不该称为中心。所以在我的题目中，"中心"一词暂且打了引号。

为什么提出文化和思想的策源传播"中心"？或许很多人会认为这是一个非常"虚"的目标。为了畅想今后的 35 年，应该回顾过去的 35 年。所以，我从过去 35 年中野村集团面向上海市政府提起的一些重大建议的例子谈起，看看上海不断迈向更高目标的轨迹。

1. 20 世纪七八十年代：提出建立具有全国影响力的"开放窗口"

1978 年，野村集团面向国家经委和上海市政府，提出应在中国大陆的经济中心城市中，率先建立能够快速实现对外经济开放，集聚外国资本和技术的"特殊开放区域"，上海应是首选。1979 年，上海虹桥经济技术开发区开始规划，并于 1986 年成为第一批 14 个国家级经济技术开发区之一，是中国最早和唯一专注于现代服务业的，也是面积最小的国家级开发区。1984 年，为了让在上海"创业"的海外与境外公司及外国业务人员有临时的工作和生活环境，野村集团与上海市政府合作，投资建设上海花园饭店，于 1985 年开工，1990 年开业。

2. 1989—2015 年：25 次面向上海市长的年度建议

上海是非常开放、愿意听取和吸收国际各种层面声音的城市。1988 年，当时的上海市市长朱镕基倡导建立一个让全球有影响力的企业家向上海献计献策的国际化咨询平台，"上海市市长国际企业家咨询会议"（IBLAC）应运而生。1989 年 10 月 9 日，IBLAC 召开筹备会，野村集团代表提议每年聚焦一个上海市在发展过程中凸显的核心问题进行集中的开放式讨论，并在之后的 25 次年会上发表咨询建议。在整个 27 届年会中，不乏面向未来的主题。如 1997 年的"上海如何面向 21 世纪"、2002 年的"如何把上海建设成一个世界级城市"、2013 年的"如何提升上海城市软实力"等。

3. 2004 年：提出打造浦东"科技创新副中心"

2004 年，野村综研受浦东新区政府委托，开展浦东新区"十一五"规划重大课题研究，旨在对浦东新区的发展机遇和挑战进行梳理的基础上，提出今后 5—10 年的战略发展目标。我们提出浦东应为上海建设全球城市而提升自身的国际级功能和水平，通过国内外和区内外的广泛的协同合作实现优势互补，为保持持续的全球竞争力而着力培育创新精神与环境。提

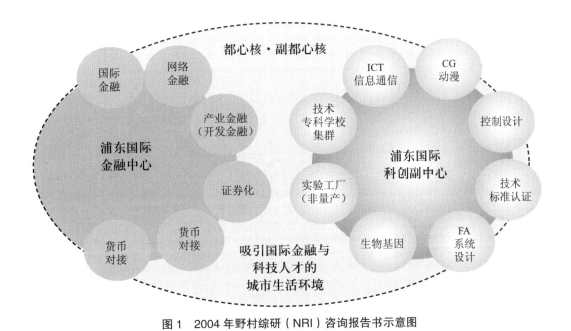

图 1　2004 年野村综研（NRI）咨询报告书示意图

出浦东在建设国际金融中心的同时，应注重打造国际科技创新中心功能，并在上海市的城市功能与空间结构上，形成"浦东国际科创副中心"。因为当时的首要目标毫无疑问是建设国际金融中心，但金融和科技、金融和ICT是密不可分的，因此提出了"副中心"的概念。

4. 2009 年：提出形成"四个中心"基础上的"三个中心"

2009 年，野村综研受上海市政府委托，开展上海市"十二五"规划重大课题研究，旨在明确上海初步实现"四个中心"路径的基础上，提出2020 年上海的战略发展目标。我们认为面向 2020 年，上海应该开始进入从"物质资本到制度资本的蜕变"，从"流量革命到存量革命的蜕变"，进而面向从"内容影响力到精神影响力的蜕变"。如果上海不能在精神层面和思想层面有大作为的话，上海也许永远不会是一个真正的世界级城市。我们提出的上海 2020 年的发展目标是：在初步建成"四个中心"以及以"金融为基础的服务经济格局"的基础上，初步形成"全球创新城市、世界文化城市、国际责任城市"。这是和上海的城市精神、价值取向相吻合的。

面向 2050 年，时间跨度很大，中间会出现什么巨大变革，会发生什么颠覆性的、非连续性的变化，我们无法预料。但是，不管发生什么变化，具有全球影响力的城市，必须被具有全球影响力的人才所认可、选择和喜爱。

我举一个例子来说明现在的上海是如何被认可和选择的。

森纪念财团和上海的专家合作，每年编制《世界城市综合排名》。这个排名的特点是做了很多采访，从而区分出上海对不同人群的吸引力是什么样的？（见表 1）表中的数字越小，代表吸引力越大。对企业家而言，上海是非常繁荣、有经济活力的城市；而根据研究人员、艺术家，特别是生活者的反馈，上海的吸引力则并不突出。

表 1 2015 年世界主要城市综合实力分类排名

	企业家	研究者	艺术家	观光客	生活者
纽约	4	1	2	3	3
伦敦	1	2	3	1	2
东京	8	3	8	6	8
上海	7	26	14	8	31

资料来源：森纪念财团城市战略研究《世界城市综合排名》，2015 年。

一个城市若要被具有全球影响力的人才所认可、选择和喜爱，就必须始终具备一些非常基本的东西。越想谋长远，就越需回归本源。回归本源，就是不断地夯实基础，不然就没有未来。城市是不是足够安全、生活是不是足够安心、社会是不是足够安定？这些不管是面向10年、20年、30年，都是至关重要的。

基于以上的回顾和思考，我提出一张上海面向2050年的愿景畅想图（见图2）。

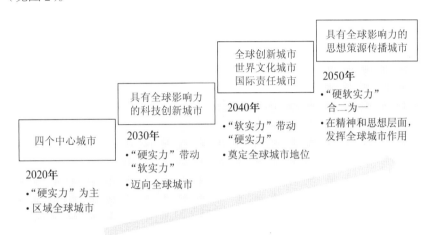

图2　上海面向2050年的愿景畅想图

2020年，上海实现"四个中心"的目标，在面向2020年这个阶段，主要以强化硬实力为主；2030年，硬实力已经发展到可以带动软实力的阶段，迈向全球城市；2040年，上海在创新、文化、责任上，能起到全球影响作用，软实力已经发展到可以带动硬实力的阶段；2050年，上海的软硬实力融为一体，成为屹立于世界城市之林的、具有全球影响力的文化与思想策源传播"中心"。

2050 年的上海——第一个全球性的 21 世纪城市

谢祖墀

高风咨询董事长

上海未来发展的定位该如何？ 2050 年的上海会变成一个怎么样的城市？在此我想跟大家分享一本最近一位美国人凯文·凯利所写的新书《必然》。在座有不少的人知道凯文·凯利，他在硅谷工作长达 30 多年之久，一直在观察、分析科技的发展是什么，他毫无疑问是该方面的权威。不少中国的创业家尤其是在互联网和科技方面的创业家都把他奉为科技之神，他对未来的科技的潮流把握都非常准确，这本书全球第一版在中国 2015 年 12 月率先以中文出版，早于美国的英文版。故此它不仅仅是一本书，是宣布了一个新时代的来临。科技方面的创业家也是面对新时代的来临，这个来临也跟近日在乌镇举行的"世界互联网大会"相关，很多谈到的问题，节奏以及我们谈到的论调都是跟我们的目标是非常相似的。其实我们看到一个新的时代的来临，尤其是更有冲刺力、更有信心的互联网时代的来临。对凯文·凯利这本书的内容，我做了一个简单的总结：我们目前看到的，在全球，在中国发现有这些重要的事情，"形成、流通、共享、追踪、使用、互动、屏读、重混、过滤、知化、提问、开始"，很多读者对于这些词语有的可能理解，有的可能还不太理解，因为里面很多阐述的知识都影响了我们日常工作和生活的方方面面。

我个人之前就做过思考，2050 年上海究竟是什么样的情景，其实每个人都不会很清楚，但是我们每个人都应该想一下，在 35 年之后，到时候中国毫无疑问是最大的经济体；到时候人民币与美元毫无疑问是全世界流通量最大的两种货币，同时，我觉得在其他的方面，全世界都能互联沟通，无处不在，人工智能非常普遍，我们人与人、物与物之间的物理距离大幅缩小，现在还是有很多不是以知识工作者为主导的职业，但是我估计到时会有大量的知识工作者出现，而且他们工作的能力和创造力是很强的。到时我们的资源非常分散，但是在分散之余又非常集中；到时全球的技能变得复杂，这句话可以这么理解，也就是说在人与人的社区里，从物理的层面来说人与人之间是分开的，但是在虚拟的世界里我们又因为新科技的发展和产生聚在一起。人类的寿命将大幅增长，目前根据权威数据人类的平均寿命为80多岁，我觉得到时候人类的寿命平均延长到100岁将不是梦。

中国人将会经历历史上一个伟大的起航时刻，从现在起持续到未来几十年，在这个大前提之下，新常态下的中国我觉得将会具备以下几个因素：企业家精神和创新意识；中产阶级和精英阶层为代表的思想文化启迪；中国政治的演变将会与中国的大环境以及中国与世界其他国家和地区的关系保持同步；未来30—50年可能是中国复兴的黄金时代。

中国的优秀人才，其实不断在反省，究竟我们是谁，我们中国人，究竟是谁。在习近平主席主政期间，未来中国将更开放更自信。未来的35年后上海究竟将成为一个什么样的全球性21世纪的大城市，我觉得大概是以下情况，虽然不一定完整或正确，但是我们可以从多方面去描述它。我觉得我们的文化、社会、科技、大环境、小环境，以及我们自己，都在这个过程里。一个全新的21世纪的城市，其实应该是追求精神层面方面的发展，也就是说所谓价值观的建立，这种价值观的建立不但是中国的，也是全球的。另外一点，政府将会扮演怎样的角色？35年后上海会建立一种新的生态和环境，政府的角色将会是促进、投资和参与。我觉得在这个过程里面，我们在共同做的事情，也就是追求"上海梦"，我们的"上海梦"其实是"中国梦"的一部分，"中国梦"也是"全球梦"的一部分。我们要追求我们的责任，要成为有意识、有责任的上海的创新的市民，同时我们所有的上海市民终将会成为我们的全球公民。

2050 年的上海——从经济金融中心到人才中心

琼安娜

中国欧盟商会上海总经理

感谢今天有此机会，与现场这么多的学者和专业人士一起分享大家对上海 2050 年的发展期望和愿景。这是一件令人激动又充满挑战的任务。令人激动是因为我们有幸出席，为设计上海的未来贡献一份力。充满挑战则是因为，在这样一个瞬息万变的世界，要想预言未来 35 年的商业和生活变化，是非常困难的，就像 10 年前我们根本想不到智能手机购物能像如今这样普遍。

但我们相信，虽然周围环境不断变化，但是有些事物恒定不变，那就是人们对繁荣、安全、充实的生活的永恒追求。从城市的角度来看，一个城市要想可持续发展，就必须提供一个稳定的宜居环境和多种发展机遇，吸引人才聚集。一个城市的成功发展可能依赖其自然禀赋和经济竞争力，但它最终还是要依赖居民的智慧。

过去的 30 年，上海一直是不可替代的国家经济和金融中心。由于中国在全球经济中的崛起，并将自身优势与新机遇相结合，如今的上海正大步向一个国际经济、金融、航运和贸易中心转变，我们相信，这一目标将在 2020 年之前达成。目前中国不断向价值链上游移动，上海要在 2020 年之前成为全球科创中心这一计划也让我们倍感激动。根据整体发展态势，预计上海将在 2050 年发展成为占据全球价值链顶端的全球人才中心。

中国的两位数经济增速时代已经过去了，在不久的将来也不太可能再次出现。现在的中国已经进入"新常态"这一新时期。这意味着我们必须适应逐渐放缓的经济增长速度。同时，这也意味着中国正在摆脱以往的出口导向型增长模式，在全球经济中重新定位自己。上海试点自贸区的建立为上海"四个中心""四个率先"的目标实现提供崭新的动力。一系列的政府管理精简化，贸易便利化和金融自由化政策已经生效，预计未来还将有更多政策出台。上海市政府致力于在 2020 年之前，将上海建设成科学和创新中心，到时，我们将看到一个为创新企业提供资金、技术支持，营造法治环境，制定人才政策的创新型企业友好城市。

但是，上海这一过渡过程充满挑战，改革也绝非坦途。2015 年 4 月，李克强总理曾说道，"旧动力减弱，新动力不足"。上海正在努力寻找新的发展动力。我们今年对上海的 600 家企业进行了商业信心调查，40% 的企业表示 2015 年企业盈利没有增加，有的甚至低于去年。四分之一的企业不看好未来两年盈利前景。这样一来，寻求扩大中国区业务的公司将会更少。因此，上海迫切需要在未来五年，即在"十三五"规划期间，加快推进改革计划和行动议程的实施。

未来 35 年上海可持续发展的关键是如何实现 2020 年上海既定发展目标，利用好流入的资金、贸易和信息流，进一步鼓励创新发展和人才吸引。根据我们的观察和研究，提出以下几点建议：

首先，促进创新的非常重要的一点是为所有竞争者提供一个公平、开放的竞争环境。创新有一个综合性生命周期。它从研发资金投入开始，经过试生产，批量生产，最后以消费和再投资结束。诚然，融资是创新的第一步，对中小企业尤为重要。但是，我们往往过分强调融资，而低估整个创新产品的生产和销售的重要性。说到生产和销售，就会涉及市场准入的问题。

虽然中国（上海）自由贸易试验区对国外投资商已实施负面清单制度，对确保更广泛的市场准入是长足的进步，但我们仍然发现，还有很多的市场准入壁垒存在，使国外竞争者与国内竞争者的竞争优势不平衡。除了这些针对国外投资者的壁垒，我们还发现，在获得资金和与政府互动方面，大型国有企业相对中小企业优势明显。在欧洲，中小企业是经济健康可持续发展的"支柱"，因为它们能够灵活应用新技术、新模式，不断寻求创新商业解决方案。因此，如果一个市场拒绝民营中小企业，就是在拒绝创新。长远来看，这种市场模式将阻碍经济的发展。

其次，除了开放市场准入，政府的激励措施和法律法规的制定对于促进创新和吸引人才来讲，也非常重要。具体来讲，为了产品研发，上海需要营造一个更为友好的环境和实施更为严格的知识产权保护法律法规，需要有独立的法院，配备专业知识扎实的法官，从而让投资商和个体确信，不论是知识产权，还是商业和其他法律纠纷，他们的权利都会得到保护。

我们的众多成员企业表示，中国，尤其是上海，有能力可以吸引更多欧洲企业来华投资，来华企业的研发能力也仍有提升空间。根据我们今年的调查，具备全球研发中心的企业中，68%没有中国研发中心，而位于中国的欧洲企业的研发中心，42%主要用于产品本地化。与此同时，我们的会员企业还表示，外资企业在中国申请高新科技企业身份受限，对于参加国家资助的发展项目也同样受限。

因此，外资企业也就无缘国家资金支持，也不能充分促进中国和上海的创新举措。如果没有外资公司的参与，上海要想转型成为一个国际创新中心，是不现实的。

知识产权保护法的执行对创新型企业的生存也至关重要。上海市政府为知识产权保护法的实施和切实执行作出很多重大举措，中国欧盟商会对此也非常欢迎。虽然这些举措的切实影响还有待评估，但已经建立的专门的知识产权法院和知识产权监管机构，已经为知识产权保护法（包括专利、商标和版权）的实施和切实执行提供了一站式的便利服务。这是个好兆头，表明上海在为创新提供必要的保障措施，这个政策方向是正确的。

第三，在吸收人才方面，上海也出台了新的出入境管理法规，包括为外籍技术人才放宽签证制度。这一政策也是朝正确的方向迈进。但是，有些对于年轻从业者的政策，仍然过于保守：如果外籍毕业生不具备两年工作经验，则必须是中国本土大学毕业，才有资格申请外国专家签证。这也就是说，国外大学毕业的外籍人才必须具备两年工作经验才能来华工作。至今还没有迹象显示上海会签发外国实习生签证，这样一来，还没从业的外国毕业生也就没有机会接触了解中国的文化、就业市场情况和商业环境。我们明白，劳动力市场政策不可避免会对国外应届毕业生在华就业提出一定的限制。但这样一来，一些公司希望吸引国外最优秀的人才加入他们中国的研发业务的计划就受到了阻碍。这些国外实习生只是暂时来上海工作，不会和中国毕业生抢工作。

如果你有机会参观大企业和学校的科研实验室或科研机构，就会发现，这些地方最大的一个特点，就是多元化的科研团队。这是因为，实现创新的最自然的环境，就是不同年龄、不同文化、不同民族背景的人才汇聚一起，大家在知识、经验和创造力上取长补短。如果上海想要实现在2020年转型成为全球创新中心的远大目标，就要坚定不移的加快技能型人才的签证政策的改革步伐，尽快扩大签发范围。例如，可以签发一种特殊的签证类型，让年轻的外籍科学家和研究人员能来华工作，让外籍科学家能来华参与短期的联合研发合作项目。只有外来人才能够轻松来沪、居住、工作，上海才有能力在 2050 年发展成为人才高地。

最后，就是我们的很多成员企业都提到的网速和一些网站的访问权限问题。2015 年 5 月的一次成员企业调查中，57% 的企业认为，网络速度慢和一些网站访问权限受限对公司业务造成了负面影响。虽然像百度和新浪这样的中国主流网站网页加载速度很稳定，但公司职员在访问许多国外网站时，还是有网速过慢或不稳定的情况。更具体地讲，企业信心调查中的24% 的受访企业表示，网速过慢降低了办公、研发和生产效率，31% 的受访企业表示无法检索信息，科研活动受到影响。

全球搜索引擎对科研和创新发展十分必要，而其访问权限也受到限制。这些网络限制影响了个人和企业的新产品、新技术和新工艺的研发，无法跟进全球发展动态。网络限制也阻碍上海吸引更多人才，因很多优秀研究人员因为网络限制，很难搜索到开展相关工作的学术论文，对此颇为反感，不愿来沪工作。事实上，中国网络问题一直没有得到改善。全球网络速度平均峰值排名中，中国 2014 年已经从第 96 位下降到第 113 位。这不仅会对上海研发工作的进行产生负面影响，还会对上海的总体经济发展形成阻碍。

严格的移民政策、网络限制，以及本周又出现的污染问题，使得上海虽然拥有优良的基础设施，也无法成为国际顶尖科学家们工作的首选城市。

总结来说，作为上海这个美丽城市 2400 万居民中的一员，我们很荣幸能够见证上海转型为全球金融、贸易和创新中心。我们相信，上海将在2050 年成为一个更加宜居，对跨国企业和国际人才更为开放的城市。与此同时，我们也知道，要想实现这些目标，还有很多工作要做。但是我们相信，上海市政府将采取正确的应对措施，推进前瞻性的政策的执行。中国欧盟商会，协同我们的成员企业，将做好充分准备，支持并推动上海 2050宏伟目标的实现，与各方共同努力，为目标的进一步制定和实施贡献自己的力量。

2050 年的上海——全球最健康的城市

吴人伟

强生中国主席

　　作为医疗健康产业的代表，我今天想和大家一起展望一下 2050 年上海医疗健康事业的发展愿景。事实上，强生一直在关注民众的健康水平，并持之以恒地为推动上海医疗健康水平的提高作出积极的贡献。

　　谈到 2050 年上海的健康愿景，我曾经问强生的员工，让他们描绘一下他们想象的 2050 年的健康生活将是一个怎样的景象。其中，一位 90 后同事的回答非常有意思，启发了我很多的思考。

　　他是这样描述的：2050 年的一天，上海将举行第 55 届国际马拉松赛。上海国际马拉松赛已经成为国际的顶尖赛事。当时，他已经年近六旬，作为一个长跑爱好者，他已经和几个朋友一起报名，参加上海马拉松业余选手的比赛。那天起床后，可穿戴设备根据最近的睡眠质量和身体状况，以及当天的天气情况，包括风速、气温、湿度等指标，告诉他非常适合参加比赛。（当然，我相信，2050 年上海的天气状况里，已经排除了空气污染的指标。）虽然在业余选手的比赛里，我的这位同事也没有拿到名次，但他还是开心顺利地完成了比赛。比赛结束后，他马上联系他的健康管理师询问自己的健康状况，医生通过可穿戴设备传来的实时健康状况监测信息，及个人历史健康档案，告诉他当时的身体状况非常良好，并提供他高强度运动后的专业健康建议。

　　在描述里，他还提到，到了 2050 年，健康管理师可以通过远程医疗，为民众提供各方面的健康咨询和有效预测患特定疾病的几率。比如说，对于糖尿病、冠心病及有肺癌家族患病史的高危人群提供健康管理咨询，并提供科学的健康饮食建议。由于医疗技术的进步，实施了有效的健康管理，上海在 2050 年已经成为全球最健康的城市。

　　听完他的故事，我想了很多（我也快 60 岁了），主要在想为了实现这一美好的愿景，我们现在应该怎么做？到 2020 年或 2030 年，上海应该实现什么样的目标?

我认为,上海已经完全有条件推动以下几个方面的工作:

首先,上海应建设覆盖全体市民的健康管理体系。健康管理体系在未来医疗卫生系统中扮演一个很重要的角色。上海可通过社区健康管理中心与大型医疗中心相结合的综合健康管理体系,充分利用大数据,从疾病预防、早期诊断、健康指数监测、疾病治疗到康复护理为市民提供全生命周期的照护,更有效地提高医疗资源利用效率、降低医疗成本,惠及民生。比如说:我们可以为每位市民在社区健康管理中心建立个人健康档案数据库,实施分级诊疗制度,使市民的健康管理将变得非常便利;我们可以通过社区健康管理中心和社会公益组织,对市民饮食、锻炼、生活习惯进行提醒和干预,向市民提倡更为健康的生活方式;我们可以通过免费接种疫苗、定期检查,以实现疾病的早期预防,因为疾病预防是市民健康管理的核心;我们可以通过可穿戴设备提供的实时健康监测数据及个人健康大数据分析,由社区健康管理中心的专业健康管理师提供实时的健康建议。

其次,上海应建立多层次的医疗保障体系,政府提供覆盖全市人民的基本医疗保险,同时充分利用商业健康保险,以覆盖基本医疗保险以外的部分支出,使患者能够得到更多的便利和服务,满足不同层次的医疗需求。同时结合医疗救助体系,降低人民群众对医疗费用的负担。2014年,上海个人自付比例平均为33.9%,我们希望到2050年,这个比例可以降低到10%。

在基本医保的投入方面,政府可以逐渐加大对医疗的投入,提升医疗总费用所占GDP的比重。另外,由于社区健康管理中心的预防和健康管理做得好,政府医疗费用将着重于预防而不是治疗,从而提高投入的效率。我们应该鼓励并监管商业健康保险的发展。比如,为市民购买商业健康保险提供税收优惠。我们还应该促进医疗保险对医院的医疗行为的干预,以进一步提高医院管理效率。

第三,上海应积极推动创新药品和创新治疗方法的广泛使用。上海将建设成为科技创新中心,创新药品和治疗方案的广泛应用带给患者的价值不可估量,这不仅能帮助患者更快、更方便地获取创新医药,同时也能够为上海医疗行业的创新带来更多的活力与可能。

上海可以通过与国家药品注册部门的合作,采用WHO优良审查实践(GRP)和ICH药品全球法规的指南及申报技术要求,在风险评估基础上,简化临床试验申请资料的要求,合格的新药在12个月内可以批准上市,与美国和欧盟同步，确保上海市民在疾病治疗过程中可以享有全球同步的创新药物和治疗方法。

在建设具有全球影响力科技创新中心战略的指导下，上海应积极推动创新生态环境的建设，鼓励开放式创新模式。政府应加大对基础研究领域的投入，强化上海作为创新源头的科研实力，并且制定相关的激励政策，激发市场的创新。尤其对于干细胞培养、3D 打印用于人工器官移植，基因测序，分子诊断用于早期预防和诊断，精准医疗、个性化治疗用于疾病治疗等 21 世纪创新技术，政府应该从资金、政策上给予大力支持。

另外，我们应该制定相应的政策，以鼓励创新，支持创新产品的开发。比如，参照其他国家的经验，采取基于创新程度的定价方法，对于创新药品给予高溢价鼓励，以调动创新的积极性；为保护创新成果和创新产品，建立有效的知识产权保护机制。

最后，上海应更为合理地配置医护人员数量，大幅提高医护人员的工作技能和地位。上海将能创造一个为医护人员的发展和执业环境提供便利的环境。随着多点执业真正开展，医护人员拥有多个执业场所，其职业成就感得到提高，同时有助于吸引优秀人才，扩充专业医疗从业人员的储备。医生和护士的福利待遇需要与他们的付出相吻合，尊重其市场价值，随着人口的老龄化，对医护人员，特别是护士的需求会大大提高。例如，护士的人数由 2012 年每万人 15 名左右，提高到 2050 年每万人超过 115 名护士（这是老龄化社会日本 2012 年的数字），不仅加强医疗护理，更要加强社区健康管理中心的预防、健康管理和老年照顾等工作。由于医护人员的数量增加、工作和沟通能力的提高，以及医疗保险制度的完善，使医患之间能够建立和谐的关系。

要做好以上几个方面的工作，需要政府各部门之间，以及政府、企业和医疗机构等各方形成共识，齐心协力，共同将 2050 年的上海建设成为全球最健康的城市。

强生植根中国 30 年，无论是过去、现在还是将来，都将全力以赴地推动上海乃至中国的医疗健康事业的发展。

展望未来，我们认为，一个更健康的未来，离不开创新。因此，强生正积极为上海成为具有全球影响力的科创中心献计献策。2014 年底强生在上海建立了亚太创新中心，该创新中心是强生深化外部合作战略的主要窗口。强生密切与创新企业、学术和科研机构，以及优秀人才的合作，通过提供资金、专业知识和技术，加速将雏形创新转化为医学临床应用的新产品和治疗方案，在满足中国市场需求的同时，将源自中国的创新推向国际市场。

前面我提到，早期预防和诊断对于提高疾病的治愈率功不可没，强生也正在此方面积极探索，结合医疗器材和制药领域的专长，研发出变革性的创新诊断方案。强生将在中国建立全球肺癌研究中心，从疾病预防、诊断和精准治疗三个方面，以病患为中心，研发整体创新解决方案。我国肺癌发病率每年增长 26.9%，肺癌已成为我国首位恶性肿瘤死亡原因。我们希望以更便捷高效的方式，让高危人群可以定期地进行精准的筛查，最终使肺癌成为一个可预防、可治愈的疾病，造福病患，减轻其对中国社会的健康威胁。

在帮助上海建立多层次的医疗保障体系方面，强生就中国健康筹资机制和商业健康保险与国家有关机构共同开展研究，以满足患者对不同层次健康需求。

另外，在提升社会对医护人员的尊重方面，强生启动了"健康社会"项目，以表彰对人民健康作出突出贡献的医生和护士。

前不久，我在一本医学期刊上看到一项新的研究成果，指出中国人的平均寿命大大延长，2015 年比 1990 年时平均延长了 8 年半，上海市民的平均寿命已达到 82 岁。如果我们能够建立完善的健康管理体系，加之各方的积极努力，我相信人们的预期寿命在未来还能够继续延长。到 2050 年，我的 90 后同事在他 60 岁，甚至更大年纪的时候，还能够参加上海的马拉松比赛，完全是一个能够实现的梦想。

面向未来的上海和塑造未来的教育

王 颐

哈佛中心上海执行董事

高等院校，尤其是研究型大学，作为重要的知识、创新源泉，对于所在城市的包括区域经济、发展，应该起到重要的作用。

美国的中心城市匹兹堡，曾经是美国重要的钢铁大城。20世纪80年代，由于经济转型和当时美国经济危机，让匹兹堡钢铁产业遭受了重创。在过去的三四十年里，匹兹堡实现了非常成功的转型，重新成为一个充满活力的城市。

这个奇迹，从当地的角度来看，非常重要的一部分原因是来自高等教育，尤其是匹兹堡的两所著名大学：匹兹堡大学和卡耐基梅隆大学。匹兹堡大学校长曾经讲过，匹兹堡成功复苏得益于多重因素，大学是她复苏的芯片。技术成果转让方面，这个大学取得了重要成就，在匹兹堡通过技术转型，创立了300多家公司，给当地经济发展作出了非常重要的贡献。在校园建立联合创新中心，吸引著名科技企业，包括英特尔、苹果、迪士尼、谷歌等美国非常著名的大企业，都纷纷到匹兹堡建立分部。借助于高等教育的资源，匹兹堡从原来依赖于钢铁的单一的产业，变成了一个拥有金融服务、高等教育、卫生医疗、交通物流等多种产业的一个现代化城市。

从这点来讲，对上海的启发，有以下几个方面：

首先，对上海2050年力争成为具有全球影响力的科技创新中心的目标，还是需要加大对基础建设的投入，尤其是大学层面。未来在跨学科的研究方面，应该是我们推进的一个重点。

应用科学和跟实体经济的联动，这方面的创新离不开我们基础研究的土壤。对此，政府也已经提出统筹推进世界一流大学和一流学科建设的目标，并开始着手落实。本地大学根据自身优势，考虑到学科布局的重要时点上，我们也应该更多地考虑跨学科的研究。

以哈佛大学为例。我们的校长在今年也建立了哈佛全球研究院，第一个地点设在上海——上海哈佛中心。希望通过哈佛全球研究院在哈佛大学推动跨学科的合作，这方面虽然哈佛有很好的基础，但是仍然还有很多工作需要做。我们以中国环境研究为突破口，组织了由工程、经济、公共卫生、政府等多个院系教授所组成的研究团队，他们正在从事中国的环境，尤其是空气质量相关的、跨学科的研究。

虽然这个项目刚刚开始，但是研究团队里面的教授对中国的环境已经有十几年研究经验。也与清华大学等多家国内机构有非常紧密的合作。我相信，这样的跨学科的、跨地域的国际合作，也应该成为上海大力推动的研究方向之一。

其次，上海的教育国际化，值得我们进一步推动。

上海大中学校在推动国际学生学者交流方面，已经取得了很多成就。我有以下几点建议：

第一，进一步推动高中和大学教育课程的进一步开放。学校需要更加包容、多元的教育内容，在更大范围内允许学生了解、探讨对于同一问题的不同见解。在一些跨学科的领域，应该为推动跨学科的学习和研究创造更好的条件。

第二，建议考虑本地大学建立用英文教学的本科学位课程。在过去的十几年时间里，以阿姆斯特丹为代表的多家荷兰公立大学，都建立了以英文教学的本科通识教育的学院或者项目。这些做法对于荷兰吸引来自全球的优秀人才到荷兰学习，并且推动荷兰相关的教育创新和其他领域的创新，起到了非常积极的作用。荷兰的这种模式，也逐渐开始为欧洲其他国家所仿效。在去年德国弗莱堡大学，也开始成立了全部用英文教课的本科通识教育学院。如果上海希望吸引来自全球的学生到中国接受教育，而不只是学习语言，那么，我们本地大学需要设立以英文教学的、符合国际标准的本科或者研究生学位项目或课程。这对中国本地大学而言，在课程内容和师资方面，都会有很大挑战，但是值得去尝试一下。

第三，吸引优秀的教育机构和教育模式到上海来落地。上海纽约大学是上海吸引世界优秀学府在本地落地的重要事件和成功案例。我们认为，目前世界上有非常多的教育方面的尝试、创新，尤其是线上教育，不管是哈佛还是麻省理工学院成立的 edX，还是斯坦福的 Kecera，包括中学阶段的可汗学院（Khan Academy）等，都有非常多的优秀的创新模式，值得我们积极参与。为把上海打造成全球领先的教育中心奠定一定的基础。

我们希望，通过打造良好的教育环境，上海能够在教育模式、基础研究、应用研究、创新创业等各方面取得更大的进展，从而加速实现上海成为国际大都市目标的进程。

2050 年的上海——最智慧的城市

张小平

德勤管理咨询合伙人

我们可以畅想一下，2050 年的上海必然是一个智慧的上海。而这种必然性，可以从以下四个方面的趋势去预测：

第一，人口增长给城市带来的压力会越来越大，环境变化、极端气候的频繁出现，要求我们的城市必须具备满足人类的基本需求，也就是安全性的需求，从而拥有更好的抵抗风险的能力。

第二，城市经济发展，需要有更好的商业环境。好的商业环境，不仅可以吸引大企业，也能够支持我们本地企业，特别是中小企业的发展。而创新机制，是商业环境的一个重要组成部分。这种创新机制，可以加强我们城市的竞争力。越来越多的颠覆性创新，不仅来自成本更低、更灵活的新兴企业，也来自大企业的跨界竞争。大企业对平台的争夺，将更加激烈。

第三，科技的发展，已经到了一个临界点。我们看到物联网技术在深度、广度上的应用，我们看到机器人和无人机开始进入大规模的商业化的运用，人工智能领域在过去十几年已经取得了突破性的进展，特别是具备深度学习的能力。科技发展为企业带来一些新的业务模式创新。

第四，工业化文明发展到今天，已经带来了很多人文的反思，就是我们如何不要成为机器的奴隶，而要成为机器的主人，让城市变得更智慧，人类变得更进步。发展进程中，人类文明可不可以站在一个更高的高度上来做？

这些方面的趋势，也要求我们重新思索一下智慧城市的建设和发展的路径。我们认为，智慧城市的建设有以下几方面的特征：

第一，智慧城市是通过人力资本与社会资本在传统基础设施，如交通、计算机通信技术等现代基础设施的有效投入，而实现的一种可持续的城市经济发展、高品质的生活质量感受。

第二，智慧城市的转型目标，是能够产生的具体价值目标。不管是居民对高生活质量的感受这种无形的价值，还是国家、社会方面形成的有形的经济价值。

第三，智慧城市的发展，要对自然资源合理利用。在需求方，我们需要更加节能低碳地使用资源，供给方则需要提供更多可再生的重复利用的资源。

第四，智慧城市的建设，是一个过程，而不是一次性的建设结果。而这种过程取决于城市的成熟度以及感受的实际痛点。

有三类城市。一类是类似于欧洲的传统城市，其次是一些发展中的新兴城市，还有就是正在转型的中国很多城市。而上海，具备了这三种城市的很多特点。这就需要我们智慧城市的发展，要从更高层次上进行规划。

我们可以从五个维度理解、规划未来的智慧上海：

（1）基础设施层面，包括硬性的，如道路交通、信息交通、网络以及软性的城市管理能力、领导力、创新机制等。强有力的执行力可以保证服务交付以及人们在科技、政府事务中的主导作用，确保共同的理解。

（2）在这个基础上，有一个互联互通的城市系统，如智慧医疗、智慧安全、智慧能源、智慧水系统等。这种互联互通需要把合作作为基本的需求，而对大智慧的利用，则成为关键。

（3）在这些互联互通的城市系统基础上，再产生不同的生态系统，例如公共服务的生态系统，包括学校、医院、紧急服务等；社会企业的生态系统；私营企业的生态系统；社区生态系统等。而这些生态系统中，我们可以看到政府不再是一个主要的驱使者，而只是关键的执行者，从而真正达到"大音希声，大象无形"的格局。

（4）智慧城市的主导者是人。而人又可分为四类：居民、创客、游客、雇主。这些人需要有平等的机会、健康的环境，可以让创新和互相帮助成为人们追求幸福的源头。

（5）智慧上海最重要的一个推动力，就是实现各类不同的生活目标、追求，以及生活质量：安全性、可持续性、财富积累性、选择的自由，而且应该可以成为清晰、可衡量的一种价值观念。

科技变革、社会变迁与城市治理

范德尚

北京大学全球治理研究中心副主任兼秘书长

当今世界正在发生复杂而深刻的变化。从 2008 年次贷危机到全球金融危机，以及西方国家主权债务危机；从占领华尔街运动、阿拉伯世界动荡，到《查理周刊》遭恐怖袭击事件凸显出的价值观冲突……人们发现，全球化进程中的世界是充满动荡、不满、冲突和对立的世界。整个世界的政治、经济形势复杂多变。同时，以美国硅谷为代表的世界经济发展出现新的转型，科技变革日新月异，人类社会政治、经济呈现出新变化，价值观念引发的冲突和对立日趋复杂。

面对复杂而深刻的变化，我试图从科技变革的视角解读科技创新如何对人类社会政治、经济、社会等产生影响，重点探讨信息技术变革对当今社会的政治、经济、社会带来的影响。最后，结合当今科技变革对社会造成的影响，对城市治理的提出一些建议。

1. 人类历史上科技变革对人类社会的影响

回顾人类历史，人类社会采取什么样的政治权力分配模式，经济生产采取什么样的方式，社会阶层的划分，大都与人类社会所处时代的科技发展水平有着密切的关系。

农业社会阶段，人类的科技发展水平主要体现在农牧业方面。人类科技创新主要体现在动植物的培育和对季节气候变化的认识和把握上。与人类农业社会阶段科技发展水平相适应，社会的经济生产方式主要是以手工业和以家庭为单位的自给自足的自耕农生产方式；在政治权力的分配模式上，国王和贵族掌握了社会权力，并用以维持社会秩序和公平正义，典型政治权力模式是君主制。社会阶层的划分为国王、贵族、自耕农和手工业者。

随着蒸汽技术、电气技术出现，人类社会步入工业化社会。人类社会政治、经济、社会阶层的划分随着科技变革又出现新的变化。人类社会的经济发展方式由家庭手工业和自给自足自然经济开始步入工业化大机器生产时代。社会阶层开始分化，科技变革带来的大机器生产把传统的家庭手工业和自给自足的自然经济冲垮，破产的自耕农和手工业者被迫进入工厂为掌握机器、技术和工厂的资本家工作，整个社会日益分裂为两大对立阶级：掌握矿山、资本、机器的资产阶级和出卖劳动的无产阶级。针对工业时代变化，马克思敏锐地将社会阶层分析为两大阶级，即资产阶级和无产阶级。在政治权力的分配方面，随着资产阶级的兴起，资产阶级要求在国家权力运行过程中获得对其利益保护的发言权。政治权力的分配变化在英国和法国分别以不同的方式实现了向君主制立宪和向资产阶级共和制的转变。

2. 当今科技变革对当前社会的影响

以信息技术为核心科技变革正在对当今人类社会的政治、经济、社会阶层分化带来深刻的影响。经济发展方式由工业化大机器生产进入深度融合知识、技术和信息的智能化生产时代。传统行业在科技变革的影响下或走向衰落或被迫转型升级，依托高层次人才的新的研发型企业开始出现。

科技的变革同时也造成社会分化和新的社会问题。以美国为例，美国汽车制造产业的工人在 20 世纪后期随着美国制造业外迁开始失去工作。奥巴马总统上台以后，致力于让美国的制造业回归，解决产业工人的失业问题。不幸的是，自动化技术和智能技术正不断用智能机器人取代美国产业工人的岗位。这就是技术变革带来的力量，由此也造成了越来越多的社会问题："占领华尔街"反映出了极少数富人和绝大多数穷人之间的对立。

在政治权力分配方面，新的财富所有者想要融入国家的权力决策和运行体系之中。依靠专利和技术而崛起的硅谷的新贵出于其利益会对美国国家权力分配和运行提出什么样的主张？亚马逊等电商巨头会提出什么样的要求？回顾人类社会政治权力分配的变化，从君主制到共和制，未来政治权力分配和运行的形态是什么？这是值得思考的问题，因为这是一个正在经历着深刻而复杂变化的世界。

正如美国奥巴马总统在 2011 年国情咨文中所言："当代世界已经发生改变，对许多人而言这种改变是痛苦的，繁荣一时的工厂已经关闭，熙熙攘攘的商业街如今已经门可罗雀。对自豪的美国人而言，他们感到游戏规则已经发生改变。他们的感觉是正确的，规则已经发生改变，技术革命已经使人们生活、工作、经商的方式发生改变，原来需要 1000 个工人的钢铁厂，现在只需要 100 人了。有因特网连接服务的地方，任何公司都可以开商店、雇用员工、销售产品。"四年前奥巴马描述的美国的景象，我们在今天的王府井、中关村、南京路、东莞等地也同样看到……

3. 当今时代背景下的城市治理的思考

第一，科技变革和全球化时代的城市治理需要价值观和灵魂。在科技变革日新月异，信息技术不断发展的背景下，一个城市、国家需要有自身的核心价值观来凝聚力量，增强认同。上海作为容纳了黄皮肤、白皮肤、黑皮肤的一个国际化大都市，更需要有精神层面核心价值观方面的共识和认同。这个核心价值观是什么？首先，它能够界定上海不同于其他国际化大都市，这需要从上海历史文化中去发掘，需要从黑头发、黑眼睛、黄皮肤的民族历史文化中去推陈出新；其次，它能够吸引汇聚全球优秀的人才来到上海工作生活，并获得一种归属感；第三，它能够把黄皮肤、白皮肤、黑皮肤的人们包容在一起，把不同肤色的人们凝聚起来在上海创新创业；第四，它要体现对社会公平正义的尊崇，对人的价值的认可，对环保、节能、绿色理念的追求。

对上海来说，这方面很重要。上海作为国际化都市，未来必须提出一种理念，超越不同文化核心价值观层面的对立和冲突，使之更为开放、包容。

第二，城市治理同时需要基层经验和全球视野。中国是有着数千年农耕社会的文明，有着悠久的历史和文化底蕴。改革开放 30 多年来，中国取得了巨大的成功，成为了世界第二大经济体。中国日益与世界融为一体，世界也越来越离不开中国。长期以来，我们的社会强调基层经验，无论官员、学者还是企业家，需要从基层做起，"修身、齐家、治国、平天下"理想中蕴含了注重基层的价值，一屋不扫何以扫天下？以官员选拔为例，在村长、镇长、县长、省长乃至国家最高领导层，这无疑体现了基层经验的价值取向，几千年来的农耕社会，这种价值观无疑是正确的。同时，当国家的经济体量达到世界第二的时候，我们有 60% 多的石油和很多重要矿产资源要从阿拉伯世界或世界其他地方进口，这就需要中国社会的精英阶层，无论是政府、学者还是企业家，走出去，了解外部世界，处理好中国与外部世界的关系。因此，我们除了需要具备村长的基层经验，还要站在地球之上，了解世界各国的历史、文化、宗教、核心价值观，来处理好国与国之间的关系，发挥中国在国际社会应该发挥的作用，在维护自身利益的同时，促进人类的共同福祉。

上海作为国际化大都市，界定自身在全球的身份定位，处理与国际其他大都市的关系，汲取国际其他城市治理经验教训，确定全球化背景下上海城市治理的思路，选择上海未来城市发展国际化、差异化的战略，基层经验固然重要，全球化视野同等重要。

第三，城市治理需要把握当今科技变革对社会造成的深刻影响和挑战。如前面所述，当今科技变革正在对社会造成深刻持久的影响。以信息技术为例，互联网的出现使得消费者和生产厂家进行直接的网上信息交流，许多中间服务商及员工正在消失。同时，智能机器人技术的出现，机器取代人力，很多产业工人正在消失。失业已经并将日益成为政府需要面对的社会问题和挑战。根据上周 CNN 的报道，作为"金砖四国"之一的巴西，以及南美的阿根廷、委内瑞拉，由于经济下滑，国内政治正发生变化，巴西总统面临被弹劾的危险。因此，当我们在拥抱互联网、新技术，推动创新的同时，要考虑这种技术变革对所其导致的失业群体的影响以及解决的方法。当熙熙攘攘的南京路、王府井、中关村因技术变革变得门可罗雀时，当机器换人的口号甚嚣尘上时，面对越来越多的失业群体，国家、城市治理显得尤为重要，和谐社会的构建更是任重而道远。

第四，城市治理需要发挥两只手的力量。面对科技变革带来的社会问题和挑战，城市治理需要发挥两只手的力量：一种就是看不见的手，市场的力量，另一种是有形的政府的政策之手的力量。

奥巴马在 2009 年就职演说中谈到政府和市场关系时曾反思："市场到底是好还是坏，是一个无需争论的话题，它创造财富、扩展自由的能力无与伦比，但是这场危机（美国 2008 年以来的经济危机）告诉我们，如果缺乏监管，它的力量就会失去控制，而一个国家如果一心偏向其中富裕阶层，就不可能保持长久的繁荣。我们国家经济成功从来都不只是单纯依靠扩张国内生产总值规模的结果，而是依靠普遍的繁荣，依靠我们让每个心存希望的公民公平享有成功机会的能力，这并非善心而致，而是因为他们是实现共同繁荣的必由之路。所以，我们今天提出的问题并不是我们的政府是大是小，而是是否运转有效，它是否能帮助美国家庭获得薪酬体面工作，负担得起的保障以及享有尊严的退休生活，凡是有利于实现上述目标的事，我们都要不断推进，凡是不利的，我们誓要把它画上句号。"

在当今科技变革和全球化所带来的社会问题、失业问题、贫富差距问题层出不穷的情况下，政府的有形的政策之手的调控显得尤为迫切和重要。

在上海城市治理未来愿景中，如何通过"看不见的市场之手"和"有形的政策之手"来对城市进行有效治理？这将成为上海未来 30 年能否成功发展成为全球繁华大都市，引领国际化大都市发展的重要因素。

2050 年的上海——一个日本经济从业者的视点与期待

小栗道明

日本贸易振兴机构上海首席代表

上海与日本的交流有着非常悠久的历史。通过长期不断的交流，上海和日本也加深了对相互的理解，我确信这是一个双赢的结果。正因如此，鉴于到目前为止两者的深远交流，作为一个致力于为促进日中经济交流的日本人，我想谈一谈对"2050 年的上海"的看法。

虽说在上海不足三个月，但我自己这 20 年来所做的，都是和促进日中经济交流有关。而我和中国结下缘分的契机就是上海。

恰好是 20 年前的 1995 年，我第一次访问中国就是到这里——上海。当时，浦东新区已于 1990 年开始开发，而 1992 年的邓小平南巡讲话更加快了改革开放的进程，上海也迎来了日本企业的第二次对中投资热潮。

沉醉于上海的城市活力和生活在这里的人们的热情，使我充满对上海，以及整个中国未来发展的信心，这也使我决定了把自己的人生投入到促进日中经济交流中去。

我现在所属的日本贸易振兴机构，是为协调日本和世界经济发展为目的，促进日本和世界各国的贸易、投资而成立的政府组织。而我任职的上海代表处正好是 30 年前的 1985 年设立的，从设立以来一直致力于扩大上海和日本的经济交流。

正如这 30 年来上海的社会、经济发生的巨大变化一样，我们日本贸易振兴机构开展的工作内容也与时俱进。设立当初一个重要的工作就是对中国企业的技术援助。但后来随着改革开放的扩大，日本企业纷纷来华投资。所以 20 世纪 90 年代到 21 世纪头十年，支持、帮助日企来华投资又变成了我们工作的中心。在 2010 年的上海世博会上，我们作为日本馆的运营机关，围绕"心之和，技之和"的主题，积极推广了日本技术和文化。而自 2000 年到现在，上海作为一个被全世界高度关注的市场，我们又把引以为傲的安心、安全、高品质的商品和服务介绍进来，并开展企业间的商业对接。如今，有实力的中国企业纷纷挺进海外市场之际，我们又开始加大对中企在日投资的支持力度。

回顾过去的30年可以看出，日本和上海从当初的单方面经济交流逐步变成相互交流。展望未来的30年，我确信双方的相互交流将进一步扩大。而为了能使人员、货物和资本的交流更加顺畅，我想重要的是上海应该从软、硬两方面来完善基础设施。

说到基础设施的软实力代表，首推贸易、投资自由化的制度框架——FTA。它的构建发挥着重要的作用。现在，日中韩之间的自由贸易协定谈判正在进行，而亚太地区的区域全面经济伙伴关系、跨太平洋伙伴协议的进展，也将为实现亚太自由贸易区助一臂之力。随着这些自由开放的贸易、投资体制的确立，上海作为国际经济、金融、贸易、航运中心城市，期望今后30年仍继续发挥先导者的示范作用。

而在硬件基础设施方面，上海既有的航运、高铁、高速公路会进一步扩大，希望与世界各国的人员来往更加活跃。

欧洲、东南亚的经济一体化正在稳定发展，国界线已不明显。展望2050年，日本、中国，以及整个亚洲各国间也应该在人员流动、开展经济活动方面有必要更加自由化。在亚洲一体化的进程中，我想上海应发挥更大的作用。

在这里，我想探索一下上海2050年的发展方向。翻看上海的历史，就是一部和世界息息相关的发展史。这也能从现存的许多历史性建筑，来充分说明上海与世界各国的联系之广。所以考虑上海今后的发展，扩大、深化与世界各国的交流是不可欠缺的重要因素。期望上海继续作为对世界各国人民极具吸引力的、外国人更加活跃的开放之都。

当然在展望2050年的上海时，也使我联想起到"两个百年"之一的中华人民共和国成立100周年时（2049年），建成富强、民主、文明、和谐的社会主义现代化国家、达到中等发达国家水平的目标。为实现这个目标，上海应起到怎样的作用才是重要的呢？

在2015年10月26日—29日召开的中国共产党第十八届五中全会上，为完成"十三五"规划（2016—2020年）中的目标，提出了"创新、协调、绿色、开放、共享"的发展理念。我想这也为上海实现奋斗目标指明了方向。

下面就是我在展望2050年的上海之际，对这五个发展理念的理解。

第一是创新。创新是发展的源泉，不管是社会、产业、技术、制度、文化、理论等等，任何方面都要创新。而虽然实现创新有几个不可或缺的因素，但考虑到不管什么创新都是由人实现的，所以怎样培养优秀的人才，怎样吸引优秀的人才，对上海来说非常重要，由此更加完善高等教育体系也变得必要。当然实现创新，维持自由、民主的社会环境也很重要。

第二是协调。在城市层面的协调中，城市和农村、经济和社会、第一二三各产业间的协调将变得重要。在产业面的协调中，特别是第二产业和第三产业、大企业和小企业间的协调是不可或缺的。虽然现在，上海的第三产业的发展非常迅猛，在 GDP 所占的比例也逐年加大，但第二产业也是不可缺少的。所以不光是大企业，也包括围绕在周围的中小企业群，上海应该继续保有和其相匹配的、成为核心的第二产业。

第三是绿色，也是日本到现在为止从城市发展中得到很多启发的理念。日本在经济发展中也曾面临过严重的环境破坏，人们从中学到了和环境共生，企业也努力开发环保产品。我想绿色发展最重要的还是每个公民的环保意识和为此的教育、启发。从我自己这 20 年对上海的了解，建筑物已非常漂亮，但走在马路上，乱扔的垃圾还是能随处可见。常常会听到去过日本的中国游客，谈起日本的城市印象都说干净整洁。我想日本之所以能保持清洁，是每一个公民从小起就养成了对自用物品的整理、整顿的习惯，和不给别人添麻烦的教育有很大关系。为了保护和生活在地球上每一个人都息息相关的空气、水、土地等共有资源，首先重要的是引导教育市民从爱护身边的环境做起。

第四是开放，关于开放，前边我也提过，构建自由、开放的贸易，经济体制是重中之重。以 2013 年 9 月设立的中国（上海）自由贸易试验区为例，上海作为中国改革开放的先行者，在深化改革中发挥着重要作用。展望 2050 年，双向开放更加重要。我希望上海的企业和市民可以更开放地拥抱世界，和世界共同发展。虽然现在日本贸易振兴机构加大对中企的对日投资支持，但和对上海投资的日企相比，到日本投资的上海企业仍然很少。考虑到 2050 年在世界各国投资的上海企业会越来越多，希望日中投资差距也会大幅缩小。当然为吸引更多的中国企业来日本投资，我们也会努力保持日本经济的发展。

最后是共享，这是中国为实现和谐发展、共同富裕目标的非常重要的理念。包括上海在内中国的各大城市在这 30 年间快速发展，但也造成了巨大的贫富差距。上海作为改革、发展的先行者，如果不能实现共同富裕的话，那么在地域辽阔、复杂多样的全国更无从谈起。因此我想，对"两个百年"的奋斗目标而言，上海在今后 30 年的发展中怎样实现共同富裕担负着重要的使命。

回顾两千多年的日中交流史，作为"一衣带水"的两国，我们相互学习、共同发展。于 2050 年的上海，我真心希望日本能作为重要的合作伙伴，成为分享共同发展成果的国家。

积极行动亦实现上海 2050 年辉煌

彭捷宁

美中贸易全国委员会上海首席代表

在准备今天的发言稿时，我回忆起近期与美中贸易全国委员会成员单位的调研，我认为，回顾成员单位的意见，并分析已经出版的关于上海未来发展的报告，将是非常有益的。预测一年后的情况已经对最有才华的研究者构成挑战，要提前 35 年预测则更是如此。

在准备这个问题的过程中，我研读了肖林主任 2014 年 12 月发表的一篇文章。他在文章中提出了上海未来 30 年发展的三点预测以及上海要在未来保持其领先和成功地位需要克服的一些挑战。过去几周我仔细思考了这些观点，我想，在肖林主任的框架下，对于引导上海未来发展，我有以下建议：

在未来 35 年影响上海发展的关键因素中，有一条不在上海自身的控制能力以内：那就是国家经济结构调整以及中国继续深化经济体制改革。改革的方向会对上海未来发展带来无法预知的挑战和机遇。过去三年，通过全面启动的中国（上海）自由贸易试验区，我们已经看到这些变化所产生的影响。就像我经常告诉我们的成员单位，中国（上海）自由贸易试验区在很多方面是一个误称，它更像是投资便利化和深化改革的试验田。通过运用准入前国民待遇和负面清单管理制度，中国（上海）自由贸易试验区在管理外商投资上建立起了全新的框架。这个模式随后在中国其他三个自贸区被采用。中国政府决定，到 2018 年在建立起国家级负面清单制度。中国（上海）自由贸易试验区现已扩围，上海政府将浦东新区的陆家嘴金融片区、金桥开发片区和张江高科技片区也已囊括进来。展望未来，上海要实现到 2050 年成为一个开放和受欢迎的投资目的地的目标，应该继续深化自贸区的负面清单制度，并将其适用范围扩大到整个上海市的范围。昨日国务院公布政策，要进一步放开外国投资在电子商务和各服务行业的限制，以及实行人民币账户自由化，这将是特别重要的推动因素。

肖林主任在 2014 年全球城市的主旨发言《关于未来 30 年的三个思考》中提到的另一个观点是关于城镇化对上海未来的影响。他指出，未来上海将面临人口老龄化和人口质量下降的挑战。中期内应采取许多的行动，以应对最具挑战性的问题，并确保上海对外国直接投资来说仍然是颇具吸引力的目的地：

　　一是提高法定退休年龄。上海和中国将有可能遭受越来越大的老龄化问题，会影响中国的社会安全体系。2015 年 3 月，中国人力资源和社会保障部部长尹蔚民表示，中国将逐步延迟法定退休年龄。该计划预计于 2017 年推出，2022 年开始正式实行。中国相对偏低的法定退休年龄对于在华经营的跨国公司产生了明显的影响。一旦员工达到 65 岁的法定退休年龄，他们就不能再合法地与公司继续签订劳动合同。

　　二是减轻户口政策对人才的束缚。中国的城镇化进程已制定了一项雄心勃勃的计划，允许按章纳税并缴纳当地社保基金到一定年限的居民获得当地户口。2015 年 5 月，上海发布《关于加快建设科技创新中心的 22 条意见》，其中有一条就是专门针对简化合格人才的户籍制度。美中贸易全国委员会成员单位表示，在研发和技术领域，获得当地户口对于留住顶级人才具有至关重要的作用。我预计到 2050 年上海户籍管理制度将发生很大变化，但在中期还有许多措施可以实施，以增加上海人才储备，并助力上海发展高附加值的制造业和服务业经济。

　　最后，为了使上海成为未来投资高地，上海的经营许可程序应当更加透明、价格应当更加便宜、批准手续应当更加便利。在过去 30 年中，上海在简化行政许可程序方面已经取得了长足的发展，但是仍有提高的空间。我给大家分享一个初创企业如何在美国加州山景城注册营业执照的例子，这是一个位于硅谷市中心的城市。

　　在山景城申请营业执照非常简单。申请者只要填写一份一页纸的营业执照申请表并同时提交一次性申请费，申请费根据经营范围不同有所浮动，最低为制造企业 32 美元，最高为软件开发 102 美元。申请表一旦提交，在两个星期之内将会得到回复。与上海不同，山景城没有运营资本最低限额、注册外汇牌照责任义务以及公众安全检查等方面的规定。这些获取营业执照上的便利是硅谷保持其美国最具创新能力地区地位的一个关键因素。

　　不仅对硅谷来说是如此，对于美国来说，获取营业执照的便利性也是其成为世界最具经商便利性的地区之一的原因，根据世界银行发布的

《2015 年全球营商环境报告》，美国在该项上的排名位列全球第 7 名。

为自贸区内的内外资企业注册提供同等待遇，消除企业注册资本最低限额规定以及明确申请企业营业执照的审批时限，将使上海自贸区成为在整个中国实施许可证自由化的有效试验田。未来 30 年上海的发展将为深化经济改革、提高营商便利性和引领全中国的改革开放提供前所未有的机遇。

创新型工程师在上海 2050 年发展愿景中的角色扮演

来咏歌

泰科电子（上海）有限公司亚洲区政府事务与企业责任高级总监

　　我们都知道上海市政府发布了一个雄心勃勃的关于"加快建设具有全球影响力的科技创新中心"的方案，要在 2030 年形成科技创新中心城市的核心功能。"创业易，守成难。"从现在到 2030 年，我们有着明确的发展目标和政策支持。那么从 2030 年到 2050 年还有 20 年的时间，我们要如何保持上海的创新生态环境能够随着全球政治经济技术发展趋势而动，继续保持一个有全球影响力的科创中心？

　　创新的主体在于人。而对于大部分企业来说，工程师就是我们创新的主体，创造出新的产业、新的流程、新的解决方案、新的工艺和新的产品。TE Connectivity 连续 5 年蝉联汤森路透全球百强创新机构，我们近年来做了一些有关工程师创新的研究。我们认为有些工作不必等到 2030 年，而是从现在就可以开始了。

　　从 2014 年开始，我们与中国工业和信息化部电子科学技术情报研究所进行合作研究，并发布年度《中国工程师创新指数研究报告》。这个报告以全国 1219 位在职工程师的调研数据为基数，从地域、行业、工程师年龄段、工程师性别、优秀工程师等多个维度选取数据，并与全国平均数据进行综合对比，以此建立中国工程师创新的各类指数，以量化的角度对这一课题进行全景呈现。该项调查在样本的选取范围上覆盖了国有、外资或合资、私营、集体等各个类型企业，在行业领域上涵盖了汽车制造、通信、机械设备制造、能源化工、医药制造业等主要行业，使研究结果既全面，又具备较强的说服力。

　　我们的研究显示，87.8% 的在华工程师表示了较有兴趣或有很高的兴趣投入到创新活动中。工程师们普遍希望能够发挥内在的能量，实现较高价值，为社会作出更大贡献。而我们又把工程师创新这个链条根据因果关系分成了两个部分的指标。"因"这个部分包括：创新环境、创新能力和创新活动，而"果"这个部分则是指创新绩效。

整体而言，中国工程师对自己的创新活动充满着自信，而这种自信很大程度来自于"因"这个部分的改善，而这种改善又来自于宏观层面的国家政策；中观层面的企业、大学、科研院所的协同发展；以及个体微观层面的工程师工作条件。在对个人创新能力的评估中，工程师们对自己的创新能力也较为认可。而在"果"，就是创新绩效方面，中国工程师尚且处在量的加速扩张时段，要实现质的重大突破，将工程师的创新热情真正转化为生产力，乃至形成全球竞争力，仍然需要一定时间的积累。

细看工程师们对外部各因素的反馈情况，以下几点显得尤为重要。

（1）在创新环境中，工程师需要在研发经费投入和职业培训方面获得更多的企业支持。

（2）在创新能力中，工程师的工作经验和教育经历在创新过程中起到了重要作用。

（3）在创新活动中，企业能否给工程师提供创新的机会及是否有机会参与或领导高精尖项目或国家宏观方向项目可能对工程师创新能否取得成效起着重要作用。

不难看出，不论是企业还是政府，如果能在刚才提到的这几个重要指标方面为工程师们创造出更有利的环境，将会大大提升工程师的创新能力。

回到我在开篇时提到的问题：从2030年到2050年的20年间，我们如何使上海保持一个有全球影响力的科创中心的地位？根据目前的调查结果，我们建议政府及企业可以从这几个方面着眼。

首先是城市的发展战略。根据上海市的规划，到2030年以后，上海将建成国际经济中心、国际金融中心、国际贸易中心、国际航运中心和全球科技创新中心。我们希望政府可以在长期的城市发展战略中，在2030年以后，继续明确先进制造业的地位。不是说到那时上海一定要保留有多少家工厂，而是说上海要留住制造业企业，留住并突出制造业企业的研发、管理、商贸这些功能，让制造业企业在国内外的工厂变成实际上的"内包"加工车间。

这样，鼓励制造业的创新政策将从设立创新中心过渡到帮助设在上海的创新中心对分布在国内外的"内包"加工车间的服务，包括工程师的借调、外派安排，各种授权收入的税务安排等。

此外，我们的调查显示，在被问及政府的哪些政策对工程师创新活动的影响程度较大时，接近 60% 的工程师认为，知识产权保护政策影响最大。同时，我们还需要有相应的劳工政策的支持，比方说职务发明的法规等。

作为大型企业来说，除了解决工程师们认为是创新遇到的最大挑战之一——设备及经费投入的问题，也应该努力把创新作为企业文化输出至整个供应链。与此同时，企业也希望通过多种形式与政府进行多种形式的交流，对政策的实施提供反馈。

根据我们的调查，60 后工程师是当前的创新主力。那么，现在的 90 后工程师或是在校大学生在 30 多年后，就是 2050 年，就将成为创新主力。在当前对 90 后的工程师来说最重要的是三个"E"，就是"Experience"经验、"Exposure"曝光和"Education"培训机会。企业要有足够的耐心培养新人，同时我们希望政府可以出台政策进一步鼓励校园招聘、鼓励企业打造多样的实习生（internship）和学徒工（apprenticeship）计划。

还有一点，我们注意到一个所谓"研而优则仕"的现象，就是工程师随着研发成果的增加而相应承担起管理的职责。这种安排诚然体现了对人才的尊重，但是并不是每位优秀的工程师都愿意成为或会成为一位优秀的经理，并不是每位优秀的项目管理人（project manager）都愿意成为或会成为一位优秀的团队管理人（people manager）。所以，TE 打造了一个和管理人才平行的工程师职业发展职级，工程师可以不断地得到职级提升，而不必去管理团队或者从事任何行政事务。当某位工程师晋升到主任工程师或者主任研究员的职级时，他／她的薪酬水平及在职待遇将等同于商务总监级别。这样，既帮助公司留住核心创新人才，也可以让工程师全心投入创新工作。

最后，我想谈的是希望政府可以帮助引导社会观念，鼓励更多的女性从事工程师的职业。目前，男女工程师比例失调是不争的事实。调查显示，在华女性工程师工作年限超过 20 年以上的，仅占女性工程师调研样本总量的 2.9%。而在华男性工程师工作年限超过 20 年以上的，占男性工程师调研样本总量的 18.9%。

但也许社会低估了中国女性工程师的创新能力及创新的成效。女性工程师需要的是一套完善的创新激励机制，以保障女性工程师的创新潜力得到充分发挥。调查结果显示，普遍认为女性工程师在专业技术能力及沟通能力方面是强于男性工程师的。此外，女性工程师在创新应用能力及知识广博程度方面也强于男性工程师。

　　细究是哪些因素制约了女性工程师创新能力的发挥？主要是社会文化观念和企业用人机制。女性工程师所拥有的创新资源低于男性工程师。所以企业在研发经费及培训方面、参与创新项目的机会方面都应适当的考虑女性工程师群体的存在和参与，给予与男性一样的均等机会。而政府同时也可以帮助引导社会观念，利于女性工程师得到更多的重视和资源。

2050年全球货币格局以及上海国际中心地位

乔依德

上海发展研究基金会副会长兼秘书长

国际货币体系，包含了很多要素，比如资本的跨境流动、汇率制度安排、流动性的提供，但是其中最主要的，是货币本位。

离2050年还很远，但我有两个假定。我觉得第一个假定是比较可靠的：

第一个假定，2050年中国肯定会成为全球最大的经济体。

英国《经济学人》2014年8月份预测，假定中国GDP增长是7%，美国2.25%，人民币升值3%，估计到2021年中国就是最大的经济体。现在看来这个预测比较乐观。如果重新计算，假定中国5%，现在到2023年，2023—2044年是3.3%。2014年美国前财长劳伦斯—萨默斯等人有个报告，认为一国的经济增长迟早会回归到中位数。他对中国经济估计是最低的，我就取他这个最低值，即前面几年是5%，后面是3.3%。美国还是2.25%。这样计算结果，大概到2044年，中国还是会赶上美国。所以可以得出结论：2050年，中国是最大的经济体。

第二个假定，中国会全面融入全球金融体系。

资本账户完全开放，资金可以自由移动。这对上海成为一个国际金融中心非常关键。完全浮动汇率，资本市场双向开放，我们国家的金融机构就像美国一样，会在全球布局，人民币将成为一个重要的国际储备货币。

虽然有上述假定，但还有一些不确定的因素：

其一，科技金融对金融集聚的影响。

科技金融对金融的效率提高是很明显的，但是对金融集聚效果不清楚。互联网金融提高了效率，但是可能在某种程度上减少了对实体金融机构的需求。回过来想，如果中国那些大银行现在在上市，它们的估值会不会还会那么高？这是一个大的问号。因为那个时候分行多，估值高，现在分行多，估值就没有那么高。说到智能（机器人）金融，美国 ETF 规范性的产品都可以用智能机器来操作，收取的管理费很低。物联网金融，我看不清楚，据说对很多物质可以进行抵押，直接跟金融连接。但我个人认为，相比较，互联网金融对金融的影响比较大。

其二，全球金融危机再次爆发的可能性。我认为还是有可能的。

以前有人说，有两件事情是肯定的，一个是死亡，一个是收税。金融危机以后，这种说法又改了，变成金融危机总归要爆发的，这个爆发以后，后面的格局怎么样，看不清楚。这次金融危机爆发反而加强了美元的地位，和预想的不同，但是下一次会怎样，没有人知道。

国际货币的网络具有惰性或者惯性。1872 年美国在经济规模上已经超过英国了，直到 1944 年美元才替代英镑成为最大的货币。尽管英国和英镑的地位在下降，但是伦敦的地位并没有下降。

还有我们国家进行金融监管体制改革，关于混业监管、分业监管，现在讨论很多，中央、地方对金融监管如何分工，它的结果对上海到底有什么影响，这需要进一步的研究。

对于政策支持力度，目前我们还看不清楚。因为邓小平早就说过，上海要搞国际金融中心，但是现在看不清楚。这有一点像"排排坐，吃果果"，很多东西在各个地方进行分配。当然也有一种说法，让市场自由选择，其实这个说法是不对的。市场早早在 1949 年以前就选择过了，那时上海就已经是"远东"最大的金融中心了。而且，现在的金融和 100 年前的金融不同，它是高度管制的，既然是高度管制，政府就要起主导作用。既然中国银行可以从上海迁到北京，那为什么不可以从北京迁回上海呢？这其中有很多不确定性因素。

其三，最关键的是，上海国际金融中心地位可能的演变。

第一，国内金融改革，第二，人民币地位，第三，上海国际金融中心地位的演变。金融改革是汇率、资本账户、监管体系，人民币地位主要看全球外汇储备占比、储备货币的地位，到 2020 年我们的汇率应该可以"清洁浮动"，而现在是"肮脏浮动"，即有管理的浮动。资本账户基本开放，或者有管理的开放。监管方面，中央跟地方会有适当分工。外汇储备占比方面，现在人民币是只占全部的 1%，到 2020 年可能达到 5%。美元欧元之后，人民币可以排在第三，现在人民币进了 SDR（特别提款权），报纸说现在人民币已经排名第三，这是错的，因为这只不过是权重，在 SDR 中第三，但是真正的地位没有第三，可能是第五、第六。2020 年应该达到第三，到时能完成 2009 年国务院提出的目标，与我国经济实力、人民币地位相适应的国际金融中心，但还不是具有"国际功能"的一个国际金融中心。到 2030 年，汇率浮动、资本账户应该完全开放，各个方面分工应该比较明确，中央跟地方，到底是混业还是分业。人民币占比可能达到 10%，美元还是排在第一，欧元跟人民币可能并列。因为欧元在 1999 年刚启动时，占外汇储备比例是 12%，现在是 20%。值得注意的是，欧元有很多假象，很多数字都是欧盟国家内部的。如果到 2030 年人民币能够和欧元并列，上海国际金融中心的地位可以达到全球第二层次，相当于东京、新加坡或者香港。到 2050 年，外汇储备占比可能会达到 20%—25%，美元还是会比较高，大概 40%—50%，因为现在美元外汇储备 64%，可能有一定下降，那个时候美元、人民币应该是并列第一，欧元第三。希望上海到那个时候能够进入全球国际金融中心的第一个层次，和纽约、伦敦并驾齐驱。

Towards Shanghai in Future 30 Years: How to Invigorate the Innovation Capability Well Matched with the Status of a Global City

Chen Yougang

Partner of McKinsey&Company, Head of MGI Greater China

Among all world-level cities across the globe, besides exceptional economic power, they all have extraordinary innovation capability. To become another new global city in future 30 years, it's imperative for Shanghai to invigorate world-level innovation capability.

It can be easily found from New York and London—two well recognized international economic centers—that an international economic center must be an innovation center with good innovation environment, diversified innovation activities and abundant innovation achievements. Depending on the success of Silicon Alley, New York has emerged as the major scientific town in the eastern coast, which is honored as "Capital of New Science in the US". New York has created a borderless hi-tech park in the downtown through tax cut program, public private partnership and refined supporting facilities. Currently, there are more than 500 start-ups in Silicon Alley, where number of jobs related to science and technology ranks No. 2 across the US. The Silicon Alley also becomes the investment hotspot for venture capital (VC transaction volume has surged by 32% from 2007 to 2011; in Q3 2012, it shot up by 44% with total investment rising to $ 218 million) and the major economic growth engine for New York since the financial crisis in 2008, which is recognized as the fastest growing IT heartland in the US in succession to the Silicon Valley. As early as 1990s, London has taken the lead to put forward the slogan of "Capital of Creativity" by leveraging its talent resources and advantages as a metropolitan. By using platform building and financial support to create high-quality and healthy innovation environment, it has supported and promoted the development of these sustainable cultural and creative industries with high added-value. London has now become one of the world Top 3 Advertising Industry Centers, one of the world Top 3 busiest filmmaking centers and international capital of design, where cultural and creative industries have also become the second largest pillar industry only next to finance.

In Asia, Shanghai's peer cities as competitors have also made outstanding achievements in innovation. Singapore regards innovation as the engine to drive economic transformation and considers intelligence capital as the key for its development. The government has vigorously increased investment in scientific research and development fund, expanded the talent team for science and technology, developed hi-tech industries, built scientific parks and attracted MNCs to engage in technological development. Singapore has become the international scientific research center and the innovation center in Asia through reasonable layout and effective execution by the government.

It can be seen innovation capability and economic status is complementary. The key proposition to become a global city is about how to invigorate the innovation capability of the city.

Current performance of Shanghai in innovation capability is not optimistic. It is lagging behind Beijing and Shenzhen in many aspects and facing with many bottlenecks, for instance inefficiency in commercialization of innovation achievements, deficiency in innovation atmosphere and entrepreneurship and shortage of fundamental environment for innovation.

Compared to other Tier 1 cities in China, Shanghai is lagging behind Beijing and Shenzhen in many aspects of innovation activities. For example, number of patent application for Shanghai in 2011 was only 1 439, equivalent to 55% of Beijing, 18% of Shenzhen and 12% of Tokyo; in terms of investment in innovation, number of investment cases in Beijing doubles that of Shanghai and the investment size is 2.5 times of Shanghai. The major causes are shown as follows:

Firstly inefficiency in commercialization of innovation achievements: Shanghai has been making large investment in scientific research for years. In 2010, number of R&D personnel per million people was 2.5 times of that of

Japan, and share of R&D investment in GDP also doubled that of UK. However, it still fell behind international advanced cities in terms of commercialization of innovation achievements and ratio of hi-tech industries. Front-end investment in scientific research may surely hasten the innovation and development of technology, but the essence of a science and innovation center lies in integration of innovation chain and value chain as well as how to convert the achievements into real value.

Secondly deficiency of innovation atmosphere and entrepreneurship: Shanghai only ranks No. 21 in the world in terms of entrepreneurship. Among Top 500 private enterprises in China, only 19 enterprises are based in Shanghai, lagging behind neighboring provinces in the Yangtze Delta area (123 for Zhejiang, 98 for Jiangsu). SOEs and foreign enterprises are still the major contributors to Shanghai's economy, while private enterprises are seriously inactive and the market is lack of vitality.

Thirdly fundamental environment for innovation to be improved: Shanghai has shortcomings in openness of innovation resources, creation of innovation ecosystem and soft environment. In the large backdrop of digital era, Shanghai government has taken the first step in data collection and consolidation, but there is still large room for improvement in data disclosure and encouraging public use of data. The linkage among innovation subjects is insufficient and there is no effective linkage platform among enterprise of different types, between enterprise and R&D institutions and between innovation enterprises and capital. At the same time, environmental problems and air pollution have caused negative impacts on talents and investment, so there is still a large gap between Shanghai and other cities in terms of internationalization and openness.

In order to explore Shanghai's advantage in innovation, we need to deep dive into different innovation prototypes, identify Shanghai's position and leverage its heritage of "simultaneous development of industry and commerce" as Capital of Industry and Commerce to make efforts in engineering and technology based and customer centric innovation.

Innovation doesn't simply mean "invention". By looking at the all types of successfully commercialized innovation, we can divide innovation into four major prototypes: (1) R&D oriented innovation, i.e. to develop new products by commercializing fundamental research products; (2) engineering and technology based innovation, i.e. to design and develop new products by integrating technologies of suppliers and partner; (3) customer centric innovation, i.e. to solve customer problems by innovating products and business; (4) efficiency driven innovation, i.e. to reduce cost, shorten production time and improve quality by optimizing the production processes.

As the Capital of Industry and Commerce, Shanghai shall leverage its heritage of "simultaneous development of industry and commerce" to focus on creating the innovation commercialization platform with the main functions of converging creativity, accelerating application and creating value, rather than deliberately seeking for hastening the basic ideas and invention of original nature. By relying on existing industrial basis, e.g. automotive and airplane manufacturing, Shanghai may further encourage innovators to develop products by designing the platform and integrating dealer network technology and advance along the path for engineering and technology based innovation. Additionally, Shanghai has highly developed service sector as well as huge and dynamic consumer market, so the potential for rapid commercialization of new products and service offerings cannot be underestimated. Shanghai shall guide innovators to understand market needs, preference and underserved segments through customer interaction, develop new products and business model on this basis and continuously practice the customer centric innovation.

Looking into the future 30 years, we are confident that Shanghai will become a global leader in innovation. To this end, Shanghai government shall take steps in the following four dimensions to fully activate the innovation capability of the market and improve the soft power of the city.

Firstly, support entreprenures and allow the market come into play.

One of the most important tasks for the government should be creating the environment favorable for existence and development of entreprenures. Shanghai government shall promote supporting projects like start-up accelerator and business incubators and allocate fund to set up venture capital guidance fund. Early financing is surely important for entreprenures, but as the investor, the government shall pay attention to avoid bias to the winner (or loser) or push out financing of private sectors. To solve these issues, Singapore government selects to partner with independent VC players to avoid direct investment of the government.

The government shall also streamline the procedures to encourage innovation. For instance, the drug approval process in China is 7 or 8 years longer than that of the US, which partly explains why Chinese enterprises almost only produce generic drugs. In order to create tangible convenience for enterprises, Shanghai government may negotiate with industry representatives and jointly conceive the idea for reducing bureaucratic obstacles.

It's beneficial for expanding market competition and innovation if Shanghai government continues to promote reform in industries dominated by SOEs: due to market monopoly and leadership tenure system, many SOEs are lack of the momentum to develop innovation from long-term perspective. One feasible approach is to introduce international competition and make SOEs grow in competition like private enterprises. For example, Huawei just improves its innovation capability in competition with international rivals and partnership with global customers.

Secondly, become the demanding customer for innovation.

In areas where the government is the major purchasing customer, become a customer with high standard and rigid requirements, continuously improve technological standard and support competition, so as to promote innovation and progress. For example, the UK government organized bidding to seek for method to deal with hospital infection, thus generated the approach to reduce pneumonia cases disseminated via ventilating system and solved such common issue in ICUs.

Thirdly, use indicators that may measure the effectiveness of innovation.

Shanghai government uses those easily quantifiable indicators, e.g. R&D investment and number of patent application, to measure innovation benefits and set up goals. However, excellent performance on these indicators hasn't been fully converted into high-quality innovation achievement. In order to forcefully encourage innovation, policy makers need to factor in measurement method outside of traditional indictors like R&D spending.

Fourthly, cultivate strong regional innovation cluster.

Industrial cluster in the same geographical location can help innovators, research institutions and investors to form partnership, so as to facilitate innovation. A strong industrial cluster is the cradle for innovation achievement. Shanghai plays an important role in international trade and it is also adjacent to manufacturing cluster in the Yangtze Delta, so that it can leverage these advantages to build the industry center for life science and engineering.

Meanwhile, Shanghai government may strengthen innovation by encouraging cross-cluster cooperation. For example, data analytics software developed by Beijing may be used in health monitoring brand produced in Shenzhen, while such branded product may also be used in mobile clinical test by life science companies in Shanghai, so as to accelerate new drug R&D commercialization process.

In order to improve the global competitiveness of innovation industrial cluster, Shanghai government shall make great efforts in solving life quality issues for top talents, especially scientific research and engineering innovation talents. Currently, judged by some "soft indicators" for living quality e.g. air quality, housing condition, transportation etc., there is still certain gap between Shanghai and world-level cities like New York, so Shanghai government shall focus on these prioritized areas.

Creating the Circular Economy Advantage

Qian Wei

Managing Director of Resource Service Accenture, Greater China

Shanghai government puts forward in its "13th Five-year Plan" that it will keep several bottom lines in the next 5 years, and the ecological bottom line is one of them. China has made great economic achievements over the past three decades, but its' development model has been largely relying on the linear model under the "take—make—waste" principle, which has brought many negative effects at the same time. For example, the induced air pollution, water pollution and the constantly cutting available land, affect Shanghai's city competitiveness. For a city that lacks natural resources like Shanghai, the linear model based on the "take—make—waste" principle is out of date, and building a circular economy is becoming an evitable choice to achieve sustainable development. The circular economy can create value without the growth limitation by adoptinging disruptive technology and business model.

The growth model favored by economies and indeed most companies for a long time—based on the availability of plentiful and inexpensive natural resources—is living on borrowed time and, so are companies that rely on it. However, we are rapidly approaching a point at which the linear model based on "take—make—waste" principle is no longer viable: when, due to rising global affluence, the availability of many non-renewables cannot keep up with demand, the regenerative capacity of renewable becomes strained to its limits, and the planetary boundaries become threatened as never before.

If nothing is done to address the situation, total demand for limited resource stocks (like biomass, fossil energy, and many metals) is expected to reach 130 billion tons by 2050. That's up from 50 billion in 2014 and it will result in more than 400 percent overuse of the earth's total capacity—a feat that's physically impossible. Even with a relatively optimistic forecast for technological innovation and improvements in resource efficiency, demand for limited resources will be 80 billion tons with an overuse of around 40 billion tons by 2050 (Figure 1). The economic impact of resource scarcity on this scale would be devastating.

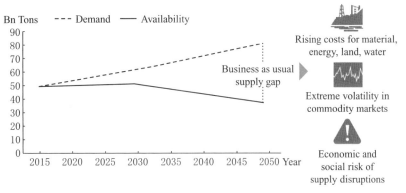

Scenarios include limited resource stocks only and therefore differ from total material conrisumption. Most notably exclude construction mineral volumes (e.g. sand and gravel) where scarcity is not on issue.

Figure 1   Resource Supply / Demand Imbalance(2015—2050)

What's the alternative? The answer is the circular economy.

1. The Circular Economy: The End of Business as Usual

Circular Economy—an alternative model decoupling growth from scarce resource use—allowing companies to innovate to enable customers and users to do "more with less". In a circular economy, growth is decoupled from the use of scarce resources through disruptive technology and business models based on longevity, renewability, reuse, repair, upgrade, refurbishment, capacity sharing, and dematerialization

Companies no longer focus mainly on driving more volume and squeezing out cost through greater efficiency in supply chains, factories and operations. Rather, they concentrate on rethinking products and services from the bottom up to "future proof" their operations to prepare for inevitable resource constraints.

Take a conventional power drill as a telling case. A power drill is typically used for less than 20 minutes at every turn while customers need to drill a hole in the wall—the market supplies various tools collecting dust most of the time. If, instead, users had convenient access to a high-quality tool only when needed, they could save money and time while the product could be optimized for longevity, component reuse, recycling, GPS tracking for finding the nearest tool, user communities for advice, mobile payments to simplify pick-up and drop-off. This thinking can be applied to anything from DIY tools to trucks, buildings, printers, etc.

Once a business goes circular, every aspect of it must be configured with the use and return in mind in addition to production and selling. In this sense the circular economy brings about a massive re-alignment of customer and business incentives—no more intentionally designing products to break down, for obsolescence or disregarding externalities.

Many companies across the globe have already adopted circular principles to close the loop on energy and material through efforts such as renewable energy investments and recycling. What's making this space truly exciting? Pioneering innovators have realized the circular economy is not only about resource supply and use efficiency, but indeed even more about evolving their business models to transform the nature of resource demand from the customer's point of view, as in the case of the power tool. Research by Accenture has identified more than 100 truly disruptive companies applying circular economy thinking and new technology to transform in ways that seriously threaten incumbents. We call the competitive edge these companies gain the "circular advantage". Net-net, the circular advantage comes through innovating for both resource efficiency and customer value—delivering at the heart of a company's strategy, technology and operations. Take Nike for instance, which has worked for years on ways to balance the dual demands of resource productivity and value delivered to customers. This pursuit has fostered numerous innovations that have boosted the performance of products in the marketplace while reducing the products' environmental impact.

One example is Nike's Flyknit™ technology, which enables the company to create a shoe upper out of a few single threads. The result is a less-wasteful (by 80 percent) production process that renders a better-fitting and lighter shoe that can help boost an athlete's performance.

Our research reveals three key things businesses need to understand and to successfully play in the circular economy: (1) The emergence of five circular business models available to companies; (2) The role of five new business capabilities required to deliver them; (3) The disruptive power of ten digital and engineering technologies enabling changes.

2. Five Business Models Driving the Circular Economy

At a conceptual level, then, there is a strong and intuitive business case behind the circular economy both in the short and long-term: What company wouldn't want to reduce its dependence on increasingly scarce and costly natural resources while turning waste into additional revenue and value and sharpening their customer insight and value proposition? But at a practical level, it's not easy. The fact is most companies today are simply not built to capitalize on the opportunities the circular economy presents. Their strategies, structures and operations are deeply rooted in the linear approach to growth—it's in their DNA. That's why companies seeking the circular advantage will need to develop business models that are free of the constraints of linear thinking. These models are not just about doing "less bad", but they are about driving positive impact "through growth". That's a concept business and economies can get behind. There are five underlying business models that Accenture has identified in its analysis of more than 120 case studies of companies that are generating resource productivity improvements in innovative ways (Figure 2).

These business models have their own distinct characteristics and can be used singly or in combination to help companies achieve massive resource productivity gains and, in the process, enhance differentiation and customer value, reduce cost to serve and own, generate new revenue, and reduce risk.

(1) Model 1: Circular Supplies.

The Circular Supplies business model is based on supplying fully renewable, recyclable, or biodegradable resource inputs that underpin circular production and consumption systems. Through it, companies replace linear resource approaches and phase out the use of scarce resources while cutting waste, and removing inefficiencies.

This model is most powerful for companies dealing with scarce

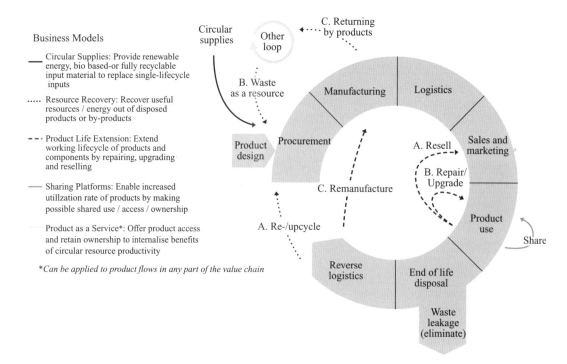

Business Models

— Circular Supplies: Provide renewable energy, bio based-or fully recyclable input material to replace single-lifecycle inputs

···· Resource Recovery: Recover useful resources / energy out of disposed products or by-products

– – · Product Life Extension: Extend working lifecycle of products and components by repairing, upgrading and reselling

— Sharing Platforms: Enable increased utilization rate of products by making possible shared use / access / ownership

Product as a Service*: Offer product access and retain ownership to internalise benefits of circular resource productivity

Can be applied to product flows in any part of the value chain

Figure 2　The Five Circular Business Models

commodities or ones with a major environmental footprint.

Royal DSM is one player at the forefront of adopting the Circular Supplies business model to fuel its shift from a virgin material supplier to a company that reuses materials and provides new eco-friendly ones. One example: The company developed cellulosic bio-ethanol, a byproduct of co-fermenting sugars derived from crops. Such bio-based chemicals have great potential to reduce waste and net CO_2 emissions compared with fossil fuels. The cellulosic bio-ethanol has created a new revenue stream for DSM from a feedstock that was previously considered very low value, and the company anticipates it could eventually create upwards of 70 000 related jobs.

(2) Model 2: Resource Recovery.

Resource recovery transforms waste into value through innovative recycling and upcycling services. Solutions range from industrial symbiosis to integrated closed loops recycling and Cradle-to-Cradle designs where disposed products can be reprocessed into new.

This model, which enables a company to eliminate material leakage and maximize economic value of product return flows, is a good fit for companies that produce large volumes of by-product or where waste material from products can be reclaimed and reprocessed cost effectively.

In the food sector, the Resource Recovery business model allows US grocery chain Kroger to convert food waste into renewable energy. The 150 tons of food waste the company produces each day at its Food 4 Less Compton distribution center—which used to be seen as a major cost in terms of lost revenue, disposal fees and emissions—now provides inexpensive, clean energy. That energy in turn powers a 49-acre campus that houses Kroger's offices as well as the distribution center.

The company relies on an "anaerobic digestion" system that converts food waste into biogas that runs the campus's micro-turbines and boilers replacing virtually all of the natural gas previously used. To date the initiative has yielded an 18 percent on Kroger's investment.

(3) Model 3: Product Life Extension.

Product Life Extension allows companies to extend the lifecycle of products and assets. Values that would otherwise be lost through wasted materials are instead maintained or even improved by repairing, upgrading, remanufacturing or remarketing products. And additional revenue is generated thanks to extended usage. Using this model, a company can help ensure that products stay economically useful for as long as possible and that product upgrades are done in a more targeted way.

This model is appropriate for most capital-intensive B2B segments (such as industrial equipment) and B2C companies that serve markets where pre-owned products are common or whose new releases of a product typically generate only partial additional performance benefits for customers over the previous version.

By embracing the Product Life Extension business model, Google is addressing the obsolescence challenge in the mobile phone arena: What to do with devices when they no longer suit a customer's needs? The company's Project Ara initiative focuses on reinventing the smart phone by breaking it down into replaceable modules that can be assembled and customized according to user requirements. With the ability to swap modules, users can easily alter their phone with basic skills and tools and repair the phone more easily and inexpensively by replacing only what is broken instead of the entire phone. By maximizing a phone's useful lifetime,

Google reduces the need for virgin resources to make new phones while minimizing the amount of E-waste generated. A possible complement to this design principle could be an online marketplace where users can trade phone modules to extend the lifecycle of components and recapture residual value.

(4) Model 4: Sharing Platforms.

The Sharing Platforms business model promotes a platform for collaboration among product users, either individuals or organizations. These facilitate the sharing of overcapacity or underutilization, increasing productivity and user value creation. This model, which helps maximize utilization, could benefit companies whose products and assets have a low utilization or ownership rate.

However, today it's most commonly found among companies specializing in increasing the utilization rate of products without doing any manufacturing themselves, putting considerable stress on traditional manufacturers.

Ride-sharing company Lyft Inc. is revolutionizing one segment of the travel market with the Sharing Platforms business model. Lyft's co-founders realized that cars making trips within cities were vastly underutilized; they estimated 80 percent of seats were empty. The company helps fill those seats by enabling, via its mobile app, individuals who need a ride somewhere to request one from someone who has a car. Pickup and ride fee (typically 20 percent to 30 percent lower than a comparable taxi fare) is paid through the app, of which Lyft takes a 20 percent cut. The business model appears to resonate not only with customers but with investors as well: The company in April 2014 announced a new round of funding worth $250 million (for a total of $333 million thus far), which the company says will help fuel Lyft's ongoing domestic—and, eventually, global—expansion.

(5) Model 5: Product as a Service.

The "Product as a Service" business model provides an alternative to the traditional model of "buy and own". Products are used by one or many customers through a lease or pay-for-use arrangement. This business model turns incentives for product durability and upgradability upside down, shifting them from volume to performance. With a Product as a Service business model, product longevity, reusability, and sharing are no longer seen as cannibalization risks, but instead, drivers of revenues and reduced costs.

This model would be attractive to companies whose products' cost of operation share is high and that have a skill advantage relative to their customers in managing maintenance of products.

Circular business models are disrupting industries around the world. In fact, our research revealed successful adoption of these business models has exploded in the past decade. Take Airbnb for example. The company allows users to rent rooms or entire homes from members through an online site. Founded in 2008, the company has overtaken both Inter Continental Hotels and Hilton Worldwide as the largest hotelier (offering more than 650 000 rooms) and has been growing bookings and revenues several hundred percent per year.

Initially, market disruption through circular business models was driven by startups. Now large multinationals are making serious moves as well. H&M collect garments in all stores to close the textile loop, BMW and Cisco Systems are extending the life of used products through refurbishment and resale, Philips offer "light as a service" to cities and municipal governments, Amazon.com textbooks as a service, Daimler's Car2Go (a car sharing service) had 600 000 customers in 2014 heading for $100 million in revenue and Wal-Mart is making a push into the $2 billion market for pre-owned videogames through an in-store trade-in program.

Another interesting development around circular economy: the emergence of ecosystems forming around pioneering organizations—both start-ups and long-established firms. Drinks manufacturer Carlsberg Group and a subset of its global suppliers have joined forces to develop the next generation of packaging optimized for recycling and reuse while, at the same time, retaining or improving quality and value. The cooperation has been formalized through the "Carlsberg Circular Community", which has set targets to include 15 partners and have at least three products Cradle-to-Cradle certified by 2016. At an Accenture event at the World Economic Forum in 2014, Jorgen Buhl Rasmussen, Carlsberg's CEO, said: "I saw there is a business case, it's in the interest of consumers and also of the planet and society".

3. Ten Transformational Technologies Make Circular Business Models Possible

Business model innovation offer companies powerful options for embracing the circular economy. But many of the models, if not most, would not be possible without the support of innovative new technologies—especially digital ones such as social, mobile, analytics, cloud and "machine to machine" technologies In our research we identified 10 disruptive technologies commonly used by the leading circular economy companies (Figure 3). These technologies fall into three categories: digital (information technology), engineering (physical technology), and hybrids of the two.

Digital technologies play an important role in establishing real-time information exchanges among users, machines and management systems. These technologies are intrinsically customer-focused and provide the information and connections needed to maintain a relationship far beyond the point of sale. Two examples in telecommunication are Vodafone and Verizon, which through in-mobile functionality and analytics, enable customers to automatically get a quote for the buy-back value of a used phone and support in returning the phone

		Circular Supplies	Resource Recovery	Product Life Extension	Sharing Platforms	Product as a Service
Digial	Mobile			▣	▣▣	
	M2M				▣▣	▣
	Cloud				▣	▣
	Social			▣	▣▣	▣
	Big Data Analytics	▣			▣	▣▣
Hybrid	Trace and return systems		▣	▣▣	▣	
	3D Printing	▣		▣		
Engineering	Modular design technology		☼	☼		☼
	Advanced recycling tech	☼	☼☼			
	Life and Material sciences	☼☼	☼			

Based on 120+case studies and 50+interviews
Number of icons in respective boxes indicate relative importance.

Figure 3   Disruptive Technologies used by Pioneers to Launch and Operate Circular Business Models with Speed and Scale

to a nearby store for instant reimbursement.

Such connections enhance remote visibility and control of assets, which are especially critical for the "Product as a Service"," Sharing Platforms" and "Product Life Extension" business models. By altering the way businesses and consumers interact with physical and digital assets and enabling dematerialization, digital technologies can transform value chains so they are decoupled from the need for additional resources for growth.

Engineering technologies—including advanced recycling, modular design, and life and material sciences—enable the manufacturing of new goods from regenerated resources, as well as the actual collection, return, and processing of goods and materials and cost-efficient collection of used assets for remanufacturing. Making these technologies especially important for running Circular Supplies and Resource Recovery models.

Hybrid technology is partly digital and partly engineering. It can establish a unique type of control over assets and material flows. It allows a company to digitally identify the history, location, status and application of materials and goods while, at the same time, support ways to physically collect, treat and reprocess them. For example, 3D printing allows for the local manufacturing of downloadable digital designs into physical objects—which is what Chinese company Winsun New Energy Co., has done. The company uses 3D printing to print houses in less than a day using recycled material—at a cost of less than $5 000 per home.

4. Five Capabilities of Successful Circular Leaders

Along with new technologies, new capabilities are essential for adopting a circular approach. From our research, five capabilities stand out as particularly important for successful implementation.

Firstly, business planning and strategy. From focusing on maximizing throughput and sales margin to participating in continuous product and service loops to boost revenue. Doing this requires not only concentrating on a narrow definition of the core business, but also participating in collaborative circular networks engaging suppliers, manufacturers, retailers, service suppliers and customers. It's vital to engage the full circular chain in one way or another to understand where and how value is really created and build up activities around that.

Secondly, innovation and product development. Companies' focus shifts from designing for single use to designing for many life cycles and users while optimizing the environmental effects of the materials used. Adapting products to generate revenues not only at point of sale but also during use as well as low-cost return chain and reprocessing are key design challenges. On the software end companies often need to mature PLM capabilities by expanding system definition and scope to repair, in-service and return activities.

Thirdly, product recycling and its impact on environment. In sourcing and manufacturing, companies will have to make sure that production is not only efficient, but that no resources are lost during the process and that the company can significantly scale up and maintain sourcing volumes from return chains. The latter often means shifting from large-scale sourcing from few suppliers to sourcing from many, heterogeneous and small-scale sources. This requires flexibility in production so that inputs of different qualities and origins can be used in production of valuable products, instead of dumped or incinerated.

Fourthly, sales and marketing. Companies will have to complement their chief focus on generating demand and fulfilling customer requirements with generating greater revenues from the use of products and services instead of the purchase of them. They also need to develop new ways to engage and incentivize customers to use and dispose of their products properly, especially if adopting service-based models where customers no longer have direct ownership of products and, as a result, less incentive to take proper care of them. Likewise, aftersales service will continue to support service levels, sell spare parts and manage channel partners, but will also have to become a much more active participant in managing the lifecycle of the product and maximizing its retained value. All-in-all, in a circular economy, sales and marketing is all about deepening the understanding of the use phase of products and feeding back revealed preferences from the markets so that products and services can be adapted for circular use.

Fifthly, disposal and collection. At the end of the process—holding the entire loop together—are reverse logistics and return chains, or disposal and collection. Reducing logistics and waste management cost, retaining customers with good return programs, and complying with government regulations will continue to be key concerns for this function. But it also must be effectively designed to manage opportunity-driven take-back/ buy-back from the markets and facilitate local reuse. A key capability, then, is quality control and determining the optimal return and reprocessing chain.

By doing so, they can initiate the transition to a new way of doing business that radically improves resource productivity, enhances differentiation, reduces costs and risks, creates robust new revenue streams, and enhances the customer value proposition. So what does it take to get started? Addressing the following five key set of questions can help CEOs and top executives frame the issues surrounding the journey toward circular advantage in their own organizations:

(1) Opportunity: Where are the opportunities for adopting circular economy approaches in our value chain and what can be done to shape our company's journey?

(2) Value: What's the real core value and essence of what we deliver to customers, and how can circular business models help us rethink how we deliver that value?

(3) Capabilities: What improvements will we need to make to our operating model and capabilities to support a circular economy business model and customer proposition?

(4) Technology: What are the technology trends—science, engineering and digital that really matter to our business when it comes to circular economy and what is their potential to disrupt the value chain?

(5) Timing: How do we time our initiation and adoption rates and the level of ambition of our circular economy approaches to create a portfolio and give us options and agility?

Moving toward a circular economy can be daunting. Yet, by adopting circular economy principles, more and more companies are gaining real competitive advantage: Getting ahead of rivals by innovating for both resource efficiency and customer value—and creating change at the intersection of a company's strategy, technology and operations. In the face of runaway resource scarcity and rising customer and policy expectations for better, more sustainable products, there's never been a better time to start.

While companies obviously are key to fostering the shift to a circular economy, governments should not play a minor role. Governments in general still need to make much greater—and more rapid—progress in creating a policy environment that nurtures circular business models. Policies like: shifting taxation from labor to resources, setting specific recycling targets for industries, making companies responsible for products throughout their life cycle, implementing tax premiums for the use of regenerated resources, and creating an international standard definition of waste.

Predicting the Future: The Global Trends and Strategic Options

Zhang Yunling

Director of International Studies, Chinese Academy of Social Sciences(CASS)

To predict Shanghai in 2050, you have to first of all predict about China, Asia, Asia Pacific, and the world as a whole, that is, you have to put Shanghai into perspective. Of course, it is difficult to predict the future in 30 years as there are a lot of variables, but some big trends are predictable.

Let's compare comprehensive economic strength of countries in 2050. According to the US Intelligence Committee's forecast on the big trends by 2050, China's GDP will be much higher than the second, the US followed by India, i.e. of the world's three major economy, two are located in Asia, all of the three are in the Asia-Pacific region. This forecast may affect people's thinking about the future.

In the regard of the future development of the world, the greatest change takes place in China. Speaking of 2050, we immediately think of China's "two-step" Initiative: the first step is to build a moderately prosperous society by the year of 2020, and the second step is to build China into a developed country in 2050. To become a developed country, it is not just about the increase of economic aggregate, but more importantly about social and political maturity. As a developed country, China will become a secure society of common prosperity; and it should establish a mature political system and national governance institution. China must go its own way of building socialism with Chinese characteristics, which is a contribution to the world, also an alternative to the current developed capitalist system.

China intends to be a new type of country, refraining from the traditional conventional powers; an important manifestation of which is to reflect the "oriental thoughts" of harmony and cooperation in national governance and participation in world affairs. While building a new international relation and order, China needs to strike a balance between inheriting the legacies of existing system and promoting its adjustment and reform.

From a global point of view, what the earth should be like in 2050? Pessimists might think that we are in a new era of war, conflict, and competitions among powers. Optimists believe that we enter an era of peaceful development, win-win, and mutual interdependence. Globalization has led to interdependence, we are all in the community of destiny, President Xi Jinping proposes to build the region and the world of common destiny, which is based on the traditional Chinese ideas of pursuing peace and harmony under the heaven. The so-called community of destiny means that we live in peace and harmony, thinking about survival and development altogether with consultation and cooperation. If so, we may be able to avoid war, and human civilization may enter a new era, which is the best result.

We must also take note that the world is in a period of great change which has multiple significances. Let's look at the change of national strength. Generally speaking, from World War II to now, the world's biggest change is the rise of developing countries, which now account for half the world's total economic aggregate, or a greater proportion if calculated using purchasing power parity(PPP). From now till 2050, the greatest potential for future development should be those developing countries, such as China, India, Indonesia, Brazil and so on, which will change the world economic landscape dominated now by the developed countries.

Another point is the transformation of development pattern. Most developing countries cannot enter the post-industrialized era as they need a brand new concept of sustainable development. In future development, global issues will be more and more prominent, and climate change is probably the largest variant. The World Climate Conference in Paris reaches a consensus to harness global warming. From this agreement, we can see very clearly that the best solution to the challenges facing a common destiny is for everyone to regard this responsibility top priority. Climate, resources, markets, rules, etc. all based on "responsibility" for global governance, which, in my mind, is probably a big trend affecting world development in the future. Meanwhile, the new industrial revolution driven by new technologies is deepening and diffusing. Information Technology, smart technology, new energy, aerospace are raging, which produces two effects: First, it creates a new driving force for economic development, so that the world economy will enter a new development period; the second is to change the economic growth structure, energy-saving, environmental-friendly and efficient industrial sectors will witness rapid growth. These factors will affect greatly the future development of the world.

In the transition, China as a big country with an ambition to realize national rejuvenation can play a significant role. Not long ago I visited Iran, a seminary professor advised that not only did Iran attach importance to China's economic achievements, but more importantly, China provided a different choice for the world. This statement makes sense. Currently, it seems western democracy is the only recognized political regime; anything else is regarded being bad. China adopts a different political system, if successfully developed, which could provide another successful model for the world to choose from. It has very far-reaching significance and the key is for China to do its best to make the harmonious philosophy and the spirit of benignity, integrity, benevolence and tolerance and principles of fairness, justice and civilization the new universal values.

In my opinion, to make a forecast about 2050, the most noteworthy aspect is to understand those big variables which are difficult for us to assume. What in the end is the world's largest variable? I believe it is uncertainty presented in all aspects, economic, political, global, and regions. In any future planning, it is necessary to factor in uncertainties as influential variables. In other words, facing such a changing world with increasing uncertainties, we need to come up with several plans.

Obviously, when we plan the future of Shanghai, there are several dimensions to take into account: trends in China, trends in the world, the new competitive trend, and possible trends in the fields of unknown. From the perspective of economic development, the next few years will be the times of structural adjustment; therefore, Shanghai should take the lead in restructuring and become a winner in new and open competitions.

As a future-oriented city, Shanghai must move towards being an innovative, smart, livable city and build its own attractiveness. Innovation is the driving force for future development; open and innovation will enable Shanghai to be the source of innovative ideas and technology; smart is the key for Shanghai to be an avant-garde, fully utilizing information technology, internet and high-tech to build a highly efficient city governance and operation system; livable city will be the label of Shanghai as a city's main attraction is reflected providing a livable (green, convenient, diverse and colorful environment to the residents).

What would the future Shanghai be like? I think Shanghai should be "large in scale-small in urban area-multi-dimensions in space". Would the future of Shanghai be like New York, London or Tokyo? None of them. Shanghai should be a global city with its own features, having its own characteristics and images. Generally, it must complete the transition from a manufacturing city to a service-oriented city, from a manufacturing center to an innovative center. Shanghai should play a pioneering role in the following three steps: that is, when China become an overall well-off country in 2020, ranks first in terms of economic strength in 2030 and be one of the most developed countries in 2050.

Shanghai in 2050: A World-Leading Innovation Hub

Jane Wang

PwC Leading Partner of Retail Consumption Duty for Asia Pacific

Globalization and technological change are deepening interaction between nation states, creating a networked whole in which all face the same challenges and complexities.

This is why Shanghai—already China's biggest city and its economic engine—has been tasked with establishing itself as a center of technology innovation with global influence. "Shanghai in 2050", a taskforce initiated by the municipal government, aims to set out the development challenges and strategic choices the city faces as it picks up the gauntlet.

In the 1950s no more than 30% of the world population lived in cities, according to the UN. Today the figure has risen to 50% and by 2030 there will be 4.9 billion urban dwellers worldwide. Rural migration will mean exponential urban growth continues—with another estimated 72%—increase in city population by 2050. This will exert tremendous implications for city infrastructure, both in developed and emerging countries. There will be huge investment demand for smart city infrastructure, especially in emerging economies. For Shanghai, in particular, these implications are most noteworthy:

(1) Mega-cities may become more powerful than small nation states;

(2) Higher trade volumes will require further big infrastructure investment (e.g. ports and airports), while populations will need better education, healthcare, employment opportunities and a social safety net;

(3) Higher density living will require better access to information and more sophisticated social media.

Also, Shanghai will need to maintain its unique edge, specifically in the following dimensions:

(1) Instead of endless expansion, the city should focus on transforming from a labour-intensive economy to a knowledge economy powered by services;

(2) It should enhance connectivity and synergies among cluster of cities in the Yangtze Delta, improving the agglomeration's overall economy;

(3) Shanghai's history is unique and efforts to preserve and promote its openness, inclusivity and willingness to embrace the best of what the world has to offer will surely pay off handsomely in the long run;

(4) The government should be committed to maintaining its open, responsive and transparent approach, working to engage citizens in city affairs and enabling them to contribute to a Shanghai that has classic appeal and innovation at its core.

For China as a whole, now featured with a "new normal" for economic growth, the old resource-intensive development model will no longer sustain. Establishing a center of technology innovation to deepen China's role in the "co-opetition" of today's global economy is therefore imperative. Shanghai is stepping up to make this possible.

1. The Business Landscape

Shanghai is already a global economic centre, driven by a combination of State Owned Enterprises (SOEs), Privately Owned Enterprises (POEs) and Multinational Corporations (MNCs). Fostering a business community that increases connectivity between each of the business types is an excellent way to encourage innovation. Cross-pollination of opportunities will enable new start-ups to tap into the expertise, processes, and networks of established companies in the city, providing a distinct advantage, especially during early phases of development.

New York offers a good example of how this can work. Wall Street firms have been encouraged to create partnerships with city authorities that link top executives and budding entrepreneurs. These partnerships have resulted in support ranging from leadership coaching to sharing access to customers. Given the wealth of world-class management in the city, establishing a "Partnership for Shanghai" program to connect seasoned executives with start-ups, and innovative initiatives can add tremendous value.

It is also worth noting that SOEs contribute approximately half of Shanghai's current GDP, and as a result their significance in driving innovation cannot be understated. Shanghai's government will play a key role in shaping the future landscape, as companies look to an environment in which firms from each pillar engage with optimal efficiency. And with true innovation often requiring ten years or more to come to fruition, defining long-term metrics that guide innovation are going to prove advantageous. Consequently, the development of benchmarks for both organisational and individual influences on innovation may become increasingly widespread.

In addition to connectivity, Shanghai has a lot to gain from its many incubators. There is a good case for continuing to build more, while increasing promotion of existing sites to attract the best innovators. Opportunities also exist with incubating new businesses in mature companies. For instance, creating smaller teams within an overall corporate structure can facilitate "in-house entrepreneurship." Being flexible on where incubation takes place is an important factor for success.

Looking ahead, by developing an innovation ecosystem that connects SOEs, POEs, MNCs, and start-ups, the Shanghai government can help the city achieve unique competitive advantages that will help it become a hub of innovation with global influence.

2. Smart Investment

Start-ups will always require access to funding, and Shanghai has excellent supply of venture capital (VC) and private equity (PE). The task will be to ensure that the market is enabled and optimised to identify and invest in innovations. Such innovations could cover technology, products and services, processes, as well as management, and can take place in both start-ups and established organisations. Due to an abundance of quick exit opportunities, investors in Shanghai have not been motivated to scour the market in search of breakthrough innovations in the same keen manner they do in other economic centres. To achieve maximum potential, Shanghai will benefit from VC professionals identifying and increasing investments in innovative ideas at earlier phases. Therefore, an imperative will be developing VC talent with expertise in recognising potential high-impact innovations, and specifically technical innovations that are ripe for commercialisation. This takes time, and also comes with a degree of risk. It's important for businesses to recognise there will be failures along the path to innovation.

Development in Shanghai could also be helped by the extension of investment and support to surrounding cities. New enterprises would initially be able to take advantage of lower operational costs, before gradually merging into Shanghai's central orbit as they develop. Greater connectivity could also help focus efforts on cultivating diverse hubs of innovation that build on areas of strength, for instance clusters in pharmaceuticals, logistics, and finance.

3. Attracting Talent

When it comes to cultivating innovation, attracting talent is critical. Today, Shanghai boasts excellent universities and research laboratories with an international field of expertise. In order to become an international centre for innovation, scaling up the talent pool will need to be among the areas of focus. In addition, by embracing technological advances, Shanghai can explore creative new ways to expand access to global talent, potentially by developing and exploiting a virtual talent pool.

A range of steps are being taken to attract talent, including plans to reduce labour restrictions. Wider initiatives in civic design will also help attract newcomers. Developing public spaces, cultural facilities, safe habitats, and advanced education facilities all help to advance appeal to innovators and their families. Further, the Shanghai government has identified policies to encourage entrepreneurship. One instance includes allowing university researchers to form start-ups while enabling university students to participate on a part-time basis. These efforts form a solid base on which to develop, by nurturing existing talent, while ensuring the city is more attractive to newcomers.

The goal is set, and Shanghai will be taking a long-term view to meeting myriad challenges that range from advancing markets, technological infrastructure, and the role of law. In particular, Shanghai has excellent opportunities in the form of optimising the diverse business environment. Shaping the business community, including SOEs, POEs and MNCs, so that there is a supportive environment for start-ups, as well as innovative initiatives within established corporations will offer substantial advantage. This, in conjunction with encouraging market investors to find and fund innovation, while scaling up the volume of talent, will see Shanghai well on the way to becoming a globally influential centre of innovation.

The government has set out its master plan. By 2020, the innovation center's framework will be ready, by 2030 the core functions will be in place and by 2050 the city will have become a globally influential innovation hub. Going forward, the key tasks will be to ensure that the market is enabled and optimised to identify and invest in innovation, and that effective steps are taken to attract global talent to the city. The ambition is there, and Shanghai will be taking a long-term view to meeting myriad challenges and opportunities on the way to becoming a global city.

Shanghai in 2050: A "Center" of Culture and Ideas with Global Influence

Ye Hua

Chairman, NRI (Shanghai)

This year, the summit's theme is "Shanghai 2050: Vision and Challenge". This is a rather meaningful and challenging title. As we cannot accurately predict what Shanghai will be like in the next 35 years, bold imagination is required.

In my vision, in 2050, Shanghai should be a "center" of culture and ideas with global influence. The word "center" is used in quotation marks because I am not sure whether the future spread of culture and ideas is central, whether it can become a center, or whether it should be called a center.

Why proposea "center" of culture and ideas? This may be regarded by many people as a rather "non-pragmatic" goal. To look forward to the future of Shanghai in the next 35 years, we should first review its past 35 years. So, I'll start with some main recommendations from Nomura Group offered to Shanghai Municipal People's Government in the last 35 years, outlining the trajectory of Shanghai's development towards higher goals.

1. 1970s—1980s: Setting Up an "Open Window" with National Influence

In 1978, Nomura Group proposed to the State Economic Commission and Shanghai Municipal People's Government the establishment of a "special open area" in an economic center in the mainland to rapidly open up to the outside world. With a view of attracting foreign capital and technology, Shanghai was a prime choice. In 1979, planning was initiated to make Shanghai Hongqiao an Economic & Technological Development Zone; in 1986, it became one of the first batch of 14 economic & technological development zones at the national level, as well as the smallest national development zone with a focus on the modern service industry. In 1984, in order to provide temporary working and living accommodations for staff members of overseas companies starting up in Shanghai, Nomura Group cooperated with the Shanghai Municipal People's Government, investing and building the Shanghai Garden Hotel. Construction of the hotel launched in 1985, and it opened for business in 1990.

2. 1989—2015: Annual Recommendations Made to the Mayor of Shanghai for the Next 25 Years

Shanghai is a very open city that is willing to listen to and take advices voices at different international levels. In 1988, Mr. Zhu Rongji, the then mayor of Shanghai, envisioned establishing an international consulting platform through which global entrepreneurs could share advice for the development of Shanghai; as a result, IBLAC was born. On Oct. 9th, 1989, IBLAC held a preparatory meeting, and representatives from Nomura Group suggested organizing annual open discussions to shed light on one prominent issue emerging in the development of Shanghai. Since then, Nomura group has made suggestions and recommendations in each subsequent annual meeting. Over the course of 27 IBLAC annual meetings, many of the topics were future-oriented. For instance, the theme in 1997 was "How should Shanghai face the 21st century", in 2002 it was "How to build Shanghai into a world class metropolis", and in 2013 it was "How to elevate Shanghai's soft power".

3. In 2004: Building Pudong as a "Sub-center for Technological Innovation"

In 2004, NRI was commissioned by the government of Pudong New Area to work on the region's 11th Five Year Plan, to identify both opportunities and challenges for Pudong New Area, and to propose strategic goals for the next 5—10 years. We proposed that in order to sustain its competitiveness in the global arena, Pudong should elevate its functionalities as a world-class city, create an enabling environment for innovation, and engage in broad collaboration both within and outside of the New Area to realize synergy. We also proposed that, while building Pudong as a global financial center, more attention should be paid to developing its functionalities as a global innovation center. Pudong should be built as a "sub-center for global innovation" to further improve Shanghai's urban functionalities as well as its spatial structure. Although the primary goal then was undoubtedly building Pudong into a global financial center, the concept of a "sub-center" was also proposed, given the inseparable relationship between technology and finance and ICT and finance.

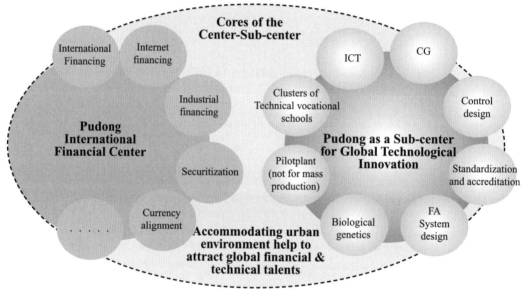

Figure 1　NRI's Report in 2004

4. In 2009: "3 Centers" Based on "4 Centers"

Commissioned by Shanghai Municipal government in 2009, NRI worked on the 12th Five Year Plan for Shanghai. We proposed strategic goals for the city by 2020 based on the completion of a roadmap for "4 centers." It was our opinion that by 2020, Shanghai should transform from "material capital to institutional capital" and from "revolution of the flow to revolution of the stock", realizing the transformation from "a content power house to a spiritual/ ideas powerhouse". If Shanghai cannot make a difference at the spiritual and intellectual levels, it will probably never truly be a world-class city. So the proposed goals for Shanghai by 2020 are to initially build the "4 centers" and establish a service-oriented economy with financial service as the basis, building Shanghai into a globally responsible metropolis featuring "innovation and vibrant world culture", which are in line with Shanghai's spirits and values.

2050 is a long way away and we cannot predict whether there will be huge changes or subversive, discontinuous changes over such a time frame. However, no matter the changes, a city with global influence means to be recognized, preferred, and liked by talents with global influence.

Let me give an example to illustrate how Shanghai has been recognized and preferred.

Table 1   Comprehensive Ranking of Main Metropolises in 2015

	Entrepreneurs	Researchers	Artists	Tourists	Residents
New York	4	1	2	3	3
London	1	2	3	1	2
Tokyo	8	3	8	6	8
Shanghai	7	26	14	8	31

Source: GPCI 2015 by Mori Memorial Foundation.

Every year, the Mori Memorial Foundation works with experts from Shanghai on the preparation of the Global Power City Index(GPCI). Through many interviews, GPCI distinguishes Shanghai's attractiveness to different groups of people. For entrepreneurs, Shanghai is a very prosperous and economically dynamic city, but it doesn't enormously appeal to researchers and artists, especially according to feedback from those who live in the city.

A city must always possess some basic elements in order for it to be recognized, preferred, and liked by talents with global influence. The more we want to plan for the long-term future, the more we need to return to basics. Returning to basics means continuously reinforcing the foundation, otherwise there will be no future. Whether a city is safe, secure, and stable enough for people to live in is crucial for a 10-year, 20-year, or 30-year plan.

Based on the above review and reflection, I propose a vision for Shanghai in 2050 as shown in the figure 2.

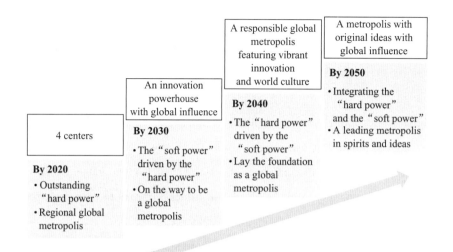

Figure 2　A Vision for Shanghai in 2050

By 2020, Shanghai will realize the roadmap for "4 centers" mainly by strengthening hard power. By 2030, Shanghai will be on the way to be a global metropolis through "soft power" driven by "hard power". By 2040, Shanghai will become a responsible global metropolis featuring vibrant innovation and world culture through "hard power" driven by "soft power". By 2050, Shanghai will become a metropolis with original ideas and global influence through the integration of "hard power" and "soft power".

Shanghai in 2050: The First Global City of 21st Century

Edward Tse

Founder & CEO of Gao Feng Advisory Company

How to position Shanghai's future development? What kinds of city it'll become in 2050? Here I'd like to share with you a new book, *The Inevitable* by Kevin Kelly, who may be known to many of you. He has worked in the Silicon Valley for more than 30 years, observing and analyzing the development of science and technology. As he's so accurate in grasping the pulse of science and technology, many Chinese entrepreneurs, especially in the fields of Internet and technology, take him as the God of Technology. The first edition of this book is the Chinese version published in December 2015 in China, prior to its English version in the United States. It's not just a book, but the manifesto for the coming of a new era. In the field of science and technology, entrepreneurs are facing the arrival of a new era, which is related to the "World Internet Conference" recently held in Wuzhen. Many topics discussed in the conference are closely linked with our goals. This new era, especially the age of the Internet, is becoming more powerful and confident. I have made a brief summary of Kevin Kelly's book: We have found these important concepts both in China and around the world, including "formation""circulation""sharing""tracing""usage" "interaction""screen pecking""remixing""filtering""intellectualizing""questioning" and "beginning". Many of you may understand some of them, but not for others. They are actually affecting our work and lifestyle in various ways.

Even before this summit, I have long been considering what Shanghai will be like in 2050. Actually no one knows the answer, but it's worth thinking. In 35 years, China will no doubt become the largest economy of the world and the amount of RMB and US dollar in circulation will exceed other currencies.

Meanwhile, our world will be highly interconnected, artificial intelligence will be common and the distance between people will be greatly reduced. Nowadays, many job positions are still not occupied by knowledge workers, but by then, there will be much more knowledge workers with great working capacity and creativity. At that time, our resources will be very scattered but highly centralized, while technologies will grow more complicated. In other words, people are separated physically in communities, but thanks to the new technologies, we are together in the virtual world. What's more, the life span of human beings will be greatly prolonged. According to authoritative data, the average life span is just over 80, living to 100 years old should not be a dream in 2050 however.

Chinese are experiencing a great time to set sail. In the next several decades, China under the new normal will be equipped with all the factors below: entrepreneurship and creativity; the ideological and cultural enlightenment represented by the middle class and the elites; political revolution in China will synchronize with the overall political and economic environment as well as its relationship with other countries and regions; the next 30 to 50 years may become the golden era for China's renaissance.

Talents in China never stops thinking and reflecting who we really are. Under President Xi's leadership, we will become more open-minded and confident in the future.

Then how will Shanghai become a global city of the 21th century in 35 years? Though not necessarily correct, we may think about it from various aspects. We ourselves, as well as our culture, our society, our technologies, our environment, will all be involved in this process. As a global city of the 21st century, Shanghai should pursue spiritual developments, in other worlds, the construction of values, which is not shared only in China, but around the world. Another question is what role will the government play in future? A new ecology and environment will be constructed in Shanghai in 35 years and the role of the government may be facilitating, investing and participating. In this process, we are all pursuing a Shanghai's dream, which is actually a part of the Chinese dream, and the Chinese dream itself is a part of the dream of our world. We should pursue our responsibilities and become the Shanghai citizens with consciousness, sense of responsibility and creativity. Finally, we will all become global citizens.

Shanghai in 2050: From Economic and Financial Center to Talent Center

Ioana Kraft

General Manager, Shanghai Chapter, European Union Chamber of
Commerce in China

Thank you for offering this opportunity to share with so many scholars and professionals our expectations and visions on Shanghai in 2050. It is both an exciting and challenging work. We are excited to be invited to participate in the design of Shanghai's future. However, it is also challenging because it is so hard to imagine how business and life would look like in 35 years in such a rapidly changing world, just as we couldn't have imagined buying almost everything with smart phones just 10 years ago.

But we believe there is something constant despite changing circumstances, which is people's eternal pursuit for prosperous, secure and fulfilling life. From the city's point of view, the development of a city is sustainable only if it can constantly offer livable environment and development opportunities for talents to settle down. The successful evolution of a city may rely on its natural endowment and its economic competitiveness, but it ultimately relies on the wisdom of its residents.

In the past three decades, we have seen Shanghai secure its irreplaceable position in China as the national economic and financial centre. Thanks to the rise of China in the global economy and its ability to match its strengths with arising opportunities, Shanghai has been able to make big steps on its journey transform itself into an international economic centre, a financial centre, a shipping centre and a trade centre and we are confident that it is set to reach its goals by 2020. We are also thrilled to see Shanghai planning to become an international science and innovation centre by the year 2020, as China is gradually climbing up the value chain. Based on the overall trend, we would like to see Shanghai in 2050 to be a city that would occupy the top of global value chain and thus become a hub for global talents.

The ages of double-digit economic growth in China have passed and it is not very likely that this growth rate will be back in the near future. China has entered now a new phase defined as the "New Normal". It means we have to get used to the gradually slowing economic growth. At the same time, it also means China is transitioning away from its previous export-driven growth model and repositioning itself in the global economy. The establishment of the China (Shanghai) Pilot Free Trade Zone has given Shanghai new momentum towards the goals set in the "Four Centers Initiative". A series of policies targeting at streamlining government administration, trade facilitation and financial liberalization have come into effect and more are to be expected. Given the Shanghai government's commitment to build the city into a science and innovation centre by 2020, we expect to see Shanghai that is friendlier towards innovation-oriented enterprises in terms of financial support, technological support, legal environment and talent policy.

However, this transition period is challenging and the reform is not an easy cause. As Premier Li Keqiang put it in April of 2015, the "the new dynamics have yet to grow strong, while the old ones are losing steam". Shanghai is struggling in finding new development momentum too. According to the Business Confidence Survey we conduct on an annual basis among our some 600 members operating in Shanghai, 40% of them see no increase or even a year-on decrease in revenue in 2015 and nearly a quarter are pessimistic about their profitability outlook within the next two years. As a result, far fewer companies are looking to expand their business in China. It is therefore urgent for Shanghai to accelerate the implementation of planned reform and initiative agendas in the next 5 years, or namely, in the period of "13th Five-year Plan" and onwards.

How to realize Shanghai's goals in 2020 as planned and take advantage of the incoming capital, trade and information flows to further encourage innovation and attract talents remains the key to the sustainable development for Shanghai in the next 35 years. Based on our observations and research, we would like to offer the following recommendations.

First of all, a fair and open competitive environment for all players is crucial to foster innovation. Innovation has a comprehensive lifecycle. It starts from investment in R&D, goes through test production and mass production and ends with consumption and reinvestment. Admittedly, funding is the starting point for innovation and it is particularly important for SMEs. However, we often overemphasize the importance of financing while underestimating the importance of production and sales for innovation in general. When it comes to production and sales, it ultimately raises the issue of market access.

Although China (Shanghai) Pilot Free Trade Zone has implemented negative list for foreign investors, which we think is a great advancement in granting larger market access, we still see many market access barriers, which make foreign players and domestic players compete on unequal ground. Apart from these barriers towards foreign investors, we also see large SOEs in an advantageous position against SMEs in terms of access to finance and opportunity to interact with government. SMEs are usually regarded as "backbone" of healthy and sustainable economy in Europe, because of their flexibility in applying new technologies and models and looking for innovative business solutions. Therefore, a market that denies access of private SMEs is not encouraging innovation. Rather, it suffocates the economy in the long run.

Secondly, besides open market access, government incentives and establishing rule of law are also important in promoting innovation and attracting talents. More specifically, Shanghai will need to construct a friendlier environment for R&D activities and ensure stricter enforcement of intellectual property right (IPR) protection. Independent courts with adequately trained judges are needed for investors and individuals to be confident that their rights are protected, not only when it comes to IP but also in commercial and other legal disputes.

According to our member companies, there is still room for China and Shanghai to attract more R&D investment from European companies and for companies to develop their innovation capacities here. Our survey showed this year that 68% of companies which undertake R&D globally do not undertake R&D in China. 42% of collected answers indicate that European companies'

R&D centers in China are mainly used for product localization. At the same time, our members have been reporting that foreign-invested companies find themselves restricted from applying for the High and New-Technology Enterprise (HNTE) status as well as participating in state-funded development projects. Thus, foreign-invested companies are not able to access to the financial incentives frameworks nor can they fully contribute to China's and Shanghai's innovation initiatives. Without the participation of foreign-invested companies, it is unrealistic for Shanghai to transform itself into an international innovation centre.

The enforcement of IPR laws is equally crucial to the survival of innovative companies. The European Chamber welcomes the important steps that Shanghai has taken to ensure that intellectual property laws and the enforcement thereof is strengthened. While we will need more time to be able to fully assess its impact, the establishment of specialized IP courts and IP supervisory authorities which now offer a one-stop shop for the administration and enforcement of IPRs (including patents, trademarks and copyrights) is a good sign that Shanghai is headed the right way when it comes to implementing the safeguards needed for innovation.

Thirdly, when it comes to access to talents, we took note of the new entry and exit regulations which include an easing of the visa regime for skilled foreign talents. They are again a step in the right direction. Nevertheless, certain guidelines announced still indicate an overly conservative approach when it comes to young professionals; recent foreign graduates that lack the two years of work experience will have to have graduated from a local Chinese university in order to qualify for expert visas. This means that talents who graduated from overseas universities will still have to present 2 years of job experience. There is still no sign of issuance of internship visa, which denies foreign talents to have a pre-job experience of Chinese culture, job market and business environment. We understand that labor market policy considerations may dictate certain restrictions to the employment of foreign fresh graduates. However, they block companies from attracting the brightest international talents to join their R&D operations in China. Interns are only temporary here and do not take away jobs from Chinese graduates.

If you ever get to take a peek inside the great corporate and academic research laboratories and institutions of the world you will notice that one characteristic they all share is a very diverse team of scientists. This is because innovation occurs most naturally where talented people of different ages, cultures and national backgrounds come together, supplementing each other's gaps in knowledge, experience and creativity. Keeping in mind Shanghai's ambitious goal of becoming a global innovation hub by 2020 then, it is adamant that the pace of visa policy reform for skilled talents is accelerated and its scope is widened as soon as possible. One further measure could be for instance, to attribute a specific visa status to allow young foreign scientists and researchers to work in China and for foreign scientists to work in China on short-term, joint R&D projects. Only if foreign talents may easily enter, stay, and work in Shanghai could we really say Shanghai is capable of become a talent high ground in 2050.

Last but not least, another issue that many of our members have raised is the speed of the Internet and access to certain websites. In a members' poll run in May 2015, slow Internet speed and the inability to access certain web pages in China were identified as negatively affecting the business of 57% of companies overall. While page loading times for main-stream Chinese websites such as baidu.com and sina.com are consistent, professionals are still faced with irregular access and slow internet speed when visiting many foreign websites. More specifically, 24% of the respondents to Business Confidence Survey reported that the slow Internet speed is leading to lower productivity in the office, R&D facilities and manufacturing. Similarly, 31% of respondents reported inability to search for information and execute research.

Access to global search engines, which are necessary for research and innovation is restricted. These restrictions on the Internet affect the ability of individuals and businesses to conduct research and develop new products, technologies and processes and set global trends. This also affects Shanghai's ability to attract top researchers as they are put off by the restrictions and the difficulty to search for scholarly papers to conduct their work. Indeed, the Internet issue in China has not improved. On the contrary, China's global ranking for average peak Internet connection speeds has dropped from 96th place to 113th place just over the past year. This will not only have a negative impact on Shanghai as a place to conduct R&D but in its economic growth in general.

Strict immigration policies, paired with Internet restrictions and pollution challenges as we have again experienced this week make Shanghai only 2nd for international top scientists despite the quality of infrastructure.

To wrap it up, as one of the 24 million residents of this beautiful city, we are honored to witness Shanghai's transformation into global hub for finance and trade, as well as for innovation. We are optimistic that Shanghai in 2050 will become more livable and more open towards companies and talents from all over the world. At the same time, we certainly know that there is still a lot of work to be done before Shanghai realizes its goals. However, we are confident that the Shanghai government will take the right measures and continue to implement forward looking policies. The European Chamber, together with our members, are well prepared to embrace and contribute to this great initiative, the further development and implementation of which will require efforts from all sides.

Shanghai in 2050: The World's Healthiest City

Jesse Wu

Chairman of Johnson & Johnson China

As a representative of the healthcare industry, I want to share with everyone here today our vision of the Shanghai healthcare sector in 2050. The fact is, Johnson & Johnson has always placed great emphasis on the state of the general public's health and is dedicated to making a positive contribution to improving Shanghai's healthcare system.

Speaking of a future vision of healthcare in Shanghai in 2050, I once asked our employees to describe what they imagine healthy living might be like in 2050.

One colleague, born in the 1990s, gave me a very interesting response that was particularly thought provoking.

This is what he said: one day in 2050, Shanghai will host the 55th annual international marathon. The Shanghai marathon will have become a top-tier international event. At that time, he will be approaching 60 years old. As a long-distance running enthusiast, he will have already signed up for the amateur marathon along with a couple of his friends. After waking up and getting ready, wearable devices will tell him that he's ideally suited to run according to an analysis of his recent sleep patterns and health, as well as the day's weather conditions including wind speed, temperature, humidity, and other indicators. (Of course, I believe that by 2050 Shanghai's air pollution will no longer be an environmental or health concern.) Though my colleague will not finish the amateur race in a ranking position, he will still be happy that he successfully completed the race. After the marathon, he will immediately contact his health consultant to inquire about the status of his health. By accessing the real-time health status monitoring information transmitted by his wearable devices as well as his personal medical history, the doctor will determine that he is in excellent condition and will provide professional advice on what to do after a high-intensity workout.

In his description, he also mentions that by 2050, health consultants will be able to provide medical advice across all aspects of health management and through remote diagnosis will be able to effectively predict the probability of suffering a particular disease. An example of this might be providing tailored health management advice and healthy eating tips for high-risk groups, including those suffering from diabetes and coronary disease as well those with a family history of lung cancer. Advancements in medical technology have made effective health management possible and by 2050, Shanghai has become the healthiest city in the world.

After listening to his story, a lot went through my mind (I'm also almost 60), mainly what should we do now in order to make this wonderful vision come true? What goals should Shanghai set for 2020 or 2030?

I believe Shanghai is already equipped to move forward in the following few areas:

First, Shanghai should build a health management system that provides coverage for all citizens. The health management system plays a very important role in the future's medical system. Shanghai can create an overarching health management system that combines community health management centers and large medical centers, and fully leverage big data to provide coverage for citizens throughout their entire life cycle in areas such as disease control, early diagnosis, health indicator monitoring, treatment, and rehabilitation. In turn this will effectively improve medical resource application efficiency, lower the cost of medical care, and improve living standards for the general population. For example: we can build a personal health record database for each citizen at the community health management centers and then implement a tiered medical system to make public health management more convenient; we can provide reminders and intervene when necessary on citizen's eating, drinking, exercise, and lifestyle habits through community health management centers and public welfare organizations, advocating an overall healthier lifestyle for our city's residents; we can provide free vaccines and regular check-ups for early disease prevention. Disease prevention is at the core of public health management; we can analyze health monitoring data from wearable devices and personal health big data for health consultants from community health management centers to provide real-time health advice to patients.

Second, Shanghai builds a multi-layered medical insurance system. The government should provide basic medical insurance that covers all the city's residents, while fully taking advantage of commercial health insurance to cover expenditures that fall outside basic medical insurance. This will make it more convenient for patients and give them access to more services, also meeting medical care needs on a number of different levels. At the same time, a medical aid system needs to be included to reduce the burden of medical expenses for the general public. In 2014, out-of-pocket medical expenses in Shanghai averaged 33.9%. We hope that by 2050 this ratio can be lowered to 10%.

In terms of investing in basic medical coverage, the government can gradually increase its investment in medical care thereby increasing medical expenditures as a percentage of GDP. Further, due to good preventive care and health management at community health management centers, government medical expenditures will emphasize prevention rather than treatment services, which will improve the efficiency of investments. We should encourage and supervise the development of private insurance. For example, we can provide tax benefits for citizens who purchase private insurance. We should also promote active intervention by health insurance companies for medical treatments performed in hospitals, to further improve hospital management efficiency.

Third, Shanghai needs to actively promote the widespread use of innovative drugs and treatments. Shanghai is transforming into a center for technological innovation. The widespread application of innovative drugs and treatments will be invaluable to the patients. It will not only help patients access innovative drugs faster and more conveniently but will also bring vibrancy and further opportunities for innovation to the healthcare industry in Shanghai.

Shanghai can collaborate with CFDA to apply WHO Good Review Practices (GRP) and incorporate the guidance and registration requirements put forth by the International Council for Harmonization of Technical Requirements for Pharmaceuticals for Human Use(ICH). Based on a risk assessment, Shanghai also can work with CFDA to simplify application material requirements for clinical trials to make it possible for qualified new drugs to receive approval within 12 months, aligning the drug approval process with the US and EU. This will help to ensure that Shanghai's citizens enjoy access to innovative drugs and treatments in lockstep with the rest of the world's treatment provisions.

Guided by the strategy of creating a technology innovation center with global influence, Shanghai can actively promote the creation of innovation ecosystems to encourage open innovation models. The government should increase its investment in basic research to strengthen Shanghai's R&D capabilities as a source of innovation and develop relevant stimulus policies to boost innovation in the market. In particular, the government should invest heavily in policies that support the nurturing of stem cells, 3D printing of artificial organs for transplant, gene sequencing, molecular imaging for use in early prevention and diagnosis, targeted therapy, customized treatments for diseases, and other innovative 21st century technologies.

In addition, we should also develop related policies to encourage innovation and support the development of innovative products. For example, we can draw on the experiences of other countries and create a pricing model based on the degree of innovation. Creating premiums will encourage and reward the development of innovative drugs. We can also build an effective intellectual property protection mechanism to protect these innovations and innovative products.

Finally, Shanghai better allocates the number of healthcare professionals and improves their skills and social status. Shanghai will be able to create an environment that is more conducive to healthcare professionals' growth and development. The increase in multi-site practices will provide more avenues for healthcare professionals to explore, giving them a greater sense of professional empowerment. This will also help attract top-tier talent and expand the number of professionals in the healthcare system. Compensation for doctors and nurses needs to coincide with their own professional investments to properly reflect their market value. As the population continues to age, the need for healthcare professionals, especially nurses, will grow exponentially. For example, the number of nurses will increase from 15 per 10 000 people in 2012 to more than 115 per 10 000 people in 2050 (Japan already reached this number back in 2012 due to its large aging population). Therefore we not only need to strengthen medical treatment and care, but also our prevention, health management, and senior citizen care at community health management centers. An increase in the number of healthcare professionals, improvements in their professional and communication capabilities, as well as a more extensive medical insurance system will help to establish a harmonious relationship between healthcare professionals and patients.

In order to lay the groundwork in the above few areas, we need to reach a consensus among the various government agencies, as well as between the government, enterprise, and healthcare institutions, so that we may all work together to make Shanghai the world's healthiest city by 2050.

Johnson & Johnson has been rooted in China for 30 years. Whether past, present, or future, Johnson & Johnson is fully committed to promoting the development of the healthcare industry in Shanghai and in China as a whole.

Moving forward, we believe that innovation is critical to a healthier tomorrow. This is why Johnson & Johnson is actively part of the discussion on how to transform Shanghai into a science and technology innovation center with global influence. At the end of 2014, Johnson & Johnson built the Asia Pacific Innovation Center in Shanghai. The Innovation Center is the main channel by which Johnson & Johnson strengthens its external strategic collaborations. Johnson & Johnson works closely with innovative companies, academics, research institutions, and top-tier talent to provide them with funds, professional expertise, and technology. The company accelerates the process of transforming innovation from its infancy stages to final products and treatments that are ready for clinical application. These innovations will meet the needs of the Chinese market and will promote China-born innovations to the international market.

I've mentioned before that early prevention and diagnosis is vital to improving the treatment rate of diseases. Johnson & Johnson is actively exploring this arena, combining its expertise in medical equipment and pharmaceuticals to develop transformative and innovative diagnostic solutions. Johnson & Johnson will establish a global lung cancer research center in China, which will search for holistic, innovative solutions centered on the patient from the three major vectors of disease prevention, diagnosis, and targeted therapy. The incidence rate of lung cancer in our country has grown by 26.9% each year; lung cancer has become the number one cause of death from malignant tumors. We hope to make it easier and more effective for high-risk demographic groups to get regular and precise screenings, eventually helping to make lung cancer a preventable, curable disease for the benefit of patients and reducing the disease's threat to Chinese society.

To help Shanghai establish a multi-layered medical care system, Johnson & Johnson has partnered with government agencies to research fundraising mechanisms and commercial health insurance programs to meet the diverse health needs of patients.

In addition, to improve societal recognition of and respect for medical care professionals, Johnson & Johnson initiated the "Healthy Society" project, which recognizes doctors' and nurses' outstanding contributions to public health.

Not long ago, I read the results of a new study in a medical journal which indicated that the average life-span of Chinese people has improved dramatically. It showed that people in China lived 8 and a half years longer on average in 2015 than they did in 1990. The average life expectancy of Shanghai citizens has reached 82 years, exceeding the national average for this same time period. If we can create a robust health management system, coupled with positive contributions from all corners of society, I believe the expected life-span will continue to lengthen in the future. It will be an entirely achievable dream to imagine that by 2050, my 60-year old (or even older) colleague born in the 1990s will be able to run in the Shanghai Marathon.

Future Shanghai and Shaping the Future Education

Wang Yi

Executive Director at Harvard Center Shanghai

As the fountain for knowledge and innovation, higher educational institutions, especially research universities, shall play an important role for the economic development of the city or region where they are located.

Pittsburgh, a central city in the U.S., used to be an important steel city. During 1980s, due to economic transformation and economic crisis then, steel industry of Pittsburgh suffered a serious defeat. However, in the past three to four decades, Pittsburgh has managed to complete very successful transformation and become a vigorous city again.

From local view, this wonder shall be mostly attributed to the higher education, especially two well-known universities in Pittsburgh: University of Pittsburgh and Carnegie Mellon University. The president of University of Pittsburgh once commented that successful revitalization of Pittsburgh benefited from multiple factors, while universities were the chip for its resurgence. In terms of technology transfer, the university has made great achievements. More than 300 companies were started through technology transfer in Pittsburgh, which have made very important contribution to local economic development. Joint innovation center was built on the campus to attract well known technology companies, so that many well-recognized U.S. companies, e.g. Intel, Apple, Disney, Google etc., have set up branches in Pittsburgh one after another. By leveraging higher education resources, Pittsburgh has shifted from pure reliance on the steel industry to a modernized city integrating financial service, higher education, healthcare, transportation, logistics etc. into a whole.

We can draw some implications for Shanghai from this case:

Firstly, in order to realize the goal of making Shanghai into a scientific research and innovation center with global influence by 2050, we still need to strengthen the investment in infrastructure construction, especially at the university level. Inter-disciplinary research shall be our priority in the future.

Applied science is linked with the real economy, so innovation in such area cannot do without the soil for fundamental research. Therefore, the government has also put forward the goal of promoting the building of world-level universities and top-tier disciplines and started to implement it. At the important time for local universities to consider the layout of disciplines by starting from their own advantages, we shall also pay more attention to inter-disciplinary research.

Take Harvard University as an example: the president built the Harvard Global Institute this year and set its foot first in Shanghai—Harvard Center Shanghai. They hoped to promote inter-disciplinary cooperation in Harvard University through Harvard Global Institute. Though Harvard has laid a good foundation in this aspect, there is still have much work to do. They made the breakthrough from environment research in China, organized a research team composed of professors from multiple faculties, e.g. engineering, economy, public health, government etc. They are now focusing on inter-disciplinary research related to environment in China, especially air quality.

Although this project just takes a start, professors in the research team have more than a decade's experience in studying Chinese environment. Meanwhile, they also have close cooperation with some domestic institutions, e.g. Tsinghua University. We believe such inter-disciplinary and cross-regional international cooperation shall become the direction for research that Shanghai shall promote strongly.

Secondly, it's worthwhile for us to promote internationalization of education in Shanghai.

Shanghai and some municipal schools have made many achievements in promoting international exchange for students and scholars. I have the following suggestions:

Firstly, Further promote the opening of courses for high schools and universities.

There shall be more inclusive and diversified contents in school education. Students shall be allowed to understand and explore different views for the same question to a larger extent. In some inter-disciplinary areas, we shall create better conditions for inter-disciplinary learning and study.

Secondly, Local universities are suggested to set up bachelor degrees with all courses taught in English.

Over the past decade, a number of Netherland public universities represented by University of Amsterdam have set up colleges or projects by using English to teach liberal education courses for undergraduates. It has played a very positive role for Netherland to attract excellent talents across the world to study there and promote innovation in education and other areas. In the last year, University of Freiburg in Germany also started to establish a college for undergraduate liberal education with all courses taught in English. If Shanghai wishes to attract global students to receive education in China, rather than study language, our local universities also need to set up undergraduate or postgraduate degrees or courses that are taught in English and meet international standards. For local universities, this will create a huge challenge in terms of both course contents and faculties. However, it will be a worthwhile effort.

Thirdly, Attract prominent educational institutions and education model to land in Shanghai.

New York University Shanghai acts as the key event and successful example for Shanghai to attract prominent educational institution to set up local base. We all know there are many trials and innovation in education across the world, especially for online education. Be it edX established by Harvard or MIT, Kecera for Stanford, or Khan Academy at middle school stage, there are many outstanding innovation models that we need to actively learn from, so that we can lay certain foundation for building Shanghai into a global leading education center.

We hope that Shanghai may make great progress in education model, fundamental research, applied study, innovation & start-ups by creating better educational environment, so as to accelerate the course of realizing the goal for Shanghai developing into an international major metropolitan.

Shanghai in 2050: The Smartest City

Zhang Xiaoping

Partner of Deloitte Consulting

There is no doubt that in 2050 Shanghai will become an intelligent city, which can be foreseen from four major trends:

First, population growth will exert greater pressure on the city. Frequent occurrences of environmental changes and extreme climate has required our city to improve its risk-resistance capability to meet our basic need for security.

Second, the development of urban economy requires a better business environment, which can not only attract large enterprises, but also support our local enterprises, especially the development of small and medium enterprises. Innovation mechanism is an important part of the business environment, which can strengthen the competitiveness of our city. More and more disruptive innovation is not only driven by lower-cost, more flexible emerging companies, but also by cross-border competition of large enterprises, as they face more fierce competition for the platform resources.

Third, the development of science and technology has reached a critical point. We have witnessed the application of the Internet to things in our every-day lives in depth and breadth, robots and unmanned aerial vehicles (UAV) are applied in large-scale commercial use, as well as the development and breakthrough of artificial intelligence in the past decade with a more mature learning ability. The science and technology development has brought about the innovation in some new business models.

Fourth, the development of industrial civilization has triggered our humanities introspection, that is, how to enable us to become masters instead of slaves of machines and how to promote city intelligence and civilization. Can we take a higher, broader and longer view? These trends require us to rethink the development path of our intelligent city.

We believe that development shall be featured with:

First, the effective investment of human capital and social capital in the traditional infrastructure, such as transportation, modern infrastructure, including the TMT technology shall be made to achieve a sustainable development of urban economy and high-quality life.

Second, clear transformation objectives, which shall aim at cultivating specific values, including the intangible value of the residents' feeling the transformation is of high-quality as well as the tangible economic value of the state and society.

Third, the rational use of natural resources for development of our intelligent city. The demand side shall be more energy-efficient in low-carbon applications while the supply side shall produce more renewable resources.

Fourth, the development of the intelligent city shall be built step by step. It is not a one-time effort, development depends on the maturity of the city as well as the pain points.

There are three types of cities: cities similar to traditional European cities, new urban cities and cities in the middle of the transformation in China. Shanghai is featured with the characteristics of the three cities, which needs us to develop a high-level plan for our intelligent city.

The plan of the future intelligent Shanghai shall cover the following five aspects:

(1) The infrastructure construction, including basic infrastructure (road and transportation system construction, information system and network development). On the other hand, the urban management capability, leadership, innovation mechanism, and strong execution are all required to ensure service delivery and the shared understanding of the leading role in science and technology, along with government affairs.

(2) The connected urban systems, such as intelligent health care, security, energy, water supply systems and etc. The connected system is based on cooperation while the use of intelligence is considered the key.

(3) Different ecological systems are formed based on the connected urban systems, such as ecological system of public services, including schools,

hospitals, emergency services, corporate social ecological systems, ecological systems of private enterprises and community ecological systems. The government is no longer a major driver but a key executor. Just as the famous Chinese saying goes: great form has no shape.

(4) The intelligence is dominated by people who can be divided into four types: residents, innovators, tourists and employers. They need to be entitled with fair opportunities and a healthy environment where innovation and helping others could be considered a dream for pursuit.

(5) An intelligent Shanghai, as the most important driver, supports the different life goals, and aspirations of its citizens to ensure a high-quality of life. Security, sustainability, wealth accumulation and choice of freedom shall become a clear and measurable set of values.

Scientific Revolution, Social Change and City Governance

Fan Deshang

Deputy Director and Secretary General of Global Governance

Research Center of Peking University

The world today is undergoing complex and profound changes. From the 2008 subprime mortgage crisis to global financial crisis, as well as sovereign debt crisis of Western countries; from Occupy Wall Street, the Arab world turmoil, to the values controversy highlighted by Charlie Hebdo... It was found that the world in the process of globalization is full of unrest, discontent, conflict and confrontation. The world political and economic situation is complicated. Meanwhile, new world economy is transforming, represented by Silicon Valley together with the rapid technological change, human social, political and economic landscape are changing, which lead to increasingly complex conflicts and confrontations surrounding values.

Faced with complex and profound changes, this article tries to interpret how science and technology innovation affect society, politics, economics, etc., focusing on the impact of information technology on today's society and politics, economics. To address the impact of technological change on today's society, this paper makes recommendations on urban governance in the end.

1. The impact of technological change on society in history

Looking back at the history of mankind, the political power-sharing model economic production mode and social class division adopted by society, are closely related to the level of technological development.

In agricultural society, the level of human technological development were mainly reflected in agriculture and animal husbandry. Scientific and technological innovation was mainly embodied in the understanding and knowledge about plants and animals cultivation and season and climate change. Consistent with the social development stage and science and technological level of the agricultural society, economic production were mainly handicraft industry and self-sufficient farming households; in terms of the distribution of political power, kings and aristocracy had the political power, and maintain social order and justice with typical political regime being monarchy. Social classes are divided among the king, the nobility, farmers and artisans.

With the appearance of steam technology and electrical technology, the industrial society arrives. Division of social, political, economic and social classes evolves with technological change. Economic development pattern began to enter the era of industrial mass production from the self-sufficient natural economy and household cottage industry. Social class witnessed differentiation as large-scale machine production brought about by technological change destroyed traditional cottage industries and self-sufficient natural economy. Bankrupted farmers and artisans were forced to work for capitalists who owned the machines, technology and factories. The whole society is increasingly split into two big antagonistic classes: capitalist who owns mine, capital and machines as well as the proletariat who sells labor as Marx saw it sharply in view of the changes of the industrial age. In the distribution of political power, the capitalists asked for voices and say to protect their interests in the operation of state power. Changes in the distribution of political power in Britain and France have resulted in the change from the monarchy to the capitalist republic respectively.

2. Today's technological change is affecting the present society

Technological change with information technology at the core is bringing about a profound impact on human society and political, economic, social stratification. Economic development pattern has transformed from the industrialized mass production into smart production with a deep integration of knowledge, technology and information. Under the influence of technological changes, traditional industries start to decline or are forced to upgrade, new R&D enterprises relying on high-level talents begins to appear.

Changes in technology also divide the community and cause new social issues. Take the United States as an example, workers in the United States automobile manufacturing business are losing their jobs along with the relocation of US manufacturing sector in the last century. After the United States President Obama took office, he is committed to Manufacturing Initiative to solve the unemployment problem. Unfortunately, automation technology and smart technology replace American industrial workers with intelligent robots. This is the power of technological change, which has resulted in a growing number of social problems: "Occupy Wall Street Movement" reflects the opposition between the wealthy few and the poor mass.

In the regard of the distribution of political power, new owners of wealth want to have the decision-making and governance power of the national system. What kind of proposition would Silicon Valley upstarts rising in patents and technology ownership make in the distribution of power? What kind of requests would Amazon and other e-commerce giants make? In comparison with the changes in the distribution of power from the monarchy to the republic, what will be the future mode of political power-sharing? This is a question worth considering, as the world is undergoing profound and complex changes.

As U.S. President Barack Obama spoke in his 2011 State of the Union: "That world has changed. And for many, the change has been painful. I've seen it in the shuttered windows of once booming factories, and the vacant storefronts on once busy Main Streets. I've heard it in the frustrations of Americans who've seen their paychecks dwindle or their jobs disappear—proud men and women who feel like the rules have been changed in the middle of the game. They're right. The rules have changed. In a single generation, revolutions in technology have transformed the way we live, work and do business. Steel mills that once needed 1 000 workers can now do the same work with 100. Today, just about any company can set up shop, hire workers, and sell their products wherever there's an Internet connection." The image Obama described four years ago can be seen in today's Wangfujing Street, Z-Park, Nanjing Road, Dongguan City etc.

3. Some thoughts on Urban Governance against today's background

Firstly, urban governance in the era of globalization and technological change needs values and spirit. In the context of rapid technological change and evolving information technology, a city and a country need to build its own core values to garner strength, and enhance recognition. Shanghai as an international metropolis that accommodates yellow skin, white skin and black skin need even more core values to build the consensus and identity. What on earth should the core values be? First, it can distinguish Shanghai from other international metropolis. These core values must be explored from Shanghai history and culture as well as its innovation from national history and culture that nurtures black hair, brown eyes and yellow skin; second, it attracts the world's best talents to Shanghai and get a sense of belonging; third, it brings together yellow skin, white skin, dark-skinned people, and brings up innovation and entrepreneurship from people of different skin colors; fourth, it should reflect respect for social justice, recognition of the human value and the pursuit of environmental protection and energy saving.

For Shanghai, it is very important. Shanghai as an international metropolis, must come up with a philosophy that transcends confrontations and conflicts among core values of different culture, making it more open and inclusive.

Secondly, urban governance also needs grass-root experience and global vision. China has a history of several thousand years of farming civilization, with a great history and cultural heritage. China has achieved great success in the past thirty years since it initiated the reform and opening up drive, and has become the world's second largest economy. China is increasingly integrated with the world and the world has become increasingly dependent on China. For a long time, our society emphasizes on grass-root experience. Government officials, scholars and entrepreneurs need to start from the grassroots, The ideal of "self cultivation, family harmony, country management and world peace" is based on the value of grass-roots, just as the old Chinese saying goes, you can't expect a clean world without cleaning your room first. For example, in the selection of government officials ranges from village head, county magistrate, mayor, provincial governor to the country's top leadership, grass-root experience matters. Such values are undoubtedly correct in the thousands of years of farming community. Meanwhile, when the Chinese GDP reached No.2 in the world, we have to import more than 60% of oil and a lot of important mineral resources from Arab world or the rest of the world, which requires Chinese elites, be it the government officials, scholars and going-global entrepreneurs, understand the outside world and properly handle the relationship between China and the outside world. Therefore, we not only need the grass-root experience, but also to stand high to understand the history, culture, religion and core values of the world, to handle well the relationship among nations and to give full play to China's role in the international community. When safeguarding our own interests, we must promote the common wellbeing of mankind.

Shanghai as an international metropolis, must define its own position and identity in the world, handle with care the relations with other international metropolis, and learn lessons and experience from other cities. To sort out the ideas for urban governance in the context of globalization, and to choose the globalization and differentiation strategy for the future development of Shanghai, grass-root experience is important, but equally important is the global vision.

Thirdly, urban governance needs to understand the profound impact of technological change on today's society and the challenges. As mentioned earlier, today's technological change is exerting profound and lasting influence on society. Take information technology as an example, the emergence of the Internet enables consumers and manufacturers to exchange information directly online; a number of intermediate service providers or agents and employees are downsized. At the same time, the emergence of smart robotics replaces manpower; many industrial workers are losing their jobs. Unemployment has been and will increasingly become a social problem and challenge for the government. According to CNN reported last week, Brazil, one of the BRIC countries, and Argentina and Venezuela in South America, are suffering from economic downturn, which causes political turmoil. The President of Brazil is in danger of being impeached. Therefore, when we are embracing the Internet, new technologies and promoting innovation, we must ponder over the technological changes' impact on the unemployed group and the solutions. When the once bustling Nanjing Road, Wangfujing, Zhongguancun become ghost towns due to technological change, when the prediction of machine substitution runs rampant, urban and state governance is particularly important for the growing number of unemployed groups, and the task of building a harmonious society is also a long way to go.

Fourthly, urban governance needs to play dual tactics. Faced with social problems and challenges brought about by technological change, urban governance need to play dual tactics: one is the invisible hand of market forces, and the other is the Government's visible hand of policy.

Obama talked about the relationship between government and the market in his inaugural speech in 2009: "Nor is the question before us whether the market is a force for good or ill. Its power to generate wealth and expand freedom is unmatched, but this crisis has reminded us that without a watchful eye, the market can spin out of control-and that a nation cannot prosper long when it favors only the prosperous. The success of our economy has always depended not just on the size of our Gross Domestic Product, but on the reach of our prosperity; on our ability to extend opportunity to every willing heart-not out of charity, but because it is the surest route to our common good. The question we ask today is not whether our government is too big or too small, but whether it works-whether it helps families find jobs at a decent wage, care they can afford, a retirement that is dignified. Where the answer is yes, we intend to move forward. Where the answer is no, programs will end."

As the social problems, unemployment issue and wealth gap caused by today's technological change and globalization become prominent, the visible hand of policy regulation by the government is particularly urgent and important.

In the vision for the future Shanghai governance, how should the "invisible hand" of the market and "visible hand" of the government effectively govern the city? This will be an important factor in the success of Shanghai in the next 30 years as the world's bustling metropolis.

Shanghai in 2050: The Viewpoint and Expectation of a Japanese Businessman

Michiaki Oguri

President of Japan External Trade Organization in Shanghai

The history of exchanges between Shanghai and Japan dated back to antiquity, and the constant communication has helped deepening the mutual understanding of each other, a win-win situation for both of us. In this regards, as a Japanese seeking to strengthen Sino-Japan economic ties, I would like to talk about my views on Shanghai in 2050.

Though my less-than-three-month stay in Shanghai is short, I have been working in related fields to promote Sino-Japan economic cooperation in the past twenty years. It is from Shanghai where my connection with China began.

Exactly 20 years ago, in 1995, I made a trip to Shanghai, that is my first visit to China. Back then, the Pudong New Development Area, since 1990, was still in development. The speech made by Deng Xiaoping during his inspection tour in the South in 1992 accelerated the process of reform and opening up and at the same time, Shanghai was embracing its second Japanese enterprises investment boom.

I was deeply impressed by the city's vigor and spirit, so confident about the Shanghai and China's future and eventually decided to dedicate myself to the promotion of Japan-China economic exchanges.

Japan External Trade Organization, as a Japanese government organ to keep Japanese economic growth in line with global economy, is designed to encourage and promote trade and investment between foreign countries and Japan. JETRO Shanghai Office I work for, was established in 1985, 30 years ago, and has been committed to promoting close economic and trade ties between Shanghai and Japan.

Just as Shanghai has experienced dramatic social and economic changes in last thirty years, JETRO Shanghai Office has been adapting itself to the new situation. Initially our priority was to provide technical support to Chinese enterprises and then the focus shifted to assist Japanese enterprises with their investment in China in the 1990s since Japanese companies flocked to China for investment as a result of China's further reform and opening up policy. During the World Expo Shanghai in 2010, JETRO served as an operator of the Japan pavilion and made active efforts to promote Japanese culture and technology with an exhibit themed on the harmony between the human heart and technology. Since the late 2000s, JETRO has been introducing to Shanghai Japan's safe, secure and quality products and services, and encouraging business cooperation between corporations as Shanghai is attracting the global attention. Right now as many Chinese companies with strength turn their attention to overseas market, JETRO is strengthening its support for Chinese enterprises' investment in Japan.

In retrospect, the last 30 years witnessed the one-sided assistance between Shanghai and Japan developing into bilateral cooperation. Looking into the next 30 years, I am convinced that the exchanges between the two sides will reach a new level. To facilitate exchange of labor, goods and capital between Shanghai and China, I think one important task for Shanghai is to improve its soft and hard infrastructure.

The first significant soft power is the introduction of the Free Trade Agreement (FTA), an institutional framework for trade and investment liberalization. It will play an important role in the future international cooperation. China-Japan-Korea Free Trade Agreement is currently under negotiation, so do the Regional Comprehensive Economic Partnership (RCEP) and Trans-Pacific Partnership Agreement (TPP) in Asia Pacific region, which will help achieve a Free Trade Area of the Asia-Pacific (FTAAP) . These free and open trade and investment systems, once established, will strengthen the role of Shanghai as an international economic, financial, trade and shipping center and an exemplary pioneer.

The existing Shanghai hard power in terms of infrastructure, including shipping, high-speed rail and highway, will be further expanded and promote active exchanges of people from various countries in the future.

Europe and Southeast Asia are making steady progress to reach the economic integration, which has blurred the country borders. In 2050, the personnel and economic exchanges between Japan, China and other countries in the Asian region should go on in a more liberalized way. Shanghai will play a greater role in this Asian integration.

Hereby, I would like to share my views on what Shanghai should be like in 2050. The development history of Shanghai is closely connected with the world history. The existing historical buildings in Shanghai fully explain the strong linkage between Shanghai and the world. In this regards, one essential element for the future development of Shanghai is to broaden and deepen its communication with other countries. I hope Shanghai will continue to be a lively and attractive destination for foreigners.

The vision on Shanghai 2050 reminds me of one of the two "centenary goals", which is to turn China into a modern socialist country that is prosperous, strong, democratic, culturally advanced and harmonious when the People's Republic of China celebrates its centenary in 2049. What kind of essential roles can Shanghai play in achieving this great goal?

The Fifth Plenary Session of the Eighteenth Conference of the Communist Party held from Oct. 26th to Oct. 29th 2015 had put forward the development concepts of "innovation, coordination, greenness, openness and sharing" in planning for its "13th Five-year Plan". I believe these concepts have made clear for Shanghai's development direction in the future.

Here is my understanding of the five development mindsets and their importance in the vision for Shanghai in the year of 2050.

The first is innovation. Innovation is the primary engine of development socially, industrially, technically, institutionally, culturally or in theoretical aspect. Though there are many essential factors for efficient innovation, how to cultivate and attract talents is the most important one since every innovation has to be achieved by people. Therefore, it is necessary of Shanghai to upgrade its higher-education system. Of course, a liberal and democratic social environment matters as well.

The second is coordination. The coordinated development in urban level requires balanced development between urban and rural areas, between economic and social sectors, between primary industry, secondary industry and tertiary industry. The coordinated development in the industrial level means coordinated development between second and tertiary industries and particularly between large enterprises and small enterprises. Although Shanghai's tertiary industry is growing very fast and its GDP ratio is increasing every year, the second industry is indispensable. Not only the big corporations located in Shanghai, but also SME groups around it are essential for Shanghai to achieve coordinated development. Furthermore, Shanghai also needs to retain the secondary industry as a core industry.

The third is greenness. One of the lessons Japanese government has learned most in its urban development is green growth. The serious environmental damage was one of the biggest challenges Japan had faced in its economic growth. In tackling this issue, Japanese have learned how to coexist with nature and enterprises, to make great efforts in producing environment-friendly products. The most important thing for green growth I believe is to foster the environmental consciousness among citizens through environment education and communication. From my own knowledge of Shanghai in the last two decades, some people still dump their trash on streets and sidewalks in Shanghai, a city with beautiful buildings. Chinese tourists who travelled to Japan would be touched with the cleanliness of each locale's streets. Japanese have grown up to organize and tidy up personal items and cause no trouble to others. I believe that's why the cities in Japan can stay so clean. To protect the natural resources such as air, water and land, accessible and vital to everyone on earth, the priority is to guide the public to care about the environment around them.

The fourth is openness, and as I've mentioned earlier it is of high priority to establish a free and open trade and economic system. Since its inception in Sept. 2013, China (Shanghai) Pilot Free Trade Zone has brought Shanghai to the frontline of reform and opening up and as a pioneer will play a major role in deepening reform. In looking forward to 2050, bilateral cooperation will be even more important. I hope the shanghai enterprises and Shanghainese will be more opening up to the world and common development in the world. While JETRO is making great efforts to encourage and support Chinese corporate investment in Japan, it is still small in comparison to Japanese corporate investment in China.

As the overseas investments by Shanghai companies will be constantly growing, I hope the investment gap between the two countries will shrink considerably in the coming 35 years. Of course, to attract more Chinese enterprises to invest in Japan, we will do our best to maintain Japan's economic power.

Last but not the least, sharing is one critical concept for China to achieve the harmony between man and nature and common prosperity. The main cities across China, including Shanghai, are growing rapidly in the past 30 years, creating a huge gap between the rich and the poor. If Shanghai, a pioneer in reform and urban development cannot achieve common prosperity, none of the other cities in the vast and diversified China will. Therefore, I believe, whether Shanghai will achieve the common prosperity in the coming three decades, the mindset of Sharing will be extremely important for China's accomplishment of the two centenary goals.

As close neighbors, China and Japan have a more than 2000 years history of exchanges and the two had learned from and benefited each other. Sincerely, I hope that Shanghai and Japan will become important partners and share achievements with each other in 2050.

Actions to Ensure Shanghai is as Successful in 2050 as It Is Today

Jacob Parker

Director & Chief Representative of Shanghai office, US-China Business Council

In thinking through my remarks today and considering recent conversations with our member companies, I thought it would be useful to review what has been published by others on the future of Shanghai to better contextualize the views of our membership. Forecasting a year in advance can be challenging for even the most talented researchers, forecasting 35 years in advance is even more so.

In the process of researching this question, I came across a paper authored by Director Xiao Lin last December. In that paper, he puts forward three thoughts on Shanghai's next thirty years and the challenges that will need to be overcome to ensure the city's prominence and success. Reflecting on these points the past several weeks; I thought I could offer some suggestions within this context that will help guide Shanghai toward the future.

One of the key factors that will impact Shanghai's development in the coming thirty five years is beyond Shanghai's control: national structural economic adjustment as well as China's continuing efforts to deepen economic reform. The direction of this reform will bring about unforeseen challenges and opportunities for the city. We've already seen the impact of these changes in the past three years with the inception of the China (Shanghai) Pilot Free Trade Zone (CSPFTZ) . As I often tell our member companies, the CSPFTZ is in many ways a misnomer; it is much more a testing ground for investment liberalization and reform. By utilizing pre-establishment principles and a negative list approach, the CSPFTZ ushered in an entirely new framework for regulating foreign investment. This model was then adopted by three additional zones. Now China stands upon the precipice of a national model negative list set to be implemented by 2018. We've already seen the Shanghai government expand the CSPFTZ to include Pudong and Zhangjiang High Tech Park in the CSPFTZ. Going forward, Shanghai should seek to further expand the CSPFTZ negative list investment pilot to cover the entire city of Shanghai to ensure that by 2050 the city is seen as an open and welcoming investment destination. This will be especially important considering the State Councilpolicy released yesterday focused on further liberalization of foreign investment restrictions in e-commerce, various service industries, and RMB account liberalization.

Another aspect raised by Director Xiao in his December paper focuses on the impact of urbanization on Shanghai's future. In Director Xiao's speech "Three Thoughts on the Next Thirty Years of Shanghai" he noted the challenges coming from an aging and less qualified population. There are a number of actions that can be taken in the medium term to defray the most challenging aspects and ensure Shanghai continues to be an attractive destination for foreign direct investment:

Firstly, raise the mandatory retirement age. Shanghai and China will have the potential to be hit by an increasingly large elderly population that impacts China's social safety net. In March of this year, the Minister of Human Resources and Social Security, Yin Weimin, announced that China will slowly extend the mandatory retirement age. The plan is expected to be released in 2017, and will only be implemented in 2022. China's comparatively low mandatory retirement ages have a significant impact on foreign companies operating here. Once a white collar employee reached 65 years old, they can no longer legally sign a labor contract with a company.

Secondly, ease the Hukou policy for qualified workers. China's urbanization plan has set an ambitious plan to allow Hukous to be transferred if a resident has paid taxes for a certain number of years and contributed to the local social security fund. *Shanghai's 22 Measures*, released over the summer, went farther, aiming to simplify the Hukou process for qualified talent. Our members tell us that obtaining a local Hukou is critical for retaining top talents in the research, development, and technical fields. Though I expect by 2050 the Hukou system will have greatly changed, there is much that can be done in the interim to both increase the availability of qualified workers and ensure

Shanghai meets its goals of becoming a top tier high value-added manufacturing and services economy.

Finally, to ensure Shanghai becomes one of the top investment locations in the future, it is critical that local licensing processes be transparent, inexpensive, and quickly approved. In the past 30 years Shanghai has made important advances in simplifying administrative processes, there is still room for improvement. To provide an example of how new businesses are registered in the U. S., it is helpful to examine the new business license registration process in the City of Mountain View, California—a city centrally located in Silicon Valley.

The process to apply for a business license in Mountain View is fairly simple. An applicant needs only fill out a one-page business license application form and submit a onetime application fee that ranges from $32 for manufacturing operations to $102 for software development. Once the application is submitted, the applicant is guaranteed a response within two weeks. Unlike in Shanghai, there are no requirements for minimum operating capital, obligations for registering foreign exchange licenses, or public security clearances. This ease of establishing a business license is one of the key reasons Silicon Valley remains one of the most innovative places in America.

This is not unique to Silicon Valley, the ease of establishing business licenses in the United States make it the 7th easiest place in the world to do business according the World Bank Report on Ease of Doing Business.

By treating foreign and domestic new company registrations equally in the CSPFTZ, eliminating registered capital requirements, and establishing clear timelines for business license approvals, the Shanghai CSPFTZ could be used as a useful pilot for license liberalization across China. The next thirty years of Shanghai's development offer unprecedented opportunities to deepen economic reform, improve the ease of doing business, and lead the opening and development trajectory for all of China.

Role of Innovative Engineers in Shanghai's Vision of 2050

Reggie Lai

Senior Director, Asia Government Affairs and Corporate

Responsibility Office, TE Connectivity

Shanghai municipal government has set an ambitious goal to build Shanghai into a science and technology innovation center with global influence by 2030. From now to 2030, there are defined goals and strong policy support to help the city achieve these goals. Nevertheless, how can Shanghai maintain as an innovation center with global influence from 2030 to 2050, despite of global political, economic and technological evolvement?

Talents are the core of innovation. For most industrial companies, engineers are the innovators that create industries, processes, solutions and products. TE Connectivity (TE) , a company that is listed on *Thomson Reuters'* Top 100 Global Innovators for five consecutive years in a row, has conducted researches on innovation of engineers. I would like to take this opportunity to share some findings.

Since 2014, TE has been releasing the annual *Chinese Engineers' Innovation Motivation Survey Report*, by partnering with the Electronic Technology Information Research Institute of the Ministry of Industry and Information Technology of China. This annual study utilizes a variety of indicators to extensively analyze Chinese engineers' innovation in the preceding year. The survey data are selected from several respects, e. g. by regions, sectors, age, gender and performance of engineers and are compared with the previous annual survey, so as to identify a variety of indices of Chinese engineers' innovation. The study is based on surveys of 1 219 engineers throughout China, from more than 20 industries including automotive, telecommunications, machinery manufacturing, energy and chemicals and information technology, and from all sorts of organizations including state-owned, foreign-owned, private owned and collective companies to ensure the findings are comprehensive and persuasive.

Our research indicates that 87.8 percent of the surveyed engineers are interested or have a strong interest in innovative activities. Generally, engineers wish to fully realize their potentials, achieve a higher self-actualization and make a greater contribution to the society. We could divide engineer innovation into two parts, namely the Causes and the Results. The Causes include innovation environment, innovation capabilities and innovative activities. The Results refer to innovation performances.

Overall, Chinese engineers are full of confidence in their innovation activities. On the Causes side, their confidence greatly comes from guiding national policies at the macro level, synchronized development among enterprises, universities and research institutes at the intermediate level, and improvement of their working conditions at the micro level. Engineers also have high recognitions of their innovation capabilities. On the Results side, Chinese engineers are still expecting quantum leaps in terms of innovation performances. To help engineers achieve major innovation breakthroughs and obtain global competitiveness, we should endeavor to transform engineers' enthusiasms into productivity.

The following points are of more importance based on the survey findings:

(1) Innovation environment—engineers require more support on R&D spending and vocational trainings from employers.

(2) Innovation capability—engineers' working experience and education background have played an important role in innovation.

(3) Innovative activities—engineers agree that participation in innovation activities, high-tech projects and national macroscopic projects greatly affect their innovation performance.

Therefore, engineers would greatly improve their innovation capacities, if both enterprise and government are able to create a more favorable environment to meet the above mentioned aspects.

Return to my opening question: how does Shanghai maintain as a global innovation center from 2030 to 2050? Based on the current survey findings, we would suggest that the government and enterprises can make efforts in the several aspects.

Firstly, the development strategy of Shanghai. Based on the plan, by 2030, Shanghai will become an international economic center, a financial center, a trade center, a shipping center and a science and technology innovation center. We suggest that the government should maintain the strategic importance of the advanced manufacturing sector in the long-term development strategy. This does not mean that by then, Shanghai must retain a certain amount of factories, but that Shanghai should retain industrial businesses especiallytheir engineering, research and development, management, and trading functions. Thus the factories actually become "insourcing" processing workshops.

Concurrently, innovation policies should shift its focus from establishment of innovation centers to provision of better assistance to established innovation centers, including secondment arrangement of engineers, tax planning of IP royalty payments, and etc.

Secondly, our study shows that nearly 60 percent of surveyed engineers think that intellectual property rights protection policies have the greatest influence on innovation activities among all government policies. Meanwhile, we also need supportive labor policies, for example, the arrangement of service inventor remuneration.

Thirdly, mega-sized companies should strive to export their culture of innovation to their entire supply chains, in addition to providing R&D funding to their own engineers. At the same time, companies also expect to maintain effective communications with the public sector and provide timely feedbacks on policy implementations.

Fourthly, based on our survey, the post '60s engineers are the main force of innovation. Therefore, the post '90s engineers and existing university students will become the main force of innovation by 2050. Experience, exposure and education are able to offer the most important development opportunities for the post '90s engineers. Companies should have enough patience to groom fresh graduates into competent engineers. At the same time, we suggest that the government release more policies to further promote campus recruitment, and programs of internship and apprenticeship.

Fifthly, we have noticed that fine engineers are constantly arranged to take more managerial responsibilities, when they progress in their research areas. This type of arrangement certainly has its reason. However, we do not expect every fine project manager is willing or able to become a good people manager. Therefore, TE has designed an engineer career development ladder which is similar to the management development mechanism. Fine engineers are able to advance their career in the engineering field, instead of taking managerial roles or engaging with administrative work. An engineer's remuneration package will be equal to a commercial director, when she or he becomes a chief engineer or a chief researcher. By this means, our company is able to retain core talents and also enables these talents to focus on innovation.

Last but not least, I would like to suggest that the government should help guide social perceptions to encourage more women to get engaged in engineering. At present, the imbalance between male and female engineers is an indisputable fact. Based on our survey, female engineers with more than 20 years of experience only account for 2.9% of total surveyed female engineers. While, male engineers with more than 20 years of experience account for 18.9% of total surveyed male engineers.

It is likely that the community has underestimated the innovation capabilities and the innovation performance of Chinese female engineers. What female engineers need is a set of thorough innovation incentive mechanism in order to ensure that the female engineers can fully realize their innovation potential. The research shows that female engineers generally have better professional capacity and communication skills. In addition, female engineers are better at innovative applications and have wider knowledge bases.

When we take a closer look, the main restrictions on female engineers' innovation capacity include social perceptions and employment policies. Female engineers have less access to innovation resources than male engineers. Therefore, companies should provide equal opportunities to females in R&D fund allocation, trainings, and access to innovation projects. On the other hand, the government should also endeavor to change the social perceptions and mindsets that will help the female engineers get more attention and resources.

Global Currency Landscape and Shanghai as an International Center in 2050

Qiao Yide

Vice Chairman & Secretary General of Shanghai Development Research Foundation

The international monetary system contains a lot of elements, such as cross-border capital flows, exchange rate regime, injection of liquidity, but the most important one is the monetary standard.

The year 2050 is very far away, I have a few assumptions. I think the first assumption is relatively reliable:

The first assumption, by 2050 China will certainly become the world's largest economy.

The Economist magazine of the U.K forecasted in last August that assuming China's GDP growth rate was 7%, the US 2.25%, RMB appreciates by 3%, by 2021 China would be the largest economy. Now it seems like an optimistic forecast. If you re-calculate, assuming a 5% GDP growth rate in Chinese by 2023, and 3.3% between 2023 and 2044, last year, former US Treasury Secretary Lawrence Summers and others issued a report, saying that a country's economic growth will sooner or later be mean-reverting. He had a lowest estimate on Chinese economic growth, so here I take this figure for assumption, which is 5% at first years and followed by 3.3%. Still 2.25% for the United States. By 2044, China would probably still catch up with the United States. It can be concluded that: by 2050, China will be the largest economy.

The second assumption, China will be fully integrated into the global financial system.

Capital account will be fully liberalized and capital can be transferred freely. This is critical to Shanghai being an international financial center. Fully floating exchange rates and two-way open capital market will enable CNY become an important international reserve currency and Chinese financial institutions will deploy across the world, just like what the United States is doing.

Even with these assumptions, there are still some uncertainties:

First, technology and finance's impact on financial agglomeration.

Technology promotes financial efficiency substantially, but its effect on financial agglomeration is unclear. Internet finance improves efficiency, but it may to some extent reduce the demand on real financial entities. Just imagine those big Chinese banks float their shares now, would they still have such a high valuation? That is a big question. Because when they were listed, the large number of branches merited high valuations, but now the more branches, the lower valuation should be. Smart (robot) finance. Standard ETF products in the United States can be operated online with a low management fee charged. Internet of Things financing. I do not know much about it. It is said that things can be collateralized. But I personally think Internet finance may have a stronger impact.

Second, global financial crisis broke out again. I think it is still possible.

Some say two things are for sure, one is death and the other is tax. After the financial crisis, this statement has changed into "financial crisis is for sure". After the outbreak of financial crisis, no one can see clearly how the world will evolve. This financial crisis outbreak strengthens U.S. Dollar, beating our expectation, but no one knows what will happen next time.

International currency network is inert or has inertia. The United States outpaced the UK on the size of the economy in 1872, but the U.S. Dollar only replaces sterling as the biggest currency till 1944. Although the position of the UK and British sterling were weakening, London's position as an international financial center did not decline.

And now China is reforming financial regulatory system; there are many discussions on mixed supervision VS specialized supervision, as well as the distribution of power between central and local financial regulators. We need further study on its impact on Shanghai.

At present we are not sure about policy support yet. Deng Xiaoping said long ago that Shanghai must be an international financial center, but no one knows how it will go. This is a bit like "waiting in line" for the power distributed across different regions. Of course, there is another saying that goes "allow the market to choose freely", in fact, this statement is wrong. As early as in 1949, the market has made a choice; Shanghai was then already "the largest financial center in the Far East". Moreover, the current financial system is different from that of 100 years ago. Today's financial system is highly regulated, so the government must play a leading role. Headquarter of the Bank of China moved from Shanghai to Beijing, why can't it move back to Shanghai? Of which there are many uncertainties.

Third, last but not least, the possible evolution of Shanghai's position as an international financial center.

Several key words, domestic financial reform, RMB Currency position, and the evolution of Shanghai's position as an international financial center. Financial reform is mostly about the exchange rate, liberalization of capital account and the regulatory system; RMB Currency position depends on the global foreign exchange reserves ratio, by 2020, we should be able to achieve a "clean floating" of foreign exchange rate, and now it is "dirty floating", i.e. managed floating. Substantially liberalize capital account, or to be free within the authority's management. There will be an appropriate division of power between central and local regulators. CNY now only accounts for 1% of the total foreign exchange reserves; it may reach 5% in 2020 next to the Euro and US Dollar. CNY is now in the basket of SDR, some newspaper say that CNY is now ranking third, which is wrong, because it is only third in terms of the weight of SDR. Its real position may be the fifth or sixth. By 2020 it will reach the third place. And China may meet the goal proposed by the State Council in 2009 to be an international financial center which is proportionate to China's economic strength and RMB status, but not the international financial center with the "full international functions".

By 2030, the free floating exchange rate and fully liberalized capital account should be the fact and division of the supervision functions between central and local regulators as well as mixed supervision or specialized supervision will be clearer. RMB ratio in the total foreign exchange reserve may reach 10%, US Dollar may still be the first currency, and RMB is on a par with that of Euro. When the Euro was launched in 1999, its proportion in foreign exchange reserves was 12%, now it is 20%. It is worth noting that there are a lot of Euro illusion as many figures about Euro are within EU countries. If in 2030, RMB ties with Euro, Shanghai would be in the world's second tier of international financial centers, equivalent to Tokyo, Singapore or Hong Kong. By 2050, the proportion of CNY foreign exchange reserves may reach 20%—25%, the US Dollar would still be relatively high at 40%—50%, as US Dollar now is as high as 64%, by then there may be some decline, both the US Dollar, and the RMB should be number one at that time. Shanghai is expected to be in the world's first tier of international financial centers, keeping pace with other global cities as New York and London.

COMMENTS & DISCUSSIONS

互动讨论

主持人·HOST

李广宇　Li Guangyu
麦肯锡公司全球资深董事合伙人
Senior Partner of McKinsey & Company

互动嘉宾·PANELISTS

邢邦志　Xing Bangzhi
中共上海市委研究室副主任
Deputy Director General of the Research Office of Shanghai Committee of C.P.C

鞠立新　Ju Lixin
中共上海市委党校研究院院长
Dean of the Academy of Party School of Shanghai Committee of C.P.C

叶　华　Ye Hua
野村综研中国董事长
Chairman of Nomura Research Instiute Shanghai

张蕴岭　Zhang Yunling
中国社科院学部委员、国际研究学部主任
Director of International Studies of Chinese Academy of Social Sciences

郑　军　Zheng Jun
IBM 大中华区华东及华中区总经理
IBM Vice President of Enterprise Business Unit in East & Central China

汪　颖　Jane Wang
普华永道亚太区零售消费品税务主管合伙人
PwC Leading Partner of Retail Consumption Duty for Asia Pacific

邢邦志：刚才听了来自国际和国内智库的专家代表对全球经济发展大趋势、城市发展规律和上海的机会与担当的诸多观点，包括上海在下一个30年里哪些地方可以有所为的建议，很有收获。这是一个大视野、长镜头的高水平的国际智库峰会，我也从中找到了工作中一直在思考的问题，想利用这个难得的机会，向有关智库专家请教。

大家对2050年的上海都充满了祝愿和期待。上海向更高能级的城市转型时，它的核心内涵是什么？核心竞争力在哪里？如果用一句话概括上海2050年的愿景，怎么描述比较好？想请野村综研的叶华先生回答这个问题。

叶华：用一句话概括2050年的上海，其实非常困难。上海有一个非常大的特点，它是一个移民城市。上海本身的历史并不长，但它在不长的历史阶段中，做了很多事情。这种力量，是中国其他城市所没有的。这是其一。

其次，上海具备做很多事情的重要的基石。即使有时候，这可能会影响它的创新。以前上海社科院的王战老师说，判断一个城市是不是文明城市，有一个非常基础的标准，就是它是否可以让大家在一个相对比较完善的规则中进行竞争，且这种竞争是不分人种、不分地区、不分国家，也不分城市的。在这一点上，上海有非常多的积累，这也是和中国其他城市很不一样的。

再有一点，刚才乔依德副会长谈到最大的经济体的问题。由于人口和面积，以及考虑到具有经济活力的城市的腹地等因素，到2030—2040年以后，上海还是不是被称作"上海"？"上海"代表的是上海市还是上海都市圈？这都无从预测。但相信到时候，"上海"一定不是当前上海的经济、文化、科技范围。

从这个逻辑来看，要把这些东西真正集合起来，使它能综合地发挥作用，同时让世界知道上海在做这方面的实验和创新，恐怕最终是要通过创业人员、上海居民等在日常中的一种城市人的精神来体现。或者说，不论是政府还是社会，要有一种精神的力量，使它在思想上能够为全球所理解，并能有所借鉴，同时得到刺激。能达到这个层面，就像习主席说的"中国梦"，它并不是物质层面的，而是要从精神层面带给大家"希望"，不仅带给中国人希望，而且要给全球人希望。这都是思想、精神层面的东西。

我在上海出生，对上海非常有感情。2050年很远，希望上海成为一个在文化层面、思想层面、精神层面上都能站得住脚的城市。一旦到了这个层面，叫不叫"上海"，其实问题都不大，也不用再谈战略、愿景，等等。这些东西已经渗透下去了。

李广宇：我特别认可您说的，可能在前30年上海发展过程中，大家把更多的注意力放在了经济发展上。那时中国还在起步阶段，还属于一穷二白的情况，大家集中精力把我们经济搞起来，这是对的。到2020年初步实现"四个中心"的目标，甚至更远的2050年，并不是经济不再重要，而是人们的关注点会越来越多元化。衣食住行都已经被满足了，除此之外就会有更高的追求。这也是为什么今天听到的很多关键词都是说价值观、我们的精神、我们的文明。那时上海是不是还只是中国人民关注的焦点？或者说，在全球范围内，大家只从经济角度关注上海的地位？中国成为世界第一大经济体，自然而然大家会关注上海是不是会成为中国第一大经济体。但是作为大家内心都憧憬的地方，可能是某些北欧城市和美国硅谷，大家憧憬的不仅仅是硅谷的富有，很多中东国家按人均财富来讲，绝对不比硅谷逊色，这个问题值得我们进一步去深思。

鞠立新：今天参加上海国际智库峰会，有很多收获，借用网络语言，叫"脑洞大开"。鉴于时间关系，我向野村综合研究上海咨询公司的叶华董事长提问，您提到一个非常重要的概念，就是上海如果成为全球城市，不仅是经济层面，也不仅是科技层面，您还提到了一个重要的目标是"世界文化城市"。到2050年，具有"全球影响力的思想的策源传播城市"。

80多年之前，上海被称为"远东的东方大都会"，30多年后，上海要怎样进一步打造"世界文化城市"和"具有全球影响力的思想策源传播中心城市"？是具备东方文化特质，还是具备西方近代现代文化特质，抑或是东西方文化交融的文化特质的全球城市？还是这两者或者多元文化融合伸展而成的、新型的、能够引领世界思想文化的中心枢纽城市？请叶董事长再具体阐述一下。

叶华：刚才说到，从文化的角度上来说，上海本身就是一个比较多元、复杂的城市。比如我们从会场走出去看到很多的高楼大厦，浦东可能是中国高层建筑最集中的一个区域。我是学建筑出身，我知道这其中没有多少建筑是我们自己设计的，当然施工配套是我们做的。我们可以回想，以前有个建筑师叫作拉斯洛·邬达克，他在上海留下了很多非常有特色的建筑。但是我们的脑子里，恐怕不会记得邬达克这个人。至少很多不是这个领域的人都不知道，也没有必要知道，但是他留下的那些建筑，已经作为上海的标记，沉积下来了。这种文化，和别的城市不一样。故宫或者西安的城墙，非常顺理成章，它们都是有特质的东西。但是上海会像一个熔炉一样，把这些东西都放在一起。

刚才说到创新，我记得上海还有一个名称，叫"冒险家的乐园"。曾经在一段历史中，上海是东亚甚至全球最活跃的一个创新城市，很多国家的人都在这里创业、创新。但是目前，在上海的作家、思想家、理论家中，我们第一时间可以想到而且能够代表现代社会的人少之又少。至少在我这个学识层面上，恐怕举不出一个例子来。除了制度创新之外，创新有一些衡量的标准，比如专利等，这些都是可以衡量的。而思想的一些东西，不好衡量，但它可以渗透下去。这是非常关键的，它没有边界。专利是有边界的，用了它要花钱，我花钱购买你的专利，并不是你影响我。当然，我可以使用。我不知道怎么能够表达得更清晰一点。

我们应该在那些没有边界、比较难琢磨的层面上进行突破。在中国，特别是上海这样的城市，利用以前的那些已经沉积下来的一些"上海精神"做出突破。这是上海和别的城市，不管是中国城市还是国外城市相比，最有特点的一个东西。如果不是这样，往往是非常容易被淘汰的，毕竟时间非常长，有35年。

张蕴岭：受主旨发言时间限制，有三个观点没有说太深：第一，世界在未来将面临很多充满未知的领域，也就是说未来 30 年左右，世界将要发生很大变化。要应对未知领域，需要非常开放的一个大的空间，让大家有一个环境去想。刚才说"冒险家的乐园"，我想起一个故事，两德统一以后，德国政府并没有重建东柏林，而是提供了一个非常广阔的空间和创新自由的环境，提供了非常廉价的房子、各种各样的优惠条件，让世界上自由的人都跑到东柏林去。现在我们讲创新，好像有一种制度性构造。北京发展也有很多约束，但上海在未知领域方面，有它的基础，比如自贸区或者很多其他事情都在上海试验。未来很多领域我们真的不知道会怎么发展，比如气候变化等。

第二，就是范式转变。人类社会、世界发展到今天，我们都意识到，传统的道路走不通。中国有十几亿人，印度有十几亿人，未来的发展潜力在发展中国家，我们必须推动整个工业化革命以来发展范式的根本型转变。这个转变，我想要从大的思路，根本的新观念来考虑。中国提出新的发展理念，来指导发展方式转变，这是一个新提法。但是很多新的理念，恐怕我们现在还想得不够。所以上海构造这么一个环境，还是有条件的。

第三，我在发言中提到，"上海"是什么？上海未来的概念是什么？它可能不是一个传统的城市概念。"city"应该是指"小城市"，而城市是代表功能性城市。将来提到"上海"可能不单单是指上海的区域范围，而是指哪个地方具有更专业、更突出的城市功能发挥。另一个是大空间的问题。未来 30 年，上海肯定还叫"上海"，但是上海的结构、内涵、功能调整，跟现在应该很不一样。上海过去主要是靠扩大发展，越做越大，将来恐怕上海的发展思路，是重生和再生。恐怕现在很多规划，还只局限于怎么扩大规模、提升范围。

新的形势下，需要一些全新的东西。就像浦东建筑，都是过去没有看到的，突然就冒出来了。所以能不能在上海创造一个创新环境？上海应当成为引领未来未知领域，应对未知领域、范式转变的一个地方。

郑军：我是土生土长的上海人，很高兴听到各位专家学者的精彩观点，学到很多东西。

我特别同意叶华董事长所讲，上海原来被称作"冒险家的乐园"，因此在这块土地上是不缺乏企业家精神的，也不缺乏创新精神。今天我们谈 35 年以后的上海，假如我们回到过去看 30 年前的上海，也就是 1985 年，那个年代上海出了很多创新的东西。我们有第一家中外汽车合资企业。这个企业的成立，定义了一直到今天为止汽车产业的产业政策。上海也有全国最大的超级商业零售企业。当然今天我们碰到很多新的挑战，因为1985年时的创新，基本是学习型的创新，而今天上海面临的创新挑战，是颠覆性的创新。

回过头看上海的产业结构和体制会发现，虽然上海有国企，有民企，有外企，但是毋庸置疑，上海跟中国其他城市比，最大的特色是国企和外企的融合。这两类企业有个特质，就是如果在各自的管理体制之内想要做一些创新和改变，有一定的困难。尤其是在当前特别关键的"跨界创新"上。

从IBM过去在中国的一些经验看，我们在各地跟很多民企，包括国企合作的时候，政府扮演了非常重要的角色。因为政府要帮助这种融合，不仅是国企和国企之间，国企和外企之间的融合。把真正的外界融合做好，那么创新的能量，城市所具备的创新的能力、能量，才会被充分发挥出来。

IBM很重视研发，有一个科学家在IBM总部曾经跟我讲过一个故事。他说IBM有很多创新的成果，是不同学科的科学家坐在一起的时候创造出来的。我认为这是未来上海要实现创新的一个非常重要的方面。政府作为一个"看得见的手"，如何在这些方面推动现有体制环境下跨界创新顺利进行，对上海未来的发展非常重要。

汪颖：我非常同意上海的特点之一是国企和外企的融合。纽约在这方面提供了一个范例，纽约大公司与纽约市政府建立了一个伙伴关系，名字叫"纽约伙伴计划"，目的就是让政府、大公司、创业者坐在一起头脑风暴或者互相帮助，从而把整体的城市创新精神提升起来。上海的条件很好，既有国企，又有民企，又有外企，大家可以互相学习。如果政府能够在这方面提供一个平台，比如叫"上海伙伴计划"，那将是一个非常棒的计划。这个计划如果运行35年，我觉得到2050年，上海就不得了了。

Xing Bangzhi: I just heard the views on global economic development trend, urban development rules and opportunities for Shanghai, including where Shanghai can make a difference in the next 30 years, from international experts of think tanks at home and abroad. It is very rewarding. This is a high-level think tank summit with vision, and I also want to put forward some of the issues that I has been thinking about in my work to solicit your ideas using this rare opportunity.

Everyone is full of wishes and expectations about Shanghai 2050. When Shanghai is upgrading to a higher level, what is its strength? What is the core competitiveness? If you are to summarize Shanghai vision of 2050 in one sentence, how should you describe it? Mr. Ye Hua from Nomura Research Institute, would you please answer this question?

Ye Hua: In fact, it is very difficult to sum up Shanghai in 2050 just in one sentence. Firstly, Shanghai has been a city of immigrants. It has a short history, but yet, it has achieved a lot. This is unrivalled by other cities in China.

Secondly, Shanghai has important cornerstones to excel, even if sometimes it might affect its innovation. I remember Mr. Wang Zhan from Shanghai Academy of Social Sciences said that there is a very basic criterion in determining whether a city is civilized, in short, whether or not it allows everyone to compete on a level playing ground, regardless of the race, region, nationality, or the city where he/she is from. In this regard, Shanghai has a good foundation, which is very different from other cities in China.

Besides, vice president Qiao Yide talked about largest economic entity just now. Considering the population and area, as well as taking into account the economic vitality of the city and other factors, will Shanghai still be known as "Shanghai" in 2030, or 2040? Will the word "Shanghai" refer to the city by itself or Shanghai metropolitan area? It is impossible to predict, but I believe that by then "Shanghai" will definitely not be limited to economy, culture, science and technology of the current Shanghai.

From this logic, to rally them all up so that they can play an integrated role, and let the world know that Shanghai is doing experiments and innovations in this area, I think, it must be reflected by the spirit of entrepreneurs and Shanghai residents in daily life, or in other words, either government or the society must have a spirit that can be understood and referenced by the world. If so, then just as the "Chinese Dream" proposed by President Xi, it is crucial to bring the "hope", not only to the Chinese people, and also to people around the world. This is ideological achievements, something about spirit.

I was born in Shanghai. Talking about Shanghai makes me very emotional. The year 2050 is very far away, I hope that by then Shanghai will be firmly-rooted in culture, ideology and civilization. Once that goal is achieved, then whether or not it is called "Shanghai" doesn't matter at all, and there is no need for discussions on strategy and vision and so on. Because they have penetrated in the daily work.

Li Guangyu: In particular, I echo with what you just said. Maybe in the past 30 years, we attached excessive importance to economic development. Because at that time, a poverty-stricken China was still in its infancy, we have to focus on our economic development. But by 2020 when we preliminarily achieved the goal of "Four Centers", and even in 2050, it is not that economy is no longer important, but people's focus of attention will be more diversified. When the basic necessities have been met, there will be more and higher aspirations. This is why we have heard many keywords today such as values, spirit and civilization. Will Shanghai still be the focus of Chinese people? Or, on a global scale, will people only pay attention to the economic status of Shanghai? China will probably be the world's largest economy, of course people want to check if Shanghai will become the city with the biggest GDP in China. But if people are asked about the place which they are yearning for, deep in their heart, the answers may be some Nordic cities and Silicon Valley. It is not the wealth of Silicon Valley that is attractive, in terms of per capita wealth, many Middle Eastern countries are definitely richer than the Silicon Valley. This is a question needs further consideration.

Ju Lixin: Today I learned a lot at Shanghai International Think Tank Summit, to describe in an Internet slang that is "brain hole wide open, meaning big eye-opener". My question to Chairman Ye Hua from NRI who brought up a very important concept, that is, if Shanghai is to become a global city, not just about economy, or science and technology, another important goal you mentioned is to be a "global city of culture" , and by 2050, to be a global city with "source of global influential ideas". 80 years ago, Shanghai was known as "an eastern metropolis in the Far East ". 30 years later, how should Shanghai build itself into a "global city of culture" and a city with "source of global influential ideas"? Will it be a city with oriental cultural characteristics, or modern Western cultural traits, or even a mix of both oriental and occidental cultures? Or, an ideological and cultural hub that may lead the world that is a melting pot for the two cultures or diversified cultures? Please be more specific, Chairman Ye.

Ye Hua: from a cultural point of view, Shanghai itself is a pluralistic and complex city. For instance, when you go out of this meeting venue, you will see lots of skyscrapers, and Pudong New Area may have the biggest concentration of China's high-rise buildings. I major in architecture, and I know that few buildings are designed by Chinese, of course the construction is done by us Chinese. There was a very famous architecture Laszlo Hudec who has designed many unique buildings in Shanghai, but not many of us know much about him, and there is no need for industrial outsiders to know about him. But his buildings have become the landmarks of Shanghai. This makes Shanghai very different from other cities. Beijing has the Forbidden City and Xi'an has ancient city walls. They are the name cards of the cities. And Shanghai is like a melting pot, a mosaic, which pieces all of them together.

Speaking of innovation, I remember that Shanghai used to have a nickname "paradise for adventurers". Once upon a time in history, Shanghai was the most active and innovative city in East Asia and even the world, people from foreign lands started up and brought their entrepreneurship into play here. But for the contemporary era, can you think of any person in Shanghai who is famous writers, thinkers or theorists? I am afraid I am not capable of naming one.

In addition to institutional innovation, there are some other measurable criteria for innovation such as patents, but some things about thoughts cannot be measured, luckily it sinks in. This is very critical, and there is boundary. Patent has a boundary. You have to pay to use it.

I do not know if you can understand that. What I mean is that we should make breakthroughs in things with no boundary and which are difficult. In China, especially in cities like Shanghai, we must make breakthroughs in "Shanghai Spirit" which has been previously deposited. This, in my mind, makes Shanghai standing out from the portfolio of cities. Otherwise, this city will be phased out in the competition against others, after all, the time span is very long, 35 years ahead.

Zhang Yunling: due to the time limit for my keynote speech, I didn't go into details about three ideas: First, the world will have a lot of unknown territory in the future, that is to say, the world will change dramatically in the coming 30 years. To cope with the uncertainties, we need a very large open space for free thinking. Just now, someone mentioned "paradise for adventurers", which reminds me of a story. After reunification of East and West Germany, German government did not rebuild East Berlin, instead, it provided a very wide space for freedom of innovation and creativity, offering cheap shelters, preferential conditions so that people in the world can come to East Berlin freely. Now when we talk about innovation, there seems to be something about institutional structure. Beijing has many limitations on development, while Shanghai has its strength in uncharted territory, that is why you see lots of experiments here such as Free Trade Zone and others. We do not really know what the future will become, climate change and the like.

Second, it is a paradigm shift. Human society and the world have developed thus far. We are all aware that the conventional road leads us nowhere. China is a country with billions of population, and so is India. The future lies in developing countries. We must push for a fundamental paradigm shift since the industrial revolution. This change must start with disruptive ideas. China puts forward a new development outlook to guide the development pattern shift, which is a new proposal. But I'm afraid that we haven't thought enough about many other new ideas. Fortunately, Shanghai is well positioned to create such an environment.

Third, I mentioned in my speech, what is "Shanghai"? What should Shanghai be like in the future? It may not be a city in the conventional manner. In the future, Shanghai may not only refer to the city proper, but the functional area. Another issue is about the space. In the next 30 years, Shanghai may also be called "Shanghai", but its structure, connotation and function may be quite different from now. In the past Shanghai mainly grows by geographic expansion. I am afraid that in the future, Shanghai will develop by rebirth and regeneration. Lots of plans still focus on geographic expansion only, I am afraid.

Under the new circumstances, we need something brand new. Just like the new buildings in Pudong suddenly come out, seems to be out of nowhere. So can we create an innovative environment in Shanghai? Shanghai should lead the future into the unknown, a whole paradigm shift.

Zheng Jun: I am a native of Shanghai, I am very pleased to hear you wisdom, it is really thought-provoking.

In particular, I agree with what Chairman Ye Hua argued. Shanghai used to be referred to as "paradise for adventurers", so this land lacks no entrepreneurship or innovation spirit. Today we are talking about Shanghai in 35 years later. But if you look back at Shanghai 30 years ago, or in 1985, Shanghai has created lots of innovative stuff. We have the first Sino-foreign automobile joint venture, which defines the automobile industry policy even to now. Shanghai also had the largest retail business in China. Of course, today we have been meeting a lot of new challenges, since innovation in 1985 was basically a learning-type, whereas innovation challenges faced by Shanghai today is a disruptive one.

If you look deeper into Shanghai's industrial structure and regimes, you will find that although Shanghai has state-owned companies, private sector and also foreign companies, without doubt, state-owned enterprises and foreign companies play a dominative role when comparing with other cities in China. The two types of companies have a drawback, that is, it is difficult to carry out innovation and change within their administrative system, especially at the special "crossover innovation".

Judging from IBM's experience in China, when IBM is cooperating with some private enterprises and also state-owned enterprises across China, the local government plays a very important role. The government wants the cooperation, not only among state-owned enterprises, but also between domestic and foreign companies. Only when the cooperation and integration is smooth, the innovative power, energy and ability owned by a city can be fully realized.

IBM attaches great importance to research and development. A scientist at IBM headquarter once told me that many innovation in IBM are created when scientists from different backgrounds sit together. I think this is a very important reference for Shanghai to achieve innovation. As a "visible hand", how should the government promote crossover innovation under the current system? It is very important to the future of Shanghai.

Wang Ying: I totally agree that one of Shanghai's characteristics is that state-owned enterprises and foreign companies are predominant. New York provides us an example in this regard, large companies in New York establish a partnership with New York City government called "New York Partnership Program", with a purpose to enable the government, giant companies and entrepreneurs to sit together brainstorming or helping each other, thus enhancing the spirit of innovation of the whole city. Shanghai is in very good condition, with state-owned enterprises, private enterprises, and also foreign enterprises that can learn from each other. If the government can provide a platform in this regard, say, let's call it "Shanghai Partnership Program", it would be excellent. If this program is run for 35 years, by 2050, Shanghai would be freaking awesome.

SUMMARY STATEMENT

总结发言

李广宇　Li Guangyu

麦肯锡公司全球资深董事合伙人

Senior Partner of McKinsey & Company

今天我们听到了很多关键词，而且频率都很高。大家讲得最多的是"创新"，从很多不同的角度，提到了人才、教育、文化、智慧城市，等等。既有宏观方面的世界和中国的宏观大势，也讲到了很多从微观层面上海在未来30年、35年发展过程中碰到的一些挑战。

站在今天看明天的时候，需要这样一种海阔天空，需要足够多的畅想，需要很多的想象力。我试图做个总结，因为意见很多，不一定把大家的所有智慧都融入进来。尽我所能把我今天听到的大家的一些主要观点做一个很快的梳理。

刚刚有人提问，如果用一句话概括2050年的上海，会是什么？我个人也是做了很多政策相关的项目，包括对未来的很多研究等，但是这真的是一个特别难的问题。

从今天往前看，不一定能看得很清楚。但是大家的一个重要共识是，上海要在今天实现"四个中心"的基础上迈向下一步的话，我们非常期待看到一个真正的、具有全球影响力的、国际公认的世界枢纽城市。20年前大家会说，要实现"四个中心"很振奋人心。经过几代人的努力，我们好不容易看到了"四个中心"的实现，35年以后，可能也没有人很惊讶。但是刚才讲的几个关键词："全球影响力"，而且是"全球公认"的，一个"枢纽型的大都市"，我想上海还是有相当大的距离。

举个简单的例子。我经常在全球飞，最关注的是天气预报。有了网络，你可以选择自己关注的城市。但是看很多世界主流媒体的天气预报的时候，你突然会发现有北京，但很多时候没有上海。这就是差距，在国际舞台上大家没有把上海主动放在枢纽中心或者是很向往的地位。未来35年，这可能也是上海应该努力的一个方向，成为一个具有全球影响力、国际公认的世界枢纽大都市。

2050年，上海在"四个中心"基础上可能有一个什么样的愿景？今天大家谈到了很多内涵性的东西，我总结了一下，应该包括五个方面：

第一，生态、健康优先。当年我们考虑"四个中心"的时候可能没有考虑到这个因素，因为那个时候我们没有感受到雾霾，没有感受到全球气候变化、环境污染能带来这么深切的影响。以至于很多人说，不管你的GDP有多少个0，或者通过多少努力个人财富有多少个0，如果没有环境和健康的环境，这一切都会归于零。那我们是不是提倡生态、健康优先，把它们放在越来越核心的议题上？

第二，能不能把上海发展成多元发展、综合性的经济体？从主体多元角度讲，IBM代表郑军说，当前上海更多是以国企和改革开放以来进入的大型跨国企业为主导的经济，那么在这个过程中，怎么释放出更多创新活力？怎么吸引更多的民营经济来上海？怎么让更多初创企业愿意把上海作为首选？不仅是中国的首选城市，甚至是全球初创企业的首选城市。如何在国企、外企、初创企业、民企四者之间，形成一个共生共荣、紧密连接的产业生态圈？我觉得这是至关重要的。从业态多元角度看，麦肯锡全球研究院院长陈有钢提到，未来是不是有第四产业的出现？未来上海会面对以服务经济为主的经济结构，但在这个过程中，上海不要放弃已经有的先进制造业，应该把现代化做得更强。

第三，是大家提到频率最多的——创新。上海怎么成为一个汇聚智慧、跨界融合的枢纽型的城市？我印象比较深的是王颐发言中讲到，教育是我们创新的"芯片"。怎么保证大量的基础研究的投入？这个过程中，政府扮演着非常重要的角色。IBM的代表也提到，很多产业不是无中生有"蹦"出来的，更多是在跨学科、跨界的融合和不断碰撞过程中，形成了很多新的产业的亮点。美国商会代表也提到，上海不缺乏企业家精神，但是怎么样有更多的工程师文化、匠人精神，也非常重要。否则上海就变得越来越"浮"在上面，而不能"沉"下来。上海在实体经济方面也要有所作为。

第四，是人才中心、人才高地。上海怎么变得更加开放、包容、充满活力？

第五个方面的核心内涵，也是最后互动讨论中越来越呼之欲出的问题，即思想、文化和价值观问题。也就是说，上海不仅在中国，在未来30年、35年中应该有很多在经济方面的话语权和经济方面的成就，更多的是怎么在思想和文化方面，也能够真正成为一个世界级的城市。

还有两个重要问题贯穿其中。一是这些内涵中，最实质的和最核心的内涵是什么？大家都讲到了，上海多元、开放、包容，是一个海纳百川的地方，这不是旧话。人们老说美国是一个熔炉；上海的伟大之处在于，它不是简单地把所有人引进来然后走出去，它不是一个很单一的上海人的面孔，上海始终是多元的，始终是多面孔的、多元化、多色彩的一个地方。我们特别希望这个特质不仅能在未来几十年中保留下来，而且在这个基础上能有进一步的发扬光大。

另一个问题是，政府在这个过程中，应该扮演什么样的角色？上海政府一直是一个有为的政府，也是从某种角度来说比较"强势"的政府，更是为城市发展做了很多贡献的政府。这个是大家有目共睹的。但是在一个更高的层次上，上海政府怎么把全社会的活力进一步释放出来？在有序的情况下，不要怕在开放的过程中出现更多有益的碰撞，或者是颠覆式的创新。这个过程中，上海政府是不是能多一点前瞻的视野、多一些冒险和勇于尝试，同时在政策执行过程中又能保持一定的延续性和稳定性。

最后我想加上一点我自己个人的一个观点。我感觉今天很多发言，更多的是站在今天看未来，都在畅想35年以后上海怎么样。其中包括很多数据分析，可能是线性的展望。反过来想，我们能不能站在未来看今天？因为我们很有敬畏之心，不敢对三四十年后做出预测，但是我们敢于畅想，也敢于站在"人"的角度看问题。刚刚有几位嘉宾讲到他们和90后互动的故事，我感触更深。在我们今天看来，90后是年轻的新兴的一代，到2050年，其实他们也接近退休年龄了。真正对这个事情有发言权的，应该是2000到2020年出生的这些人。反问我们自己，对这些人群有多少关注和研究？到时候是他们主导的社会，他们身上有什么样的特质？从这个角度思考可能对我们城市的下一步经济社会发展能提供很多颠覆性的启示。

我们也做了一些这方面的研究，我们叫他们"Generation Z"——2000年以后出生的人。他们一出生就接触互联网，是"数字土著"。很多社交媒体、云计算、人工智能，对他们来说都不是什么新鲜的事物，而是他们来到这个社会后生命中的一个部分。这些东西对他们的行为、教育和观念有着颠覆性的影响，对我们更是这样。他们会有更强烈的城市公民的意识，也会习惯于越来越快的生活节奏，同时又超强的学习意愿和接受新鲜事物的能力。他们可能会比我们这代人更追求拥抱个人爱好，追求多元化的价值体现。企业家的冒险精神，可能也会根植在他们的 DNA 中。他们在很富足的环境下成长，可能不知道什么是贫困。所以简单地对物质的追求和渴望，不会成为他们唯一或者最重要的一个动力。他们同时会非常重视合作、互助和共享。

这些特质和我们今天在座的各位非常不同。而他们，会是主导 2050 年上海的一群人。所以我希望大家能多一些对这方面的关注。我家孩子 15 岁，2000 年出生。我说到今天要来参加上海智库峰会，通常他对我的工作一点都不关心，因为他觉得太严肃。我问他，你怎么想 2050 年的上海？他说了一句特别实在的话，因为我们都是用文绉绉的，学术化的话讲，他说："我大学还是想到国外读，回不回来到时候再说。""那什么样的城市能让你回来？"他的回答再简单不过，他说："希望 2050 年上海是全球最酷的城市，如果那样，我肯定愿意回来，继续作为这个城市的一分子存在。"

作为总结，就让我们带着这个梦想，继续海阔天空，希望 2050 年的上海真的是全球公认的，大家心目中最酷的，也是环境最好最优美的一个世界性的枢纽的城市。

We've heard many key words mentioned at higher frequency today. The most frequently mentioned word by all is "innovation", but it is explained in different angles, e.g. talent, education, culture, smart city etc. Both macro trend at world and China level and some challenges at micro level that Shanghai may encounter in future 30 to 35 years are mentioned.

When we look forward to the future from today's perspective, we need such unrestrained and far-ranging imagination. I'll try to summarize what you have said, but as you've shared many ideas, I may not be able to integrate all of your wisdom in such summary. Nevertheless, I'll try my best to streamline your views I've heard today.

Just as someone asked to use one sentence to make a summary, what will it be like in Shanghai 2050? As for myself, I've also participated in many policy-related projects, including some studies for future. This is really a difficult job.

We cannot have a clear view today. But an important point is we have certain consensus that if Shanghai wants to move forward on the basis of realizing "Four Centers" today, we are looking forward to see an internationally recognized world hub city with real global influence. Two decades ago, many would comment that the idea of "Four Centers" was stimulating and with great efforts for generations, we finally see the realization of "Four Centers". But 35 years later, there will be none feeling surprised about it. However, for those key words we just mentioned, i.e. global influence, internationally recognized and a hub metropolitan, I think there is still a long way to go in this aspect.

I'll show you a very simple example. I travel a lot around the world, so

I pay most attention to the weather forecast. Of course as there is the Internet, you can select the cities you care about. But when I check the weather forecast in a number of global mainstream media, I'll often find Beijing is included, but Shanghai not. This is the gap and Shanghai hasn't been put in the position of a hub center on the international stage. In future 35 years, this may become the direction that Shanghai shall strive for.

Under the vision of an internationally recognized world-level hub metropolitan with global influence, what kind of vision will Shanghai have on the basis of "Four Centers" by 2050? Today we've mentioned many connotative contents and I've simply summarized them into five dimensions:

Firstly, put ecosystem and health as priority. When we considered "Four Centers" in the past, we failed to consider this issue as we didn't feel how profound impacts that haze, global weather change and environmental pollution might bring to us then. So that many people commented that, no matter how high the GDP was or how much individual wealth was, without environment, or healthy environment, all of them would be equal to zero. Well, shouldn't we prioritize the ecosystem and health and put them on core agenda?

Secondly, can we develop Shanghai into a diversified and integrated economic entity? In terms of diversification of subjects, Zheng Jun, representative from IBM, has said we are an economy that is mostly dominated by SOEs or MNCs since reform and opening up. Well in this process, how to unleash more vigor for innovation, how to attract more private enterprises to Shanghai and how to make more start-ups select Shanghai as their base of choice? Here I'm not only mean China, but also the preferred city for global start-ups. In this way, a co-prosperous and closely linked industrial ecosystem can be formed among SOEs, foreign enterprises, start-ups and private companies. I think it is quite critical. Additionally, we shall turn to the diversification of business format. In the beginning, Chen Yougang from McKinsey & Company's Shanghai Office even proposed if there would be any quaternary industry. In the future, Shanghai will have to focus on the service economy, however, in this process, we shall not abandon the advanced manufacturing industry we already have, but make the modernization even stronger.

Thirdly, it is the mostly frequently mentioned topic: innovation. How can

Shanghai become a hub city that gathers talents and cross-industry integration? I was deeply impressed by what Wang Yi mentioned in his speech. When it comes to innovation, education is really our "chip". How can we have more investment in basic research? The government plays a very important role in this process. IBM once also mentioned interdisciplinary and cross-industry integration. Many industries are not created out of thin air, while many highlights in new industry are generated in the process of continuous cross-industry and interdisciplinary collision. The American Chamber of Commerce also mentioned Shanghai didn't lack of entrepreneurship, but it is important for how to generate more engineer culture and craftsmanship. Otherwise, Shanghai would be "floating" on the surface and can't "keep down", and it also needs to perform well in real economy.

Fourthly, it shall be a talent center and highland. How can Shanghai become an open, inclusive and dynamic city?

Fifthly, it shall be the core of our discussion in the final interaction part, i.e. thought, culture and value. That is to say, we not only need to have more speaking right and make more achievements in China's economic domain in future 30 to 35 years, but also think about how to become a real world-level city in terms of thought and culture.

There are two important issues we also need to pay attention to. The first is that what is the most essential core among these connotations? You've all mentioned, Shanghai shall be diversified, open and inclusive and it's not an old saying. The U.S. is usually commented as a "smelting furnace", but what is great for Shanghai lies in that it doesn't simply attract everyone here and display the single Shanghai appearance outside, but that Shanghai is a diversified, multi-faceted and colorful place. We especially hope this attribute can not only be maintained in future decades, but also be further strengthened on this basis.

The second is that what role shall the government play in this process? Shanghai government has been a "promising" and somewhat "strong" government and it has made a lot of contribution to urban development. This is obvious to all. However, at a higher level, how can we further release the vigor of the society? In an orderly environment, we shall not be afraid of more beneficial collision in the process of reform, or disruptive innovation. In such process, can the government be forward looking and make more venture and trial, meanwhile maintain consistency and stability in policy execution?

Finally, I want to add some of my personal views. I feel that many speeches today look into the future in today's position and they all imagine what Shanghai will be in future 35 years. Even for some data analysis, it is also linear outlook on future. In contrast, can we look back to today by standing in the future? We really have some fear that we dare not make forecast for what may happen in 30 to 40 years. But we are bold in imagination and we also dare to start from the perspective of "human being". Some speakers have talked about the story about their interaction with the "Post-90s" generation. I am also deeply impressed. In fact, the "Post-90s" generation is a young and emerging generation today, but by 2050, they shall reach their retirement years. People having the speaking right for this topic shall be those born from 2000 to 2020. Well, we can reflect that how much attention and study have been given to these generations now? What attributes do they have in a society where they are in dominance? It may give us some disruptive implications for urban social and economic development as the next step.

We've also carried out some studies on this aspect. We call them "Generation Z", or people born after 2000. They had contact with the Internet after they were born, so they are the so called "digital natives". In this process, those including social media, cloud computation, artificially intelligence etc. are not fresh for them, but a part of life after they came into the society. These things have world-shaking and disruptive impact on their behavior, education and concept, which is also true for us. They will have stronger awareness of urban citizen, they will be more used to faster living pace and they will be more willing to learn and accept fresh things. They may pursue and embrace individual habit and more diversified value representation than our generation. The spirit of adventure for entrepreneurs may be rooted in their DNA, as they don't know what poverty is and they are growing up in a well-off environment. So the simple pursuit and desire for materials cannot be become their sole or most important momentum. They will also pay much attention to cooperation, mutual assistance and sharing.

They are really different from us, who are present today. But they will dominate Shanghai in 2050, so we hope you can pay more attention to them. My kid is 15 years old, who was born in 2000. I told him I would attend this summit. He usually pays no attention to my work, as he feels it's too serious. I asked him about his view on what Shanghai would be in 2050. What he said was very practical and he didn't use any liberal and academic words like us. He said he would like to study abroad when he goes to the university and he was not sure if he would go back or not after graduation. When I asked him what kind of city can attract him back? His answer was very simple. He said he hoped Shanghai would the coolest city then. If that is the case, he would like to come back and live and work as a part of the city.

To summarize, we shall continue our wild imagination and with this dream, I hope Shanghai can really become an internationally recognized, the coolest, the most beautiful and environment-friendly world-level hub city.

CLOSING REMARK

闭幕致辞

屠光绍　Tu Guangshao

上海市人民政府常务副市长

Executive Deputy Mayor of the

Shanghai Municipal People's Government

改革开放 30 多年来，上海整体发展一直沿着两条线索迈进。第一条线索是经济社会的发展，包括"四个中心"建设、民生改善、城市管理等方方面面，我们每年都要晒出政府工作报告、成绩单。此外还包括社会对上海发展的评价、国际对上海发展的关注。我们还有另外一条线，这条线不一定有很高的关注度，但也非常重要，那就是伴随着我们改革开放 30 多年来关于上海的发展战略研究。这条线对支撑前面那条线，起了重要的作用。

改革开放 30 多年来，上海组织国内外专家学者开展了几次城市发展战略大讨论。这些大讨论对支撑上海整个经济社会发展战略的制定，并在战略制定之后付诸实施和不断推进起着重要的作用。由于有了这些战略研讨和研究，这 30 多年来我们不断尝到甜头，因为这些战略研讨明确了上海发展战略，以及在不同时期的目标和城市功能定位。在上海发展转型的若干重大时刻，它都发挥了重要作用，产生了重大和深远的影响。所以发展战略研究这条线，虽然社会上可能不很关注，但是非常重要，而且会越来越重要。

上海发展战略研究，要解决三个问题：

（1）上海怎么定位。包括从空间上怎么定位？从时间轴上怎么定位？过去有很多形象化的说法，比如不能"就上海看上海，要跳出上海看上海"；还有人说要立足全国看上海，放眼全球看上海，说的都是从时间和空间上看上海的定位。但是今天的主题，不光是要从全国、全球看上海，要跳出上海看上海，还要"放眼未来"看上海。要从现在看未来，从未来看上海。

所以怎么给上海定位？这是发展战略一个非常重要的问题。

（2）用什么方式。今天讨论的是 2050 年——未来 30 年的上海发展战略研究，这个战略怎么具体展开？这么多年我们也在总结这方面的经验。上海要进行战略研究，必须是开放的、前瞻性的、共享的、互动的。因此，我们搭建了若干平台。比如，每年的市长国际企业家咨询会、上海国际智库峰会、上海发展研究基金会，等等。在这些平台上，通过开放、前瞻、互动、分享的交流，甚至各种碰撞的方式进行研究，使战略研究基础更扎实，从而使战略的选择、发展和推进具有更坚实的支撑。

（3）什么人来研究。今天参与上海发展战略研讨的，都是非常合适的人。一方面，你们了解上海，很多人工作在上海，很多机构业务本身就在上海，有的人还生活在上海；另一方面，你们了解全球，了解全球发展的整体状况。一方面，你们有国际经验和国际比较，包括国际其他城市的不同定位，既具备了了解某些行业和领域的专业知识、经验，又有把握整个战略发展大局方面的思考。所以在座各位参与上海发展战略研究，使我们能够吸取和分享大家的智慧，促进战略研究更有效的推进。

不断总结上述三个问题，对推进上海发展过程中另一条线索——发展战略研究，意义重大。

从古到今，中国的思想家和文学家，用很多语言来描绘为什么要进行战略研究。比如，"欲穷千里目，更上一层楼"，意思是要登高望远，才能看得更全面、更长久。还有"不识庐山真面目，只缘身在此山中"，因为在"山"中，"山"的真面目看不到，所以必须从全局角度，走到"山"外面来看。这都说明了战略研究的实质就是怎么把握大趋势。此外，"不谋全局，不足以谋一域"，说的是不谋全局，具体某个方面也做不好。"不谋长远，难以谋一时"，即没有长远考虑，短期也很难把事情做好。这都说明了战略研究的重要性。

未来 30 年，世界经济和社会发展将进入重大的转型期，特别是当前世界经济格局面临重大调整，全球的经济重心也在进行转移，科技的发展日新月异。上海作为世界六大城市群之一的长三角城市群的首位城市和崛起中的全球城市，在这个转型过程中，也面临着重大发展机遇与挑战。

这次研讨会的主题——面向未来 30 年的上海发展战略研究，是上海市委市政府确定的重大战略研究。未来 30 年上海到底是什么样的？变化因素很多，不容易把握。定下这样一个主题，反映了上海市委市政府立足于长远、放眼长远来进行战略研究的态度，也显示了上海市委市政府持续推进上海发展的决心。

重大战略研究光靠政府是很难推进的，需要汇集各方的智慧，需要专家学者对未来30年全球经济、社会、政治、科技和文化进行"畅想"，才能形成未来上海转型、发展的目标和路径，推动上海实现新的、可持续的长期发展。这对未来上海的发展具有重要的意义。

今天时间虽短，但内容丰富，意义也非常重大。我相信专家学者提供的智慧思想，有助于我们科学分析，把握未来30年世界经济格局变化和中国崛起态势对上海的影响，更好地推动上海未来30年新的发展。

In the past three decades since China's reform and opening up, Shanghai's overall development has been following two tracks. The first track is the economic and social development, including the building of "Four Centers", the improvement of people's livelihood, urban management etc. Every year we release report on the work of the government and performance results to the public. We also follow up on the masses and the world's attention on Shanghai's development. There is also a parallel track, which may not necessarily have attracted as much attention, but is also very important, that is research on the development of Shanghai for the past 30 years of reform and opening up. The latter track plays an important role in supporting the former one.

In the past 30 years, Shanghai has organized experts and scholars from home and abroad to carry out several rounds of discussion on urban development strategy. These discussions are very important for us drafting the strategies and policies on the economic and social development as well as supporting us to implement and pushing forward those strategies and policies. We continue to have the benefits from these strategic discussions and research in the past three decades. Because of the discussion on strategies, we clarified Shanghai's development strategies, targets at different stages and the functional positioning of this city. In a number of important junctures for Shanghai's development and transformation, it played an important role, and exerted a significant and profound impact. Therefore, the track of development strategy research, may not be so concerned about by the public, but is very important, and will become increasingly more so.

Research on Shanghai's Development Strategy is aimed to solve three questions:

(1) What is the position of Shanghai?

What is the position of Shanghai in space? And in timeline? In the past, there are many figurative statements, for example, we cannot "view Shanghai for the sake of Shanghai, we must think out of the box", some also say that we must look upon Shanghai from the nations' perspective or even from the world's perspective, which means we must ponder over Shanghai's positioning from time and space.

But today's topic is not just to view Shanghai's position from China's perspective and the global point-of-view, but to think out of the box and also look into the future. Not only should we look into the future standing at the current position, but also look in retrospect from some future point.

So how to locate Shanghai is a very important issue in the study of development strategies.

(2) In what way?

Today's discussion is the year of 2050-the Development Strategy of Shanghai in 30 years' time, but how should we roll out those strategies? In the many years we have also summarized experiences.

Shanghai's strategic research must be open, forward-looking, and interactive. So we set up a number of platforms. For example, there are annual International Business Leaders Advisory Council for the Mayor of Shanghai, Shanghai International Think Tank Summit, Shanghai Development Research Foundation, and so on. On these platforms, through open, forward-looking, interactive exchanges, or even some hot debates, strategic research will be consolidated, so that the selection, development, and promotion of strategy will have a stronger supporting.

(3) Who shall do the study?

Today we have involved very suitable persons to carry out the discussion on Shanghai's future development strategy. On the one hand, you are familiar with Shanghai, most of you work in Shanghai, lots of institutions present here are based in Shanghai, and some of you are living in Shanghai. On the other hand, you know the world, and you understand what is going on in the world. You have international experience which enables you to make the comparisons across countries, including different positions of other international cities. Not only do you have expertise and experience on a number of industries and areas, but you also have your own insights on the overall strategic development. So all of you participating in this research will enable us to learn and share the wisdom and promote strategic research more effectively.

To constantly sum up the three issues above serves well to the other track in promoting the development of Shanghai Development Strategy Research.

Since ancient times, Chinese thinkers, scholars and gurus describe why there should be strategic research in many sentences. For example, "Ascend further, were you to look farther." Meaning that you can only scale new heights to take long-term perspective and see a bigger picture; and "The true face of Lushan Mountain is lost to my sight, for it is right in this mountain that I reside," meaning that I can not have the whole sight for I am in the Mountain, or, in order to see the true face of the Mountain, I have to look at the outside, which explains that the essence of strategic research is to grasp the big trend. In addition, "He who doesn't study for overall situation is hardly to manage for one aspect", and also "He who has no long-term consideration is hardly to organize temporarily", meaning that without a long-term view, it is hard to meet the short-term goal. All these quotes show the importance of strategic research.

In the next 30 years, the world economy and international social development will enter a major transformation period, especially, the current world economic landscape is facing major adjustments and the world's economic center of gravity is also moving; technology development has been changing rapidly. Shanghai, as a leading city among the six mega-city clusters in the world, is first emerging to be a global city from the Yangtze River Delta. In this transition of process, it is also facing major development opportunities and challenges.

The theme of this summit, the Development Strategy of Shanghai in the Next 30 Years, is a major strategic research topic determined by Shanghai Committee of C.P.C and Shanghai Municipal People's Government. What should Shanghai be like in the next 30 years? It is not easy to imagine as there are various changing factors. We set up such a broad topic reflects Shanghai Committee of C.P.C and Shanghai Municipal People's Government's attitude to look into the future for strategic research and it also shows that Shanghai government's determination to promote the development of Shanghai.

The wisdom of all parties must be brought together and experts and scholars are kindly requested to give free rein to their imagination on global economy, society, politics, science and technology and culture in the next 30 years to come up with goals and the path for the future transformation of Shanghai. It is only by doing so that can we achieve a new and sustainable development for Shanghai in the long term. It has important implication for the future development of Shanghai.

Today, time is limited, but we have achieved a lot. And the discussion is significant in meaning. I believe that the wisdom and thoughts of experts and scholars will help in ideological and scientific analysis on the changes in the world economic landscape and will allow us to know better about the impact of China's rise on Shanghai, and I believe it will facilitate Shanghai's development in the next 30 years.

CONFERENCE REVIEW

峰会综述

2015 年 12 月 18 日，由上海市人民政府发展研究中心主办，上海国际智库交流中心、上海发展研究基金会、麦肯锡公司联合承办，举行了"2015 年上海国际智库峰会"。上海市政府常务副市长屠光绍、上海市政府秘书长李逸平莅临现场，屠光绍致闭幕辞。来自麦肯锡、埃森哲、普华永道、德勤、IBM、野村综研、哈佛上海中心、强生中国、高风咨询、美中贸易全国委员会、上海美国商会、欧盟上海商会、日本贸易振兴机构、泰科电子等 17 家国际智库专家围绕"2050 年的上海：发展愿景与挑战"的主题，对 2050 年上海发展的愿景、面临的瓶颈挑战和实现这些愿景的思路和对策建议进行了广泛深入研讨。

1. 2050 年上海发展愿景

专家们认为，2020 年上海基本建成"四个中心"后，要进一步在 2050 年建成具有全球影响力和国际公认的全球城市。具体包括：成为全球领先的创新城市（普华永道）；全球最健康的城市（强生中国）；最智慧的城市（德勤）；具有全球影响力的文化与思想策源传播中心（野村综研）；第一个全球性的 21 世纪城市（高风咨询）；全球最"酷"的城市（麦肯锡）。

IBM 华东及华中区总经理郑军、普华永道中国合伙人汪颖认为，未来上海要全面释放创新活力，实现以国企外企主导的经济向国企、外企、民企和创业企业四者共生共荣、紧密协作的经济生态圈转变，成为多种经济和产业综合发展协调的现代化国际大都市。麦肯锡全球研究院中国负责人陈有钢期望，上海将形成以创造性为特征的"第四产业"，形成与先进制造业相融合的现代服务经济。

哈佛上海中心执行董事王颐指出，上海要充分重视教育作为城市芯片的作用，汇聚智慧，打造高等教育资源的战略驱动力，建设世界一流的科研教育基地和跨界融合的枢纽城市。上海并不缺乏企业家，但只有在跨学科跨行业碰撞融合的条件下，才能发挥企业家精神，激发颠覆性创新的城市能量。中国欧盟商会上海总经理琼安娜和日本贸易振兴机构上海所所长小栗道明进一步提出，上海要构筑开放包容和充满活力的人才高地，在初步建成经济金融中心后，2050年前要进一步向具有全球吸引力的人才中心转变，为占据全球价值链顶端形成人才基础。

陈有钢、埃森哲战略咨询董事总经理钱蔚、琼安娜、强生（中国）公司主席吴人伟和小栗道明提出，上海首先要建成生态良好和健康安全的宜居城市。城市和个人发展必须建立在良好的生态和安全的社会环境基础上，这是发挥人民健康、福利和发展潜能，实现城市可持续发展的基本前提。

野村综研中国董事长叶华认为，上海要形成核心价值观和独特城市气质，积淀"上海精神"，成为具有民族性和世界性的文化与思想策源传播中心，被世界理解和借鉴，对世界启发和鼓舞，在文化、思想和精神层面屹立于世界城市之林。琼安娜和小栗道明指出，要实现这个目标，上海的企业和市民首先要以更加开放的姿态，拥抱世界，和世界共同发展。

2. 未来上海面临的瓶颈与挑战

专家们从宏观和微观层面上提出了上海在实现这些愿景过程中所面临的挑战。

北京大学全球治理研究中心副主任范德尚认为，挑战首先来自世界的不确定性，上海要应对充满着不满、动荡、对立和冲突等世界政治经济挑战，在宗教文化多元化背景下特别要应对这些挑战的复杂化趋势；同时，要适应科技日新月异带来的经济社会快速转型。中国社科院国际研究学部主任张蕴岭和上海发展研究基金会副会长乔依德强调了国内发展中的不确定性对上海发展的挑战，提出要关注上海发展环境三个新因素：（1）经济进入新常态和2050年成为世界第一大经济体；（2）在新的发展环境下，国家在全球经济中定位的调整；（3）国家维护新型大国关系和周边和平，承担全球治理责任的能力。

汪颖、高风咨询董事长谢祖墀和德勤能源与资源行业领导人张小平提醒，经济实力进一步壮大，将越来越迫切地要求形成透明高效互动的政府、公正开放的竞争环境和有保障能力的制度环境，上海在这些方面还有许多工作要做。在城市经济发展上，上海政府在继续扮演投资者、参与者和促进者角色的同时，更重要的是要学习和适应扮演"幕后英雄"角色，这是一个重大挑战。

陈有钢对上海、北京和深圳等国内外城市进行了比较，提出上海在城市创新力上面临三个瓶颈：（1）研发投入不少，但创新成果转化和高科技产业比例低于国内外先进城市；（2）国企和外企是创新主要贡献者，民企不活跃，创新氛围淡薄；（3）创新数据等资源开放和使用等基础环境欠缺，缺乏有效整合企业、机构及市场资源的平台。

此外，张蕴岭和汪颖认为上海发展面临着如大伦敦和巴黎大区类似的地理上限制，中心城区高密度的建设和人口已经接近上限。陈有钢提到了上海生态环境和开放程度上与重要国际城市的差距，以及对吸引高端人才和投资的负面影响。

3. 战略思路与政策建议

专家们对如何实现上海愿景各抒己见，提出了许多思路和政策建议，主要如下：

陈有钢建议，为实现释放创新活力的愿景，上海不应放弃"工商之都"的传统优势。要在工程技术型创新上，依托汽车飞机等制造业基础，鼓励工艺设计等创新，加强知识产权保护，汇聚创意，不要刻意追求基础性和原生性的创新。在客户中心型创新上，要依托规模大和有活力的消费市场，加强创新供需的互动、市场细分，整合营销商网络和商业模式创新，挖掘创新产品与服务商业化潜力。在激活市场创新力上，陈有钢和泰科电子亚洲区政府事务高级总监来咏歌都强调政府要摆正位置，把营造有利于创新创业者生存发展的环境作为主要任务，建立新的衡量创新指标体系（专利数量指标是不够的），让市场发挥作用的思路和建议。

为实现教育作为发展的战略驱动力目标，王颐建议上海借鉴匹兹堡复兴转型的做法[①]，加大对高等院校的跨学科研究基础建设投入，推动高中

---

① 匹兹堡的经验可概括为：加速大学技术成果转让，加强大学与科技企业合作，建立联合创新中心。

和大学教育课程开放、包容和多元化，推动教育的国际化。他特别建议建立英文教学的本科学位课程，吸引海外教育机构和教育模式。汪颖建议借鉴纽约市政当局与华尔街伙伴关系经验 [1]，利用在上海的众多世界顶尖管理人才资源，搭建政企沟通平台，建立培训和支持当地创业者的"上海伙伴计划"。琼安娜基于中国欧盟商会的调查 [2]，提出了提高网速和放宽网络限制的建议，以加强信息交流，吸引顶尖研究学者，保证创新的必要基础条件。

在建设宜居城市的愿景上，张蕴岭提出以"小城市—大城区—大空间"的空间模式，破解空间瓶颈的思路，即放弃简单空间扩张模式，按照城市分工协作要求，打造长三角世界级城市群和建设世界级城市。钱蔚突出了"发展循环经济、守住生态底线"的思路。

叶华提出了上海实现有全球影响力的文化与思想策源传播中心愿景的三个阶段和三个路经：（1）2030 年向全球城市迈进，路径是"硬实力"带动"软实力"；（2）2040 年从创新、文化和国际责任三方面奠定全球城市地位，路经是"软实力"带动"硬实力"；（3）2050 年在精神和思想层面发挥全球城市作用，路径是融合"软硬两种实力"。在具体措施上，麦肯锡全球资深合伙人李广宇提醒要关注作为未来主导者的"Z 世代" [3]；2050 年上海要"酷"，要对"Z 世代"有吸引力，这是成为文化与思想策源传播中心的重要条件。

---

[1] 纽约市与华尔街的伙伴关系主要内容是：由华尔街企业的高级管理人员为纽约市提供创业者教练培训和分享客户体系的支持。

[2] 中国欧盟商会对 600 家成员单位的商业信心调查显示，2014 年，中国在全球网速的排名从 96 名掉到 113 名，57% 的公司受到网速太慢以及网站访问限制的影响，31% 的研究人员表示无法在国外网站收取一些信息以及进行研究，这对企业的经营、生产、科研和创新都产生了很大的影响。

[3] Z 世代（Generation Z）：指 2000 以后出生的年轻一代。李广宇认为，Z 世代一出生就接触互联网，是"数字土著"，社交媒体、云计算、人工智能等现代技术是他们生命的组成部分，对他们的行为、教育、观念，有颠覆性影响；他们有更强烈的城市公民意识，习惯于越来越快的生活节奏，同时有超强的学习和接受新鲜事物的意愿。追求拥抱个人爱好和多元化的价值体现；对物质追求和渴望不会是他们唯一或者最重要的动力。

On December 18, 2015, sponsored by Development Research Centre of Shanghai Municipal People's Government, and jointly organized by Shanghai International Think Tanks Exchange Center, Shanghai Development Research Foundation, McKinsey & Company, "2015 Shanghai International Think Tank Summit" was hold. Tu Guangshao, Executive Deputy Mayor, and Li Yiping, Secretary-General of Shanghai Municipal People's Government, attended the meeting. Executive Deputy Mayor Mr. Tu delivered the closing remarks, participants from McKinsey, Accenture, PricewaterhouseCoopers, Deloitte, IBM, Nomura Research Institute, Harvard Center (Shanghai), Johnson & Johnson China, Gao Feng Advisory Company, the US-China Business Council, the American Chamber of Commerce Shanghai, European Chamber Shanghai Chapter, the Japan External Trade organization (JETRO), TE Connectivity and other international think tanks exchanged around the theme "Shanghai 2050: Vision and Challenge" , and conducted in depth discussions about the vision of Shanghai development 2050, bottlenecks and challenges faced as well as ideas and solutions to meet these proposals.

1. 2050 Shanghai Vision

Experts believe that after Shanghai basically completes the goal "Four Centers" in 2020, it should build Shanghai into an internationally recognized global city with global influence. These include: the world's leading innovative city (PwC); the world's most healthy city (Johnson & Johnson China); the most intelligent city (Deloitte); a "Center" of culture and ideas with global influence (Nomura Research Institute); the first global city of the 21st century (Gao Feng Advisory Company); the world's "coolest" city (McKinsey).

Zheng Jun, Vice President of IBM Enterprise Business Unit, East & Central China, and Wang Ying, PwC Leading Partner of Retail Consumption Duty for Asia Pacific believes that to fully release the creativity and vitality of the future Shanghai, a transition from economy dominated by state-owned and foreign companies to an economic ecosystem featuring synergy by state-owned, foreign enterprises, private enterprises and start-ups must be achieved, so as to become a modern international metropolis with integrated and coordinated economic and industrial development. Chen Yougang, Partner of McKinsey and Head of MGI Greater China expects that Shanghai should have the "Fourth Industry" with creativity as the feature and a modern service sector that is integrated with advanced manufacturing industry.

Wang Yi, Executive Director at Harvard Center Shanghai points out that Shanghai should give full attention to the role of education as the chip of a city, gathering intelligence, promoting strategic driving force of higher education resources, building a world-class research and education base and crossover integration hub; and Shanghai has no lack of entrepreneurs, but only if the sectors and industries are integrated can entrepreneurship be innovated and mobilized. Ioana Kraft, General Manager of European Union Chamber of Commerce in China, Shanghai Chapter, and Michiaki Oguri, President of Japan External Trade Organization in Shanghai suggest that Shanghai should build an open, inclusive and vibrant talent pool. After the preliminary completion of economic and financial center, Shanghai should move to be a talent center of global appeal and lay a foundation to occupy the top of the global value chain.

Chen Yougang, Managing Director of Accenture Resource Service, Greater China, Qian Wei, Ioana Kraft, Wu Renwei, Chairman of Johnson & Johnson (China) and Michiaki Oguri state that for Shanghai to be an ecologically sound, healthy, safe, livable city, cities and personal development must be based on a good ecological and social environment, which is basic premise of achieving sustainable urban development.

Ye Hua, Chairman of Nomura Research Institute believes that Shanghai should form its own core values and unique temperament, accumulate "Shanghai Spirit", become a national and a cosmopolitan cultural and ideological source that is understood and appreciated by the world, providing inspiration and encouragement for the world and standing among the strongest cities in terms of culture, ideology and spirit. Ioana Kraft and Michiaki Oguri point out that Shanghai's business and citizens must embrace the world for common development with an open mind to achieve this goal.

2. Future Bottlenecks and Challenges Facing Shanghai

Experts propose the challenges Shanghai is facing in achieving these visions from macro and micro perspectives.

Fan Deshang, Deputy Director and General Secretary of the Center for Global Governance Studies at Peking University, believes that the first challenges are from uncertainty of the world. Shanghai is confronted with the world political and economic situation with challenges such as discontent, unrest, confrontation and conflict, and must deal with these complex challenges against the background of religious and cultural pluralism, at the same time, it must achieve rapid economic and social transformation brought about by rapid changes in technology. Zhang Yunling, Director of International Studies of Chinese Academy of Social Sciences and Qiao Yide, Vice Chairman & Secretary General of Shanghai Development Research Foundation highlight the challenges posed by uncertainty in domestic development and direct the attention to the 3 factors on Shanghai's development environment (1) Chinese economy enters a new normal and by 2050, China will become the world's largest economy; (2) in the new development environment, adjustment of national economic positioning; (3) China assumes responsibility for global governance and safeguards the new relations between big powers and neighboring countries.

Wang Ying, Gao Feng Advisory Company Chairman Xie Zuchi, and Partner of Deloitte Consulting Zhang Xiaoping remind that the growing economic strength calls for a transparent and efficient interactive government, fair and open competitive environment and an ensuring institutional regime and there is much work for Shanghai to be done. On urban economic development,

Shanghai government plays the role of investor, participant and facilitator, and more importantly, it should learn and adapt to play the role of "unsung heroes", which is a major challenge.

Cheng Yougang compares Shanghai with Beijing and Shenzhen and other foreign cities and proposes that there are three bottlenecks in urban innovation: (1) Large investment in R & D is not translated into innovations and the proportion of high-tech industries is lower than advanced cities abroad; (2) state-owned enterprises and foreign companies are major contributors to innovation while private enterprises are not active with weak innovation atmosphere; (3) lack of open data access to innovation and other infrastructures and lack of effective integration platform for corporate, institutions and market resources.

In addition, Wang Ying and Zhang Yunling think that Shanghai is faced with similar geographical restrictions such as Greater London and Paris as the population and high-density construction in central city is close to the limit. Chen Yougang mentions about the gap between Shanghai and important international city in openness and ecological environment, and its' negative effects on attracting top talents and investment.

3. Strategic Thinking and Policy Proposals

The experts express their opinions on how to achieve the vision of Shanghai, offering a number of ideas and policy proposals notably the following:

Chen Yougang suggests that to realize the vision of releasing creative energy, Shanghai should not give up on the traditional strengths of being "the capital of Commerce and Industry", in terms of engineering and technical innovation, relying on the manufacturing base of aircraft and automobile industry to encourage innovation in process design; strengthen intellectual property protection to pool creativity; do not deliberately pursue basic and primordial innovation. On the customer-oriented innovation, relying on large-scale and dynamic consumer market, to enhance the interaction of supply and demand and innovation in market segmentation, integrating marketing network and business model innovation, tap potential of innovative products and services commercialization. In the regard of activating market innovation, Chen Yougang and Lai Yongge, Senior Director of Government Affairs Asia of TE Connectivity emphasize that the government must properly position itself to create a favorable environment for innovation and entrepreneurship as its primary task and establish new measurement index for innovation (index of patent number is not enough) and allow the market to play a major role.

To achieve the goal of education as a strategic driving force for development,Wang Yi suggests that Shanghai draw experience from Pittsburgh renaissance and transformation, increase investment to interdisciplinary research infrastructure in universities, promote open, inclusive and diverse courses in high school and college and globalization of education. In particular, he proposes setting up undergraduate degree in English teaching to attract overseas educational institutions and model. Wang Ying suggests drawing experience from New York municipality and Wall Street partnerships, using many of the world's top management resources in Shanghai to build a communication platform between government and enterprises and provide training and support for local entrepreneurs' "Shanghai Partnership Program". Based on European Chamber's investigation, Ioana Kraft proposes to speed up Internet and relax restrictions on Internet to strengthen the exchange of information, attract top researchers to ensure a hotbed for innovation.

In the vision of building a livable city, Zhang Yunling puts forward a space pattern of "small city—big urban area—huge space", breaking the space bottlenecks; specifically, to abandon the simple space expansion mode and build Yangtze River Delta and a world-class city cluster in accordance with the requirements of the city's division of labor. Qian Wei highlights the idea of "developing recycling economy and hold the ecological bottom line ".

Ye Hua proposes three stages and three paths to achieve the goal of Shanghai as a cultural and ideological center with global influence (1) move forward to be a global city by 2030, with the path leveraging Shanghai's "soft power" by existing "hard power"; (2) by 2040 establish Shanghai's status as a global city in the aspect of innovation, culture and international responsibility with the path leveraging Shanghai's "hard power" by "soft power"; (3) by 2050 play Shanghai's global city role in the spirit and ideological level, with the path being the fusion of "hard and soft power". On specific measures, Li Guangyu,

Senior Partner of McKinsey & Company reminds to pay attention to future leader "Generation Z" and Shanghai should be "cool" to be attractive to them, which is an important condition to be a cultural and ideological center.

ATTACHMENTS

附　件

未来纽约城市发展愿景与挑战

1. 未来纽约城市发展愿景展望

2015 年 4 月，纽约市公开发布"一个纽约"规划：建设一个富强公正的纽约，根据"成长、公平、可持续发展与韧性"的原则，为纽约市第 5 个世纪的发展制定了蓝图，以构建纽约在全球范围内的领导地位，维持并巩固其作为全球城市的领先地位。

1.1 繁荣兴旺的城市

纽约市将继续成为全球最具活力的城市经济体，在这里家庭、企业和社区都在不断发展。为了维持城市的持续繁荣，纽约也在住房、产业、劳动力、基础设施等方面采取一系列的措施。面对人口增长带来的住房需求，纽约将实施美国国内最宏大的计划，以建造更多的支付得起的住房。同时通过投资高增长行业的培训以及为就业困难的群体提供技术训练，来增加劳动力结构的包容性，以支持就业率的增长。面对新的经济趋势。纽约也大力支持创新经济的发展，建设新的高速无线网络，投资交通基础设施。最后作为区域枢纽，纽约将在交通、住房、就业等问题上与周边地区紧密合作。

1.2 公平公正的城市

纽约将建设一个包容性的、平等的经济体，为市民提供高薪的就业和机会，并保证他们生活的尊严和安全。围绕这一愿景，具体的措施包括增加最低工资、支持教育并促进就业的增长等，使 80 万纽约人在 2025 年脱离贫困。将早产儿死亡率降低 25%，提高纽约人健康服务的水平。扩大家庭公正中心以帮助家庭暴力的受害者。并促进城市范围内政府服务、信息和社区数据的整合，等等。

1.3 可持续发展的城市

纽约将成为世界上最大的可持续发展城市，并成为应对气候变化的领军力量。从前几版规划开始，纽约就聚焦于可持续发展并制定了行动计划，"一个纽约"中进一步承诺尽力减少环境足迹和有害的温室气体排放，致力于拥有最清洁的空气和水。为了实现在 2050 年温室气体减少 80% 的目标（世界上做此承诺的最大城市），纽约正将关注点从建筑物扩展到能源供给、交通和固体废弃物等其他方面。并承诺在 2030 年达到垃圾填埋量为零的目标，投资修复被污染的土地，保证纽约市民拥有很多的公园。

1.4 韧性城市

纽约的社区、经济和公共服务都已做好准备，以应对气候变化的影响和 21 世纪其他的挑战。作为具韧性城市，纽约将对不利的事件（比如飓风"桑迪"）做出反应，为所有居民提供基本的功能和服务——至 2050 年消除因重大不利事件带来的长期家庭和工作迁移。同时不断升级城市中的私人和公共建筑，使其更加高能效和应对气候变化影响的弹性能力；提高交通、电信、水和能源等设施应对严重气候事件的能力；加强海岸线防御以应对洪水和海平面上升。强化家庭、商业、社区为基础的组织建设和公共服务，以降低不利事件的影响，促进灾后的快速恢复。

2. 未来纽约城市发展将面临的挑战

步入发展的第五个世纪，纽约面临着与往常一样艰巨的挑战。在纽约经济整体繁荣的背后，居住成本持续升高，收入不平衡日益加剧。贫困人民和无家可归的人员数量仍然居高不下。城市核心基础设施——道路、地铁、下水道和桥梁——正在一一老化。保障性住房供不应求。清洁空气和水源离我们还很远，公园和公共空间数量始终无法满足市民的需求。气候变化也将成为未来的一大威胁。

2.1 人口持续增长

纽约市人口增长迅速，其中一大部分为移民。纽约市人口目前将近 840 万，创历史新高，预计在 2040 年将达到 900 万。未来人口增长主要集中在曼哈顿以外的地区，其中布鲁克林区和布朗克斯区增幅最大。人口增长将为市区基础设施造成沉重负担，为服务可靠性带来严峻考验。纽约市同时面临人口老化问题：截至 2040 年，全市 65 岁以上人口将超过在校青少年人口。这些变化将对城区带来诸多崭新挑战，从服务提供模式到城区设施设计，不一而足。我们必须优化改进社会制度与基础设施，为不断变化的人口提供公平的服务资源与就业机会。

自始至终，纽约都是一个人人趋之若鹜的热门城市，拥有丰富的经济机会和多样的种族网络。外裔居民占纽约人口总数近四成。同时还有许多受过高等教育的美国年轻人口不断迁入纽约市。

随着人口不断增长，纽约居民对公开公平的保障性住房需求随之而来。为了适应预期的住房需求、部分房屋的自然损耗，并且降低房价压力，纽约市规划在下个十年内新建 24 万个住宅单元，包括商品住房与保障性住房。

2.2 经济发展态势

纽约市的薪金岗位数量多达 420 万个，创历史新高，仅在 2014 年期间就新增了 11.3 万个私营机构（Private Sector）岗位。在经济活动方面，市内生产总值达 6470 亿美元，上次经济危机以来，纽约市的经济恢复水平超过美国全国平均水平 :2009 年至 2014 年期间，纽约市工作岗位增加了 11.5%，美国全国平均岗位增加了 6.1%。

可持续性经济发展和社会稳定的实现，依靠的是我们核心产业的持续壮大，以及各行政区与产业的经济多元化。各行政区的工作岗位增速最近也有所提升，超过曼哈顿区在过去十年内的表现。虽然就业情况因地区而异，但是就业岗位总体依然高度集中在曼哈顿区。

纽约市的传统核心产业——金融、保险、房地产，依然是本市的经济基础。虽然这些产业仅占总体就业岗位的 11.7%，但却贡献了 38.4% 的市内生产总值。这些产业还是纳税大户，为纽约的基础设施与公共服务提供资金支持，确保适应长期人口增长。

由于人口总数、游客与老年市民增加，零售、食品服务与家庭护理等产业的工作岗位持续增加。这些产业为缺少高薪岗位工作技能的人口提供了机遇，也为其获得更好的工作，向更高一级工作发展创造了可能。因为许多纽约市民就职于这类工作，所以这些岗位至关重要。虽然生活成本高昂，但缺乏专业技术的人员仍旧愿意留在纽约市工作，其中一个原因，正是此类工作可供他们从事，而且一般无需驾车便可抵达。拓展技能培训与劳动力开发项目、拓宽高等教育渠道等举措有利于帮助缺乏专业技能的人员习得晋级高薪岗位所需的劳动技能。

虽然登上《财富》全球 500 强榜单的企业中有 52 家在纽约市落户，但是雇员不足 100 人的小型企业依旧是纽约经济的主要组成部分。这些企业的雇员数量超过纽约私营机构工作岗位的半壁江山。纽约市的小型企业主在创立企业或拓展经营时经常受到法规局限，高昂的生活成本又使其难以吸引或留任年轻人才。

2.3 社会不公

在整体繁荣的背后，纽约仍将与高贫困率和持续增长的收入不均做斗争。中产阶级摇摇欲坠不再只是个地区问题，而是成为当前整个国家的危机问题，需要从国家层面解决。在过去十年内，纽约的收入差距进一步加大，超过美国平均水平——近年来，收入差距持续攀升。

在 2008 年经济衰退期间，除高薪产业外，其他行业员工的工资并未增长甚至出现下降。2009 年至 2014 年期间，纽约迎来复苏，新增 42.2 万个工作岗位。不同行业的工作岗位都有一定程度增加，低收入行业（如餐饮、住宿和零售行业）尤为明显。自 2014 年来，随着就业率下降，劳动力需求增大，越来越多的员工收入有所增加。尽管如此，员工收益却无法完全补偿经济衰退期间减少的收入。因此，低收入的人们继续在纽约这座生活成本高的城市中艰苦奋斗。由于缺少职业发展培训，低收入者和他们的家庭很可能仍然陷于贫困泥潭。认识到高、中、低技能工作都是多样化健全经济的部分，纽约市承诺支持所有经济部门范围内的工作岗位质量，提高低薪工作者的工资水将增加技能培训的机会。

这些就业和工资举措将在其他重大经济挑战的背景下展开。近一半的纽约市民仍然处在贫困线或以下水平，包括大量非洲裔美国人、拉丁美洲人和亚洲人。纽约本来就高的居住成本仍在攀升。住房供应与人口增长不相协调，导致保障性住房的极大短缺，特别是针对最底层人民。无家可归的人数达到历史新高。

随着这一情况的恶化，纽约必须开展战略投资，为弱势群体和低收入市民创造新的经济机会。我们必须增强对经济部门的支持力度，增加中等收入工作。城市就业率快速增长，对提高低收入工作者的工资水平具有实际意义。为此，我们必须竭尽全力，提高最低工资水平。我们还需要与员工和工会合作，强化员工培训，提高晋升机会并关注员工留任情况。

2.4 基础设施需求

虽然纽约是21世纪的全球城市，然而，城市中老化的基础设施却难以满足现代和活力城市中心的需求。基础设施连接着市民、社区和商务，并提供人们所需的基本服务——如饮用的水、煮饭用的煤气、家庭和商务照明的电力等以及通信和学习需要的网络连接。

大量证据证明现代基础设施和经济发展之间存在巨大关系，尽管如此，跨区域公共投资仍然无法满足资金投资需求。纽约的交通系统亟待改善和拓展，方可更好地服务纽约市民。纽约的地铁系统是美国最大的地铁系统，2013年的总载客量达17亿人次，现已接近或达到满载能力。每天，纽约市民搭乘着拥挤不堪的地铁和巴士上下班，平均通勤时间为47分钟，堪属美国最高。交通系统（包括拓展特选公车服务路线和纽约轮渡系统）直接投资以及与地区实体的合作将成为支持纽约持续发展和提高纽约竞争力的重要因素。拓展现有城市轨道交通系统需要大量的资金，然而，联邦投资却在减少。缺少维护投资，在不久后的将来，老化的基础设施将需要更多的维修费用，甚至影响纽约的长期繁荣发展。

城市中许多煤气、蒸汽、废水和水供应线路不单存在老化问题，它们甚至是采用现已淘汰的材料制成，存在重大的破裂和泄露风险。许多城市地下基础设施在地图上均未标注，使得人们难以发现问题，采取必要维修和改善。高速公路和桥梁也日益老化，风险重重。例如，布鲁克林大桥于1883年就已开放使用。

与电、气和水一样，网络已快速成为人们日常生活的中心。然而，当前22%的纽约住房缺少宽带。网络服务的负担能力已成为纽约市民使用宽带的主要障碍。提高网络支付能力以及公众宽带服务利用率，将有助于降低网络应用缺口，提高网络工具在个人、家庭和商务方面的使用。

主要挑战在于如何使用恰当的资金资源维护和更新正在老化的基础设施，并确保全市所有基础设施始终保持良好的维护状态。

2.5 城区环境状况与气候变化

近几年中，纽约通过优化空气质量、减少温室气体排放（2005年至今已成功减排19%），在环境保护方面取得长足进步。纽约减少了建筑能耗，改为采用碳排放更少的发电模式。纽约的空气质量达五十多年以来最优水平，在过去几年中，在美国城市中排名从第七跃升至第四。

已有100多块棕地得到清理重建，占地超过100万平方英尺。仅仅

2015 年完成整顿的 23 个区块，就创造了 420 多个新岗位，550 个住宅单位的保障性住房，新增税收 1.62 亿美元。一系列绿色基础设施行动计划得到落实，包括用于缓解雨水内涝、预防城区水道非法排污的生态沼池。

与此同时，长期存在的环境问题继续威胁着纽约市民的健康与生计——2012 年，每 1000 名 5—17 岁少年儿童中，就有 4 名因罹患哮喘而住院治疗。随着纽约市人口持续增长，攀升的基础设施需求将对环境造成额外压力。截至 2030 年，预计供暖燃料需求增长 14%，能耗增长 44%。纽约的住宅、商务、公共部门每天制造大约 2.5 万吨垃圾，其中仅有 15.4% 被环卫工人收集并投入循环利用。

气候变化方面：全球气候变化影响导致纽约市面临的风险日益加剧。虽然我们努力控制加剧气候变化的因素，并且取得了长足进步，但是预计局部气候影响仍然威胁着纽约市。纽约市政府同纽约市应对气候变迁小组（NPCC）通力合作，探究相关风险，确保采用最新科学技术探测气候状况，为纽约市政府提供气候政策依据。

2015 年早些时候，纽约市应对气候变迁小组发布了"建立气候韧性知识库"一文，更新了区域气候预测信息。根据这些信息，预计 2050 年代的平均温度增幅为 4.1—5.7 ℉，平均降雨增幅为 4—11%，海平面上涨幅度为 11—21 英寸。平均每年将有至少 10 天日气温超过 90 ℉。由于海平面上升，沿海地区洪灾将更加频繁、强度更大。横跨北大西洋流域的强力飓风数置也预计有所增加。

上述变化都将增加纽约市社区、企业与基础设施的风险。对纽约市民的健康威胁也将持续加剧。幸运的是，纽约市政府继续不遗余力地降低风险，正在减少温室气体排放，并且通过关键投资改造社区，开展岸线、建筑与基础设施建设。虽然还有很多工作要做，但是在与气候变化的较量中，纽约市致力于成为全球先驱，造福子孙后代。

2.6 纽约之声

只有当纽约市民参与城市建设并切实享有发言权，政府在专注倾听民意后做出更好决策时，纽约市才能真正在方方面面做到最好。我们需要创造新的交流与对话机制。只有这样，才能实现更加明智的决策，设计出更好的方案，让纽约市民充分获得工具与资源，推进城市未来建设。有责任心的纽约市民积极同政府交流沟通，能够对关键问题和政策制定提供有效帮助。

但在增加公民的民主参与方面，我们仍面临诸多挑战。超过三分之一的低收入纽约市民无法使用宽带网络，阻碍了他们同市政服务的沟通与交流。只有 18% 纽约市民参与志愿工作，低于全美国 25% 的标准，49% 市民表示对自身社区的文化服务不满。符合条件的纽约市民中，只有 66% 登记投票，2014 年选举中，实际投票率仅占 21%。

政府的方针政策与行动计划应该对广大利益相关人公开透明，包括因语言、时间滞后等障碍而无法表达言论的市民。了解到沟通对话对政策制定的意义后，"一个纽约"规划工作组持续努力收集广大民众的意见。

2.7 区域重要地位

纽约市的未来与大都市圈息息相关。城市经济带动地区繁荣，为区域交通、技能熟练工、文化资源与广泛基础设施带来好处。我们的郊区与市区面临许多相同问题，包括贫富收入差距，人口增长过快导致保障性住房供不应求，以及港口共用问题。1990—2010 年间，该地区通勤人数增长了 10.9%，人数变化最大的地区位于新泽西北部（14.3%）。与此同时，2000 年以来，纽约市的工作岗位数量增长占区域增长的八成。

本区居民每年乘坐巴士、地铁、通勤火车与轮渡通勤超过 40 亿次，每人平均 184 次。没有其他哪个美国大城市的通勤规模能与纽约媲美。区域出行线路不仅限于前往曼哈顿。2000—2010 年间，出城通勤人数增加了 12.5%，而流入城市区域交通枢纽的通勤人数增加了 9.5%。如果能使工作人员方便到达区域内的各工作地点，那么城市的宜居性和商务竞争力必将到提升。

然而，我们的发展脚步仍跟不上地区出行的需要，必须同其他地区合作伙伴密切合作，共同推进横跨新泽西哈德、长岛、康涅狄格州乃至更广区域的关键运输连接网建设。大批行政管辖区各自为政，影响更广范围的区域规划，包括交通、能源、电信及众多其他关键领域。封闭式的基础设施与服务建设难以取得理想效果。纽约市必须带头与各个区域政府共同协作。只有这样，才能确保区域协调合作，实现明智投资。

支持这一点的有力例证：纽约市政府与众多地区公共部门将在未来十年中对该区投入 2660 亿美元进行建设，例如大都会运输署（MTA）、纽约及新泽西州港务局（PANYNJ）以及众多私营公共事业公司。纽约市的第一个 10 年资金预算大约占此预期开支的 25%。这一开支将直接影响纽约市的繁荣，以及能否实现公平、可持续发展和韧性等目标。放眼下个 10 年乃至更长远阶段，纽约市致力于发挥领头作用，引导投资方向，并将投资与自身策略步骤相结合，充分利用地区开支，最大化城市效益。

大伦敦未来发展愿景与挑战

1. 未来伦敦城市发展愿景的制定依据

从一个跨河港口演变为一个繁华的国家政府及国际商贸的中心，伦敦是英国的首都，也是一个在成长中包含了城市与乡村的都市。它吸引了来自世界各地、各行各业的人口，引领了工业与科学的创新，其遗产也得到全世界的认可。贫富、新旧、城乡都在这里融汇。它是一个充满活力不断变化大都市，2036 年伦敦发展愿景也将极力延续这个城市及其人口的活力。

2. 2036 年伦敦城市发展愿景

伦敦未来可持续发展的总体愿景是成为一个顶级全球城市——为全部公民和企业增加机会，达到最高环境标准和生活质量，并引领世界应对 21 世纪城市挑战，特别是气候变化方面的挑战，成为世界城市的领军者。这一愿景可以保证伦敦最大限度的受益于代表伦敦和伦敦人民的能量、活力及多元化的特征，保证伦敦接受转变的同时推广其遗产、街区和特征，保证伦敦重视其责任及公民权利，富有同情心。

这一高水平、贯穿整体的愿景由六个细节目标进行支持。

2.1 有效应对经济和人口增长需求的社会城市

确保所有伦敦人拥有可持续的、良好和不断进步的生活质量，充足的高质量房屋及街区；帮助解决伦敦人关于贫穷和不平等的问题。

2.2 国际竞争力强、成功的城市

拥有一个强大和多元的经济，充分利用历史文化资源，发展经济发展，建设竞争力强、经济结构多样、创新和研发能力超前，让经济发展的收益惠及全伦敦人和全伦敦地区的城市。

2.3 拥有多样性、凝聚力、安全和便利居住社区的城市

增强社区归属感，为所有的伦敦人，不管种族、年龄、身份、本地居民还是访客，提供表达渠道、实现潜能机遇，为他们生活工作提供优质的生活环境。

2.4 让人愉悦的城市

珍视自己所有的建筑和街道，拥有最棒的现代建筑同时充分利用自己的历史建筑，同时将它们的价值延伸到开放的绿色空间，自然环境和水道中去，为伦敦人的健康、福利和发展实现它们的潜能。

2.5 低碳节能的世界级环保城市

致力于全球和当地环境的改善，领军世界城市气候变迁应对，减少污染，发展低碳经济，节约能源，提高能源利用率。

2.6 便利、安全和舒适的城市，每个市民都能享受就业、发展机遇和服务设施

通过方便和有效的交通系统，鼓励更多的步行和自行车交通，更好地利用泰晤士河同时支持所有规划目标的实现。

3. 2036 年伦敦城市发展将面临的挑战

3.1 人口问题

一是人口数量不断增长。伦敦人口在 2011 年达到 820 万，到 2036 年预计将达到 1011 万。即未来 25 年，伦敦将新增 191 万人口。二是人口结构发生改变。相比于 2011 年，2036 年伦敦学龄人口将增加 17%，35—64 岁的人口将增加 28%。同时，2036 年，64 岁以上的人口预计将增加 64%（近 58 万），达到 149 万。随着医学进步、生活方式改善及有助于延长寿命的新技术的出现，90 岁以上人口将增加 8.9 万人。三是人口构成多样化。非洲裔、亚裔以及其他少数族裔群体将大幅增长，这是自然增长及持续海外移民造成的。此外，大约 10% 的伦敦人存在残疾或感觉机能损伤，伦敦将会有更多的人需要行动、通道及其他方面的支持。这些都对伦敦的住房、学校、便民措施和其他基础设施提出了更高的要求，也产生了更多的老龄化人口挑战。

3.2 经济增长问题

经济与就业之间存在很强的相关性。只有保持经济增长，才能为伦敦持续增长的人口提供就业机会。到 2036 年，伦敦工作数量很可能出现强劲增长，也会面临持续的变化与挑战。必须保证当前到 2036 年期间，逐渐增加的伦敦劳动力人口（16—64 岁）能有一系列的就业机会——如果工作岗位增速低于人口增速，问题将更加严峻。作为一个经济上依靠私营企业的城市，伦敦也需要保证其社会机构和基础设施建设得到必要的公共投资，不然财政收入也将面临挑战。

3.3 持续的贫困问题

过去 20 年，伦敦总体经济表现良好，但贫困率并未下降。伦敦的儿童、成年劳动人口、退休人员的收入贫困率高于英国其他地区。在计算住房费用后，25% 的成年劳动人口和 14% 的儿童都处于贫困状态。贫困问题主要集中在有非独立子女的家庭，以及伦敦的非洲裔、亚裔少数民族和残障人士中。贫困还衍生出很多其他的问题，如劳动市场中薪资支付的问题，贫困更容易带来失业问题，导致伦敦的失业率高于英国其他地区；如住房问题，收入低的人群很难得到满足需要的住房，以致对廉租房的需求上升，廉租房和贫困之间紧密相连，使得贫困人群更难从廉租房搬到其他条件的住房居住；如贫困人口分布区域日益集中问题、健康问题、药物滥用和犯罪等。因此，伦敦的两极化越来越严重，引发了一系列社会问题，对社会治理和城市规划形成了诸多挑战。

3.4 气候变化问题

未来气候变化不可避免。根据预测，到 21 世纪 50 年代，伦敦夏季平均气温将上升 2.7 度，冬季平均降水增加 15%，而夏季平均降水将减少 18%。夏季热浪很可能成为常态，需要随时应对"城市热岛"效应。高温对伦敦的生活质量将产生重大影响。同时，伦敦也存在洪水侵袭的威胁。如果有些地区没有匹配的排洪排涝设施就会受到洪水威胁，制约着伦敦的发展规划，特别是在伦敦住房达到 2036 年预期增长的情况下。气候变化也将引发严重的用水短缺。如何保证有符合条件的合适的用水基础设施以确保家庭和企业获得灵活高效且经济的用水供给也要纳入考虑。低碳经济、能源问题，特别是电力方面有弹性的安全供给和基础设施的提供，将会越来越重要。

2030 年 "巴黎大区" 发展愿景与挑战

1. 2030 年 "巴黎大区"

法国行政区划的基本等级依次是：大区、省、市镇。巴黎大区，即巴黎大都市区，是法国本土 22 个大区之一——法兰西岛 (île-de-France)，包含了巴黎省、近郊三省和远郊四省，地处巴黎盆地的中央，位于欧洲南北交界之处，通过塞纳河与英吉利海峡及大西洋相联结在一起。巴黎大区之所以富有潜力，既由于有巴黎这个政治、经济、文化之都的繁华，也依赖于塞纳河谷，依赖于成片的绿地、可供农业生产的平原和高原、森林资源，还有曾经的皇家园林或村镇所构成的文化遗产。

2. 2030 年 "巴黎大区" 发展愿景

在全世界众多蓬勃发展的都市圈中，在大都市林立的欧洲，"巴黎大区"都享有盛名，因为它懂得如何在保留自己历史和地理环境的前提下继续扩展，懂得如何适应其地区活动与居民日益增长的多样性，并在此基础上不断追求革新，使自己长久地扮演着欧洲重要枢纽的角色。

"巴黎大区"的总体发展愿景是建设成为一个创新型、可持续发展的国际大都市，成为一个带有法国色彩的"智慧型城市"，同时也希望能将巴黎建设成整个法国经济辐射的驱动城市。"巴黎大区 2030 规划"着眼于可持续发展的理念，目标在于提升巴黎的吸引力，同时提升大区的辐射力度，将整个巴黎区域纳入新的发展模型中去。

2.1 生活多元化的大区

2030 年，巴黎大区居民生活中的不同活动场所将会更加便利。改善交通条件、提高出行效率是巴黎大区居民提高生活品质的一项根本愿望。巴黎大区并非一个同质化、高密度的城市区域，它包含了丰富多样的景观、环境和城市要件，适应着不同的生活方式。

2.2 团结互助的大区

社会与地区公平要求重现地方吸引力，这也是提升都市国际影响力的重要基础之一。为巴黎大区居民创造更好的城市条件（住房、就业、设施和服务），在各个地区提供平等的享受医疗和社会服务的机会，以及对许多地区社会、经济和环境不平等现象进行特别关注和优先治理。注重社会融合、地区互补与区域平衡。

2.3 具有吸引力和创新性的大区

巴黎大区因其面向世界而充满活力，到2030年大区将变得更有吸引力，而且每个地区都为此努力并分享其成果。巩固巴黎大区的经济地位和国际吸引力一方面要依靠其经济的多样性、稳固性和丰富性，另一方面要从整个大区层次来考虑经济发展，使未来生活的节奏更加惬意，居民间的沟通更加紧密，经济活动分布更加平衡。

2.4 具有可持续性和稳固性的大区

城市与自然间的互补相容是必要的，不同地区的优势和财富应该共享。既要让某些地区经济的快速发展惠及整个大区，也不能忽视广大农业地区、森林资源、大区自然公园和众多村庄未来的发展及吸引力的提升。将自然看作是发展的"合作伙伴"，把与自然有关的人类活动融入到自然本身的多样性中去，让都市地区更能承受压力，更持续也更能适应气候的变化，处理好城市与自然的关系。

3. 2030年巴黎大区发展将面临的挑战

"巴黎大区"的构建涉及巴黎人民生活的方方面面：交通、住房、就业、环境等，同时也涉及巴黎大区和法国的未来：科研、创新、吸引力和经济。法国政府希望将"巴黎大区"建设的成果分享给所有涉及的地区。但要实现这一目标困难重重，主要面临三个方面的挑战：

3.1 促进大区内部团结

在促进大区内部团结，尽量减少风险上，巴黎大区面临着维持人口活力、增强对增长人口的培养教育、修复地区和社会裂痕、缓解地区不平等现象、增加保障住房和公共设施供应、建立高效公平的医疗卫生健康服务体系、提高住房、工作、经济和娱乐活动等与生活质量密不可分的设备与服务等挑战。这些问题保持地区多样性、适应改造创新能力和是居民获得更好的生活的关键。

3.2 应对环境变化

和其他国际都市一样，巴黎大区必须应对能源、气候变化、生物多样性减少和食品等问题挑战。人口密集增加了遭受污染和各种危害的危险。只有建立一个更有弹性的大区，才有能力吸收并从严重的环境、经济和社会灾害或困难中重新振作。减少温室气体排放、加快能源转型、保护自然资源和生态系统、降低大区的受灾可能性以及加强对气候灾害的影响评估等问题，成为巴黎大区提供有质量的城市生活，保持对居民和企业的吸引力的一大挑战。

3.3 增强大区吸引力，帮助大区经济向生态化和社会化转变

由于是法国的经济中心，巴黎还面临着如何在保证社会和谐和环境良好的同时，保持其国际经济地位和吸引力的挑战。要保持可持续发展势头，必须重新考虑增长方式，加强巴黎大区对法国、欧洲乃至世界经济的推动作用。如何强化巴黎大区传统优点、刺激大量岗位的产生、通过经济类型和创新多样化克服经济危机、推动经济向可持续方向发展、重新平衡地区经济活力以及运用新兴电子技术作为大区开发新手段，是摆在巴黎大区面前的问题。

2030 年东京城市发展愿景与挑战

1. 东京 2030 年城市发展愿景展望

从几百年前的小渔村江户到如今的超级大都市，东京的城市发展常被作为城市化发展的正面教材。2013 年 9 月，东京获得 2020 年夏季奥运会主办权，为应对奥运会和城市可持续发展，2014 年 12 月，东京都政府颁布了新的城市规划蓝图《创造未来：东京都长期展望》，这份蓝图提出了建设"世界第一城市"的宏伟目标。

东京将 2030 年城市发展愿景定位为"世界一流大都市"，即"能为居民提供最大幸福"的城市，目标在社会福利、经济活力、城市基础设施、艺术文化振兴等各方面超过伦敦、纽约、巴黎等城市。规划列出了为实现愿景所需达到的基本目标及相关战略，进一步提出为实现各目标而计划采取的各项政策，同时制定了一个为期三年的实施计划。所有政策共通的五大视角包括：活跃经济、提高生活品质；软硬件相融合；政府与社会合作，放宽限制；积极、充分地运用尖端技术；提高女性活跃程度，提升高龄者的社会参与度。

《东京都长期展望》提出的两个基本目标是：

1.1 举办有史以来最好的奥运会及特奥会

以奥运会和特奥会的举办为契机，推动城市发展，提升东京的面貌以及奥运遗产的继承。具体包括三个城市战略：一是充分发挥东京作为成熟城市的强大实力，成功举办两大奥运盛会；二是建造以人为本、城市基础设施高度发达的大都市；三是展现日本人民的好客之心和东京的城市魅力。

1.2 解决重大课题，实现东京可持续发展

解决低生育率、高龄化、人口减少等问题。具体包括五个城市战略：

一是构建安全、安心的城市；二是构建社会福利优厚的城市；三是构建领先世界的全球化大都市；四是加强城市建设，将优美环境和完备基础设施留给下一代；五是振兴多摩和离岛地区。

2. 未来东京城市发展主要挑战

在未来的20—24年发展建设期间，东京都面对的主要挑战包括：

2.1 安全方面存在的隐患

以老年人为目标的特殊诈骗，对女性的跟踪犯罪是市民希望得到解决的问题。老龄消费者受害现象连年上升；危险药物事故多发；网上银行的诈骗汇款，越权访问犯罪等网络犯罪；暴力团伙和军火毒品走私等犯罪行为。

2.2 社会福利管理

随着父母共同工作家庭增多，育儿需求增大。截至2014年4月，8672名儿童独自留在家中，因而在育儿服务、设施、人才、儿童保护等方面，东京政府面临诸多挑战。

老年人口预计将在2025年增加到327万人，其中失智老人将从2013年的38万增加到2025年的60万人。老龄化人口的增加，使得老年人医疗、护理、预防、生活援助、住房综合社会护理系统亟待完善。痴呆症的早期发现、诊断、应对等方面也需要政府着力解决。护理人才的有效招聘率、离职率比其他行业高，呈现出慢性人才不足。东京人口众多，可利用土地资源有限，政府在建设育儿和老年人相关设施和住宅时，也面临如何通过政策红利、改建方案确保有效用地。

残障人士的生活范围单一，需要集体康复之家、白天活动场所等生活设施使这些人向社区生活过渡。东京都的残障人士2014年实际民企就业率低于全国平均水平，残障人士的自理、就业也是发展难关。

2.3 全球化挑战

经济方面：因日本进入人口下降时代，劳动力人口下降，国内需求萎缩，经济活动有可能陷入中长期不景气，为了确保可持续发展，东京需在国际竞争中胜出，牵引日本经济发展。对于如何活跃经济，东京都还面临多方面的挑战，面临引入外资，吸引人才，国际企业交流以及创新的要求。

城区建设：东京交通拥堵，为了辅助经济发展，要合理规划解决拥堵问题。

就业问题：东京非正规就业青年人仍然很多，非正规就业者比例为35.7%（216万人），呈现增加趋势。正规就业者工资随年龄增加，但非正规就业者则维持不变，缺乏接受教育训练机会，在待遇方面存在差距。即便就业，但三年内离职的青年人，在高中毕业生中约占4成，大学毕业生中约占3成。很多老年人或出于经济原因，或出于健康、贡献社会等多种理由，也希望就业。现行社会环境，劳动者很难兼顾工作和家庭，出现劳动时间长、育儿负担男女不均及护理需要增加等现象。近年来女性就业率有增加趋势，但在结婚、生育期，女性就业率下降，育儿稳定期后，再次上升，呈现 M 形曲线。少子老龄化现象导致劳动人口减少，也就要求社会更多调动女性就业积极性，消除 M 形曲线。

人才培养：以 2020 年奥运为目标，需要更多国际化人才。目前东京少年儿童的学历呈上升趋势，但与学历较高的县相比，东京学历较低的学生比重较大。小学生体力逐年提高，但两极分化严重，初高中生的体力居全国较低水平。公立学校各种活动提高了学生的工作意识和工作意愿，但也有学生对自己的生活方式和未来没有目标。

2.4 可持续发展城市建设

能源改革：东京已切实降低了能源消耗，2012 年能源消耗相比 2010 年降低约 16%，但家庭和经营机构应实现进一步节能，市民对下一代清洁能源——氢能源的期待不断高涨。为了普及一般民众，需要解决如何削减费用，放宽管制等问题。

绿色东京：东京都至今采取了很多环保绿化措施，但绿化率 2003—2013 年间基本不变。随着城市开发，树林和农地等的绿地出现减少趋势。城市化使生物的栖息受到干扰，繁育空间不断减少，外来物种入侵也对生态系统造成威胁。海水浴需求增加，下水系统需要升级，大气状况也需要改善，PM2.5 或光化学氧化剂的环境标准达标率依然很低。

城市安全：对应基础设施需要大量更新，包括下水道管线的维护和延长，1 号羽田线在内的首都高速公路至今已使用超过 50 年，出现大量破损，亟需维护和新技术的革新改造。针对低出生率、老龄化、人口减少的现象，提出有必要重组并建设紧凑型街区的城市规划建议。东京市内的建筑数量已超过了家庭数。必须考虑人口减少社会的到来以及单身家庭比例的增加，重新完善居住环境。设施老化，人口老龄化，遏制地区活力，方便性、安全性下降。

地区发展：多摩、离岛地区是东京市民生活场所，自然资源丰富。低出生率、老龄化社会的到来，防灾防震能力需要加强。另外，丰富的自然资源在开发利用的过程中，也要注重可持续性发展。

未来 50 年新加坡发展愿景与挑战

1. 未来 50 年新加坡发展愿景展望

2015 年 8 月 9 日，是新加坡独立 50 周年的纪念。

作为一个几乎没有任何自然资源的国家，新加坡在过去 50 年间实现了发展奇迹，成为亚洲人均国内生产总值最高的国家。未来 50 年，面对全球化和网络化挑战，新加坡将发展成为一个政治更公开，经济更活跃，人民更包容，环境更宜居的可持续发展移民城市，进一步将自己打造成为一个辐射亚太地区和全球的金融、经济中心。

1.1 保持新加坡全球竞争优势

一方面是保持新加坡长期稳定的政治优势，另一方面是保持新加坡作为全球物流中心、金融中心的经济优势。新加坡国土面积狭小、资源匮乏导致其在维持社会稳定和保证平等政治代表权方面的需求更为显著，通过任人唯贤制度，新加坡已成为一个成功的国家，未来要保持上下团结才能避免"内部动乱"，为经济社会发展创造良好条件。作为全球最成熟的区域中心之一，新加坡将在未来区域和世界发展中继续发挥核心作用。面对全球和亚洲不断变化的复杂的货币和金融环境以及其将对新加坡经济带来的影响，新加坡将与其他金融中心和区域经济中心建立更强大、更灵活的联系，保持经济健康运行并应对全球经济势力转移、资本流动和新型金融中心的崛起。

1.2 重新塑造国民特质

新加坡是一个年轻的国家，它几乎没有自然资源，最大的资产就是它的人民。新加坡人的特质和发展将对新加坡未来的成功扮演举足轻重的角色。新加坡公民和社会需要一种更宽容、更包容、更尊重的气质，更友好的对待所有和我们一起共享工作空间、生活空间、娱乐空间的人，无论年龄、性别和种族。采取更多措施来创造归属感，特别是在社会边缘群体当中，保持并助推文化多元性和社会多样性。通过教育年轻一代承担起个人和社会责任等措施，将"权力文化"转变为"机遇文化"。鼓励蕴含创造性和适应性的企业家精神，只有这些特质才能让新加坡在这个全球化的时代继续演变，并保持韧性。

1.3 打造可持续性和宜居性的新加坡

新加坡注重可持续发展且一直走在时代的前面。除了被评为世界上最环保的城市之一，在多个领域树立了可持续性的生活典范，包括使用环保建筑，建设生态环境，节能减排，推广利用公共交通，废品回收，改善空气质量和促进公共环境整洁等。新加坡曾是殖民地，如今已成为世界上最宜居的城市。未来 50 年，新加坡将继续打造花园城市，找到满足社会诉求、保护生存空间和维持生态环境的同时发展经济和保持优势之间的平衡。作为地区贸易和金融枢纽，民众教育程度高，见识广，新加坡有能力且应该为当地及整个区域的可持续发展做出重大贡献。

2. 未来 50 年新加坡发展将面临的挑战

新加坡在过去 50 年实现了高速发展，但未来 50 年新加坡的发展将面临主要来自三个领域的风险：

2.1 世界范围，特别是亚洲地区的地缘政治与安全风险

全球已进入前所未有的多地区、多文化的多极性时代。北美洲、欧洲和亚太地区都是具有全球或超级大国影响的世界地区。尽管当今世界经济不稳、金融紧缩、军队撤军、人口转型、社会混乱，美国、欧盟和中国都愿意并有能力在未来的几十年里维持自己世界大国的地位，而印度和巴西也将成为世界大国。

此外，全球范围内，强劲的区域一体化趋势正在加速，这意味着展望未来看得越远，区域一体化组织就越有可能成为世界秩序的主要支柱。由此，世界也会由地缘政治等级制进一步发展，尽管不会发展成为中美两国简单的两极世界，也会发展成为名副其实的分散化、成网状的多极世界。

亚洲是全世界人口最多的地区，在该地区内部也会出现多极化的动态。在东北亚，强烈的地缘政治变化和经济变化使得该地区极具影响力。展望未来几十年，东盟会迎来发展繁荣期。东盟已成为世界第四大经济

区，东盟各国总人口大约为印度的一半，但其总合 GDP 却超过了印度。重要的是，东盟各国人口构成年轻，劳动力成本更低，于 2013—2014 年超过中国，成为获得对外直接投资更多的地区。假设东盟经济共同体、亚太自由贸易区和区域全面经济伙伴关系三大组织先后按此时间线发展，到 2030 年或者更早，东盟将成为下一个世界工厂，东盟各国供应链分布强劲，向世界各地进行出口。然而，东盟内部分歧明显，成员国之间发展水平存在巨大差距，新加坡是最发达的成员国，而缅甸和柬埔寨则是最不发达的成员国。这些不断深化的经济关系必须得到利用，以推动繁荣，缩小该地区收入的严重不平等。除了使用不断增加的对外直接投资，还必须关注基础设施的发展和诸如医疗保健和教育方面的社会政策。

新加坡可以成为地区制度发展的重要参与者。尽管不是亚洲的布鲁塞尔或美国的华盛顿，新加坡实际上扮演着泛亚中心的角色。它同时得到中国、美国、印度、澳大利亚和日本的信任，并且被认为精通外交，在外交领域具备实力。新加坡的多元化使其成为亚洲的缩影，但这同时也警示着如此多元文化的 24 个亚洲国家一体化是十分困难，甚至要比战后欧洲的一体化还要难。

但是，新加坡在这一地区扮演的较为突出的角色并不意味着新加坡在东盟扮演的角色不重要。东盟经济一体化的同时，也必须推动各国团结，以谋求有意义的外交话语权。这不仅仅适用于在有争议的海域突出的海洋争议，同时也适用于新出现的挑战，比如湄公河筑坝、民族矛盾、从缅甸边境涌出的难民和其他危机等。从危机管理转变为构建稳定需付出持之以恒的努力，东盟必须考虑采取措施以便更有效地维持地区治安，比如成立共同的维和部队。这一提议已得到包括印度尼西亚和马来西亚在内的一些东盟成员国的支持。

2.2 全球经济势力转移、新兴金融中心与资本流动的风险

亚洲一体化的深化，不仅有助于确保地区的政治性和维护社会稳定，这在本区域抵御未来宏观经济的波动上更有着举足轻重的作用。尽管有旨在防止 2007—2008 年金融危机重演的新的宏观审慎措施，如今的量化宽松政策、利率差异化、货币贬值的趋势以及全球和区域层面上的新监管要求，都预示着当今世界经济并不安全。

因此亚洲国家当务之急是要加深努力——从 2000 年清迈倡议开始，不仅要扩大彼此在货币危机中的流动性，更重要的是通过长期成熟的本币

债券市场和区域性规模的金融机构使区域资本市场的长期优势得到深化，从而引导资金平稳流入该地区的中小企业和其他公司。这是在未来十年及以后使亚洲避免重蹈西方国家的结构性弱点的关键步骤。

作为亚洲最成熟的金融中心，新加坡必须在这一次关键的经济转型中发挥核心作用。新加坡需要在全球范围内有更持久的流动性，并更多地分配给亚洲内部前沿市场——无论是在巴布亚新几内亚和苏门答腊抑或是柬埔寨和缅甸。东南亚中央银行应该巩固区域债券市场，以保证长期投资的视野。最重要的是，应当将更多的公共和私人资金——无论是通过促进新加坡自身缺乏的出口机构还是银行——分配给贸易融资，让更多的亚洲企业进入全球市场，这也正是中国过去几十年来一直做的。

事实上，亚洲各国必须继续抓住的另一全球性的经济结构发展趋势应当是在现如今并可能是未来全球化的主要推动力中跨区域市场的贸易占比。譬如值得一提的目前正在谈判的 TPP 贸易协定仅仅代表着亚洲与中南美洲的不断增长的贸易的一部分。而所谓的太平洋联盟——包括墨西哥、哥伦比亚、智利等一些拉美国家——已经拥有比巴西更大的 GDP 总和以及更快的增长。东盟应继续开放区域定位，重点是建立尽可能多的互利互惠的贸易关系。

从地缘政治原因来看，新加坡是一个价格接受者，而不是价格制定者，在地缘经济学中也是如此。因此要使我国经济健康运行并最大程度利用浮动资本的流动，从美元主导的全球金融体系缓慢过渡走向一个多币种的环境是不可或缺的。在亚洲供应链面临的不断增强的竞争面前，即使是美元的当前走强和新加坡元的相应疲软也很可能不会大幅提升新加坡制造业的出口。因此无论是在新加坡还是作为区域和全球企业的枢纽，我们的竞争战略都必须以非货币因素为基础，如技术生产力和服务部门的加强。

进一步运用多种货币进行贸易结算可能对新加坡的金融战略来说至关重要。这将给新加坡金融管理局（MAS）以人民币而不是美元或其他货币持有甚至更多的资本储备带来压力。虽然新加坡已经是人民币交易和离岸人民币债券的枢纽，却仍需要在中国的资本账户自由化要求下，做好与中国同步进行大规模资本出入的准备。

全球和亚洲不断变化的复杂的货币和金融环境以及其将对国内经济带来的影响，迫切需要新加坡与其他金融中心和区域经济中心建立更强大、更灵活的联系。亚洲监管机构则需要对彼此金融市场的稳定和暴露于跨境企业债务的公司的健康运行有更好的掌控。对于新加坡来说，要想成为亚洲真正的首府，不仅要承担外交责任还得要是一个经济都市。

2.3 社会契约的演变

在具有里程碑意义的独立建国 50 周年之际，新加坡不仅要紧随区域性及全球性的政治和经济发展潮流，还要考虑其国内面临的挑战和社会稳定程度。

政府与人民之间的社会契约，是每个社会中最核心的关系之一。社会契约是政府和人民之间订立的默认契约，规定了所有社会成员的权利和义务。

然而，到了 21 世纪，全球很多国家的社会性质迅速转变，尤其是东南亚地区的国家。马来西亚、泰国、印度尼西亚甚至包括新加坡在内的一些国家中，勇于表达个人意见的中产阶层人数不断增加，地位不断上升；人们的教育程度和生活水平不断提高；社交数字媒体广为使用。这些都是造成转变的因素。

现在，新加坡政府有责任满足有想法的、见识广、愈加网络化的民众的期盼，且要与公众紧密联系，否则在不远的未来，新加坡的社会契约将会遭受不可挽回的损害。

许多民众仍认为新加坡需要强大，有能力的领导者。在目前的政治气候下，强大的领导也需要赋予公民更多权力。新加坡的领导人必须要倾听多方的观点和意见，努力制订长远问题的可持续性解决方案，而不是短期内快速修补。

政府调整的同时，新加坡人也需要改变。不仅仅需要政府满足国人的需求，国人也要有归属感和正确的公民意识，公民及其他类型居民要主动向政府提供建设性的意见，让政府认真考虑。

除了听取新加坡人民的意见，非新加坡公民的意见也同样重要，包括在新加坡学习、工作的永久居民或短期居民。在未来的日子里，新加坡需要确定对外来员工和移民的开放程度，这一争论至今仍在继续。但在一定程度上，新加坡必须依靠外来人才，非新加坡公民永远是新加坡社会组成的一部分，要特别注意不要疏远或歧视他们，否则可能对新加坡的经济增长和社会稳定产生剧烈影响。

2.4 国民特质缺失的风险

当新加坡在展望未来 50 年时，不仅要考虑未来政府的形式，同时需要考虑其国民的特质，这是一个很重要的因素。新加坡未来命运的公共话语权也需要新加坡人内部的直接参与。

新加坡是一个年轻的国家，它几乎没有自然资源，最大的资产就是它的人民。新加坡人的特质和发展将对新加坡未来的成功扮演举足轻重的角色。现在的新加坡人都变得非常物质主义，极度重视通过职业发展和财富积累来改善生活。这种发展重心导致其他一些方面被忽视，比如社会的包容性，对他人的关心爱护，以及对财富和资产增值的更为理性的追求等。新加坡无意间孕育出了一种反常的关于成就和感知成功的思维模式。以购物中心高度密集为特征的强大消费文化正刺激着人们争取更好的教育和职业技能水平，但是同时将成功的定义限定在更好的工作和薪水之中。

新加坡公民社会需要一种更宽容、更包容、更尊重的气质。新加坡的非政府组织欣欣向荣，服务领域广泛，但是现在很多组织默认采取"呼吁高层当局"的方法，通过呼吁国家而不是自我推动的方式来实现社会改革。

必须通过教育年轻一代承担起个人和社会责任等措施将"权力文化"转变为"机遇文化"。鼓励蕴含创造性和适应性的企业家精神，只有这些特质才能让新加坡在这个全球化的时代继续演变，并保持韧性。

虽然保留对国家的强大归属感很重要，但这并不意味着新加坡的国家认同应该是排他的。新加坡人对自身的文化多元性和社会多样性感到自豪，这种归属感不仅应该存在于公民和常住居民之中，也应该存在于社会的其他群体之中。

2.5 相互关联的生态、环境和气候变化问题

新加坡社会主要关注的是政治、经济和社会方面的挑战，但在独立建国 50 周年之际，新加坡还面临很多其他挑战。

例如，雾霾是最明显的环境问题。此外，尽管新加坡的水资源、粮食和能源供应是稳定的，但远远没有达到自给自足的程度。由于区域和全球环境发展前景不明，无法保证这种稳定会一直持续下去。另一个问题就是，岛国的未来面貌将是什么样子。新加坡一直称自己是花园城市，但面对人们不断增长的需求，要求提供更多更好的住房和交通基础设施，新加坡的绿地面积难以得到保证。

未来 50 年，新加坡面临的生态、环境和气候变化挑战主要源于六个方面：一是粮食供应；二是水资源供应；三是气候变化的影响；四是能源供应；五是可持续增长；六是包容性增长。这六个挑战互相关联，必须统筹应对。

New York City's Future Development: Vision and Challenges

1. The Vision of Future New York

"One New York: The Plan for a Strong and Just City" was released on April, 2015. It organized vision for New York City's fifth century around principles of growth, equity, sustainability, and resiliency. This plan is aim to build New York City's global leadership as well as preserve and enhance its role as a leading global city.

1.1 Our Growing, Thriving City

New York City will continue to be the world's most dynamic urban economy where families, businesses, and neighborhoods thrive. To meet the needs of a growing population at a time of rising housing costs, the City will implement the nation's most ambitious program for the creation and preservation of affordable housing. The City will support a first-class, 21st century commercial sector. It will foster job growth, and build an inclusive workforce by focusing investment in training in high-growth industries, as well as programs that provide skills to the hardest-to-employ. The city will support the burgeoning innovation economy, create new high-speed wireless networks, and invest in transportation infrastructure. As a regional hub, the city will work closely with our neighbors on issues including transportation, housing, and jobs.

1.2 Our Just and Equitable City

New York City will have an inclusive, equitable economy that offers well-paying jobs and opportunity for all to live with dignity and security. With the measures in OneNYC, the City will lift 800 000 New Yorkers out of poverty or near poverty by 2025. The city will do this by fighting to raise the minimum wage, and launching high-impact initiatives to support education and job growth. The city will seek to reduce premature mortality by 25 percent by ensuring that all New Yorkers have access to physical and mental healthcare services and addressing hazards in our homes. The city will expand Family Justice Centers to help victims of domestic violence. The city will promote the citywide integration of government services, information, and community data.

1.3 Our Sustainable City

New York City will be the most sustainable big city in the world and a global leader in the fight against climate change. The city will strive to minimize our environmental footprint, reduce dangerous greenhouse gas emissions, and have the cleanest air and water. The City is building on its goal to reduce greenhouse gases by 80 percent by 2050—the largest city in the world to make that commitment—by expanding from an initial focus on buildings to including energy supply, transportation, and solid waste as part of a comprehensive action plan to reach our goal. The city is committing to a goal of Zero Waste to landfills by 2030. The city will keep organics out of the landfill, which will also cut greenhouse gas emissions. The City will make major investments to remediate contaminated land, and ensure that underserved New Yorkers have more access to parks.

1.4 Our Resilient City

Our neighborhoods, economy, and public services are ready to withstand and emerge stronger from the impacts of climate change and other 21st century threats. As a resilient city, New York will be able to respond to adverse events like Hurricane Sandy, deliver basic functions and services to all residents, and emerge stronger as a community—with the goal of eliminating long-term displacement from homes and jobs after shock events by 2050. The City will upgrade private and public buildings to be more energy efficient and resilient to the impacts of climate change; adapt infrastructure like transportation, telecommunications, water, and energy to withstand severe weather events; and strengthen our coastal defenses against flooding and sea level rise. The city will strengthen homes, businesses, community-based organizations, and public services to reduce the impacts of disruptive events and promote faster recovery.

2. Challenges Faced by New York in Future Development

The challenges of our fifth century will be as profound as those we've seen in the past-Despite widespread prosperity, living costs and income inequality in New York City are rising. Poverty and homelessness remain high. The city's core infrastructure—our roads, subways, sewers, and bridges—is aging. Affordable housing is in short supply. Our air and water have never been cleaner, but our parks and public spaces don't always serve the needs of all New Yorkers. And, without action, climate change is an existential threat to our future.

2.1 A Growing Population

New York City continues to grow at a rapid rate, in large part through immigration. With nearly 8.4 million people, the city's population is at an all-time high, and is expected to reach 9 million by 2040. Growth is projected to be greatest outside Manhattan—with the largest increases in Brooklyn and the Bronx. This increased population will strain the city's infrastructure and test the reliability of services.

New York City's population is also aging: by 2040, the number of New Yorkers over 65 will surpass school-age children. These changes will create new challenges in everything from the delivery of services to urban design. We must improve social and physical infrastructure to provide equitable access to services and employment for a changing population.

Throughout its history, people have flocked to New York City, drawn by its economic opportunities and ethnic networks. Foreign-born residents comprise almost 40 percent of the total population. At the same time, many young, educated Americans are also moving to New York City.

With a growing population comes the critical need for additional affordable housing for all New Yorkers. In order to accommodate projected growth and the natural loss of some housing over time, and to reduce pressure on housing prices, the City intends to create 240 000 new housing units—including market rate and affordable—in the next decade.

2.2 An Evolving Economy

The city has an all-time high of 4.2 million wage and salary jobs, adding 113 000 private sector jobs in 2014 alone. Our economic activity, measured by Gross City Product (GCP), is $647 billion, and the city's economic recovery since the last recession outpaced the nation's, with an 11.5 percent increase in jobs between 2009 and 2014, compared to only 6.1 percent nationally.

Sustainable economic growth and stability depend on the continued strength of our core sectors, as well as economic diversification across both boroughs and sectors. The rate of job growth in the boroughs has been higher recently, outpacing Manhattan in the past ten years. While employment is becoming geographically diversified, it continues to remain highly concentrated in Manhattan.

The traditional core sectors of the city's economy—finance, insurance, and real estate—remain the foundation of our economic strength. While they represent 11.7 percent of our jobs, they comprise 38.4 percent of GCP. They also provide a substantial tax base that supports investment in infrastructure and services to ensure our long-term ability to accommodate continued growth.

Jobs in sectors such as retail, food services, and home care are increasing due to growth in the overall population, tourism, and senior residents. These sectors provide opportunities for people who lack the skills to compete for high-wage jobs, and provide access to the job ladder to advance their careers. New York City has many people in this position, and these jobs are vital. One of the reasons less-skilled people stay in New York City, despite the high cost of living, is that jobs of this kind are available and generally accessible without a car. Expanding skills training and workforce development programs, as well as access to higher education, will enable low-skilled entry level workers to gain the skills needed to move into higher paying jobs.

While New York City is home to 52 *Fortune* 500 companies, small businesses with fewer than 100 employees are a critical part of the city's economy. These businesses account for more than half of New York's private sector employment Small business owners in New York often face regulatory hurdles to starting and growing their businesses, while the high cost of living makes it difficult to attract and retain talented young people.

2.3 Growing Inequality

Despite its overall prosperity, New York City continues to struggle with high rates of poverty and growing income inequality. The crumbling of the middle class is not just a local problem, it is one that requires a national solution, and is a crisis of our time. Over the past decade, income inequality has increased in the city, surpassing the national average, expecially in recent years, it has continued to rise.

During the 2008 recession, workers experienced flat or declining wages, except for those in select high-wage sectors. The city has experienced an impressive recovery, gaining 422 000 private jobs between 2009 and 2014. While job growth has occurred across a range of sectors, it has been particularly strong in lower-paying sectors, such as accommodation, food service and retail trade. Since 2014, more workers have started to see wage gains due to declining unemployment and increasing demand for labor. Nonetheless, these gains have not fully offset the wage stagnation that occurred during the recession. As a result, low-income New Yorkers continue to struggle with the city's high costs of living. Without training to support career development, these individuals and their families are likely to remain in poverty. Recognizing that high-, mid-, and low-skill jobs are all part of a diverse, healthy economy, the City is committed to supporting job quality across all sectors—higher wages for low-wage jobs and expanded opportunities for skills training.

These employment and wage trends are occurring against a backdrop of other significant economic challenges. Nearly half of the city's population still lives in or near poverty, including a disproportionate number of African-American, Latino, and Asian New Yorkers. The city's already-high cost of living is still increasing. The supply of housing has not kept pace with the increase in population, leading to a severe lack of affordable housing, especially for those who are least well off. Homelessness is at a record high.

As it continues to grow, the City must invest strategically to create new economic opportunities for the most vulnerable and lowest-income New

Yorkers. We must provide increased support to the economic sectors that drive middle-income job growth. The city's rapid employment growth offers a real opportunity to improve the incomes of low-wage workers. To ensure that this happens, we must do all we can to continue to raise the minimum wage. We must also work with employers and labor unions to improve employee training, provide a path for advancement, and emphasize employee retention.

2.4 Infrastructure Needs

While New York City is a 21st century global city, its aging infrastructure is straining to meet the demands of a modern and dynamic urban center. Infrastructure connects people, neighborhoods, and businesses, and provides essential services—the water we drink, the gas we need to cook, the electricity that lights homes and businesses, and the Internet access to communicate and learn.

Despite a mountain of evidence emphasizing the link between modern infrastructure and economic growth, public investment across the region has not kept pace with capital investment needs. New York City's transit system is in need of improvement and expansion to provide the best possible service to New Yorkers. Our subway system, the nation's largest, had a record 1.7 billion total riders total in 2013 and is near or at full capacity. Every day, New Yorkers crowd onto subways and buses, with an average commute time of 47 minutes— the highest of any major American city. Investing directly in transit systems, including expanded Select Bus Service routes and a citywide ferry system, as well as coordination with regional entities, is key to supporting continued growth and will support competitiveness. Significant expansion of our existing rail transit system is extremely expensive and federal resources are dwindling. Yet without investments to maintain a state of good repair, aging infrastructure incurs higher costs down the road and imperils our long-term prosperity.

Many of the city's gas, steam, sewer, and water lines are not only aging, but are made of materials not in use today, and prone to leaks and breaks. Much of the city's underground infrastructure is not mapped, making it hard to pinpoint issues to make efficient repairs or improvements. Our highways and bridges are also old and at risk. The Brooklyn Bridge, for instance, opened in 1883.

The Internet is rapidly becoming as central to our daily lives as electricity, gas, and water. However, currently 22 percent of New York City households lack broadband Internet at home. Affordability of Internet services is cited as the main barrier to broadband adoption in New York City. Increased affordability and public availability of broadband service will help to close the adoption gap and increase access to online tools that support individuals, families, and businesses.

Identifying adequate funding resources to maintain and upgrade critically aging infrastructure and ensure a consistent state of good repair across the city is a major challenge.

2.5 Urban Environmental Conditions and Climate Change

In recent years, New York has made substantial headway in protecting the environment through improved air quality and reduced greenhouse gas emissions, which have decreased by 19 percent since 2005. We have reduced energy use in buildings and switched to less carbon intensive electricity generation. New York City's air quality is the cleanest it has been in over fifty years, and among U.S. cities, it has moved from having the 7th to the 4th cleanest air over the past several years.

More than 100 brownfields encompassing over one million square feet have been cleaned up and redeveloped. The 23 sites completed this year alone will generate more than 420 new jobs, 550 units of affordable housing, and $162 million in new tax revenue. Green infrastructure initiatives such as bioswales help to mitigate stormwater flooding and prevent the discharge of pollutants into the city's waterways.

At the same time, longstanding environmental conditions continue to have chronic impacts on the health and livelihoods of New Yorkers, with four out of every 1 000 children aged 5—17 years hospitalized for asthma in 2012, as the city's population continues to grow, additional strain will be placed on the environment from basic infrastructure needs, including a projected 14 percent increase in heating fuel demand by 2030 and a 44 percent increase in energy consumption by 2030. The city generates about 25 000 tons of residential, business, and institutional garbage every day, but only about 15.4 percent of waste collected by City workers is diverted for recycling.

Climate Change: The city also faces increasing risks from the impacts of global climate change. While we have made significant strides in reducing our contributions to climate change, we still expect to face local impacts that could threaten the city. In partnership with the New York City Panel on Climate Change (NPCC), the City has continued its work to understand these risks and make sure that the best available science continues to inform the City's climate policy.

Earlier this year, the NPCC released Building the Knowledge Base for Climate Resiliency, which included updated projections for the region. Among them, we can expect to see, by the 2050s, increased average temperatures (4.1°F to 5.7°F), increased average precipitation (4 to 11 percent), and rising sea levels (11 to 21 inches). The average number of days per year above 90°F is expected to at least double. Due to sea level rise alone, coastal flood events will increase in both frequency and intensity. The number of the most intense hurricanes across the North Atlantic Basin is also expected to increase.

Each of these changes will increase the exposure of the city's neighborhoods, businesses, and infrastructure. Health impacts on New Yorkers will continue to increase. Fortunately, the City continues to reduce these risks. We are reducing our greenhouse gas emissions and adapting our neighborhoods, with critical investments now underway on our coastline, in our buildings, and for our infrastructure. Much more remains to be done, and the City is committed to leading the globe in this fight, to the benefit of future generations.

2.6 New York City Voices

New York City works best when New Yorkers are involved with their city and have a say in their government, and when government listens to their voices to make better decisions. We need to create new processes for communication and dialogue. The result will be more informed policymaking and better-designed programs, and New Yorkers with the tools and resources to help shape the future of their city. Engaged New Yorkers are empowered residents who interact with their government, and can effectively help set priorities and shape policy.

There are a number of fundamental challenges to increasing civic engagement and democratic participation. More than one-third of the lowest-income New Yorkers, for example, lack broadband Internet access, which hinders their communications and access to City services. Only 18 percent of New Yorkers do volunteer work, below the national average of 25 percent, and 49 percent are dissatisfied with the level of cultural services in their neighborhood. Only 66 percent of eligible New York City voters are registered, and the voter turnout rate was 21 percent in the 2014 election.

Decisions about City policies and initiatives should be informed by broad public engagement with a wide range of stakeholders, including residents whose voices are not heard because of barriers such as language and time. Recognizing the importance of this dialogue in shaping policy, OneNYC sought and continues to seek input from a broad range of residents.

2.7 Importance of the Region

New York City's future is intertwined with its metropolitan region. The city's economy drives the region's prosperity, while benefiting from the region's transportation, skilled workforce, cultural resources, and extensive infrastructure. Our suburbs and our city face many of the same issues, including increased income disparity, the need for affordable housing to keep pace with our growth, and a shared harbor. Between 1990 and 2010, the region grew by 10.9 percent, with the greatest percentage changes in population in Northern New Jersey (14.3 percent). At the same time, New York City's job growth constituted 80 percent of the region's growth since 2000.

Every year, residents in the region take more than four billion trips, or 184 per person, on buses, subways, commuter railroads, and ferries. No other U.S. metropolitan area comes close. Regional travel is not only about coming into Manhattan. Between 2000 and 2010, the number of reverse commuters increased by 12.5 percent, compared to 9.5 percent arriving at our city's regional transportation hubs. The ability to access a broad range of employment opportunities and workers within the region enhances the city's competitiveness as a place to live and to locate businesses.

However, we are not keeping pace with this growth in regional travel, and must coordinate with our regional partners to advocate for the critical transportation connections across the Hudson in New Jersey, as well as with Long Island, Connecticut, and beyond. The fragmenting effects of a multitude of jurisdictions have hindered regional planning in our broader region, including in transportation, energy, telecommunications, and a number of other crucial areas. The siloed delivery of infrastructure and services does not produce optimal outcomes. New York City must be a leader in working with regional governments. This will ensure regional cooperation and coordination and that funds are wisely invested.

A powerful illustration of this shared responsibility is that over $266 billion will be spent in the region over the next ten years by the City as well as regional agencies, such as the Metropolitan Transportation Authority (MTA) and Port Authority of New York and New Jersey (PANYNJ), and private utilities. The City's preliminary ten-year capital budget makes up nearly 25 percent of this anticipated spending. This spending has a direct impact on New York City's capacity to thrive and meet its goals for equity, sustainability, and resiliency. Looking ahead to the next ten years and beyond, the City is committed to taking a leadership role in directing these investments and incorporating them into our own strategic process, so that regional spending can be leveraged for the city's maximum benefit.

The Great London's Future Development: Vision and Challenges

1. The Basis of the Great London's Future Plan

Throughout its history from a port to a governmental and international trading hub with propriety, London, the capital of Britain, has constantly changed and reinvented itself with both urban and suburb areas involved. As greater numbers of people move to cities worldwide, we have the opportunity to set the benchmark for successful large-scale urban living. London's strength is its diversity, dynamism and history. The diversity is based on the migrated people from all circles all over the world. The dynamism has been built on the innovations in industry and science. Its historical heritages have also gained worldwide respect. London remains to be a metropolitan with continued dynamism and changes. The plan for 2036 is set to keep the dynamism of this city and its people.

2. The Vision of the Great London in 2036

The overall plan for a sustainable development of London is to excel among global cities—expanding opportunities for all its people and enterprises, achieving the highest environment standards and quality of life and leading the world in its approach to tackling the urban challenges of the 21st century, particularly that of climate change. Achieving this vision will mean making sure London makes the most of the benefits of the energy, dynamism and diversity that characterize the city and its people; embraces change while promoting its heritage, neighborhoods and identity; and values responsibility, compassion and citizenship.

Six detailed objectives set out what this overarching vision is to achieve:

(1) A city that meets the challenges of economic and population growth in

ways that ensure a good and improving quality of life for all Londoners and help tackle the huge issue of inequality among Londoners, including inequality in health outcomes.

(2) An internationally competitive and successful city with a strong and diverse economy and an entrepreneurial spirit that benefits all Londoners and all parts of London; a city which is at the leading edge of innovation and research, while also being comfortable with, and making the most, its rich heritage.

(3) A city with diversity, cohesion, security and accessible neighborhoods to which Londoners feel attached, which provide all of its residents, workers, visitors and students, whatever their origin, background, age or status, with opportunities to realize and express their potential; and a high quality environment for individuals to enjoy, live together and thrive.

(4) A city that delights the sense and takes care over its buildings and streets, having the best of modern architecture, while also making the most of London's built heritage; and which makes the most of its wealth of open and green spaces, realizing its potential for improving Londoner's health, welfare and development.

(5) A city that becomes a world leader in improving the environment locally and globally, taking the lead in tackling climate change, reducing pollution, developing a low carbon economy and consuming fewer resources or using them more effectively.

(6) A city where it is easy, safe and convenient for everyone to access jobs, opportunities and facilities, with an efficient and effective transport system which places more emphasis on walking and cycling and makes better use of the Thames, and which supports delivery of all the objectives of this plan.

3. Challenges Faced by the Great London in 2036

3.1 Population

First, continued population growth. London's population has reached 8.2 million in 2011 and will grow to 10.11 million in 2036. In the next 25 years, the city's population will continue to grow by over 1.91 million people. Second, not only is the population likely to grow, but it will also change in composition.

Compared with 2011, London will continue to be younger, there will be 17 percent growth in school age Londoners in 2036 and 28 percent growth in aged 35—64. At the same time, people aged 64 or more is estimated to grow by 64 percent (approximately 580 000) and reach 1.49 million in total. There will also be significantly more people here in their nineties (89 000 more) as life expectancy improves on the back of medical advances, improvements in lifestyles and new technologies. Third, London's population will also continue to diversify. Black, Asian and other minority ethnic communities are expected to grow strongly as a result of natural growth and continued immigration from overseas. In addition, about 10 percent disabled Londoners or those with illness in sensation require the city to provide more support in mobility and access in needs. All these mean that London is in demand of better housing, schools, convenient facilities and other infrastructure. It also faces the challenge of more aged people.

3.2 Economic Growth

The link between economic growth and employment is quite strong. Only keeping economic growth can provide more job opportunities for continued growing population in London. By 2036, job positions may well have had a considerable increase, with both continued changes and challenges. With a growing number of Londoners of employment age (16—64) in the period to 2036, it will be essential to make sure they have the range of opportunities they need. If the growth of job positions goes slower than that of population, more severe problems will appear. A city with an economy as dependent upon the private sector as London needs growth to ensure the fabric of the city receives the investment it needs. Or, London's fiscal income will face challenges as well.

3.3 Continued Poverty

Although London's economy has been generally successful over the past twenty years, not everyone has been benefited and levels of poverty did not reduce. Income poverty rates for children, working age adults and pensioners are higher in London than elsewhere in the UK. A quarter of working age adults, and 41 per cent of children are in poverty after housing costs are taken into account and poverty is particularly concentrated in households with dependent children (working age people without children have poverty rates similar to those in the rest of the country). Deprivation is also concentrated among Black, Asian and ethnic minority and disabled Londoners. Deprivation also generates other problems including the payment of salaries in job market. It also leads to more unemployment which makes the fact that London has had higher levels of unemployment than other parts of the country. The result can be that those with lower incomes find it very difficult to access the housing they need, with many having no option but to seek social housing. This in turn can lead to social housing and deprivation being closely linked. There is a close correlation between housing tenure and deprivation in London, and people have increasing difficulty in moving on from social into other forms of housing. Deprivation tends to be geographically concentrated; problems like public health, medicine abuse and crimes appear more often. Thus, London is an increasingly polarized city, leading to a series of social problems and lots of challenges to civil management and planning.

3.4 The Challenge of a Changing Climate

We know that some climate change is now inevitable. By 2050, what we in this country think of as being a heat wave may well be the norm. Adapting to the climate change we can anticipate over the next two decades means making sure London is ready to meet the issues raised by becoming a warmer city with wetter winters and hotter, dryer summers. This includes being prepared for heat waves and their impacts and addressing the consequence of the "urban heat island" effect, the way parts of cities tend to get warmer than less developed areas, and to retain that heat longer. Both these will have major impacts on the quality of life in London. We also have to be ready to meet an increased probability of flooding and to cope with the consequences when the housing in London will have reached the estimated growth in 2036. A further problem arising from climate change will be an increasing shortage of water. It is central to promote water-use efficiency for families and companies with proper water-use infrastructure. Low-carbon economy, energy issues especially resilience and security of supply and infrastructure provision in electricity are likely to go up the policy agenda and increasingly important.

The Metropolis of the Great Paris in 2030: Vision and Challenges

1. The Metropolis of Great Paris in 2030

Administration in France is levelled as region, province and county. "The Metropolis of Greater Paris" ("Île-de-France" in French), is one of the 22 regions of France, and includes the city of Paris. The region is made up of eight administrative departments: Paris, Essonne, Hauts-de-Seine, Seine-Saint-Denis, Seine-et-Marne, Val-de-Marne, Val-d'Oise and Yvelines. The region is in an area of lowland called the Paris Basin and between the northern and southern Europe. The river Seine runs through the region and connects the place to the English Channel as well as the Atlantic Ocean. "The metropolis of Great Paris" has great potential, on the one hand due to the propriety of Paris as a political, economic and cultural centre, and on the other due to rich resources along by the Seine valley of vast grassland, science-and-technological-oriented plain, highlands and forests, as well as the cultural heritages constituted by royal gardens or towns.

2. The Vision of "The Metropolis of Great Paris" in 2030

"The metropolis of Great Paris" boasts a good reputation among many developing urban areas in Europe, because it is known how to develop based on its own history and geographic environment, how to adjust to activities in other areas and to the increasing diversity of its residents. "The metropolis of Great Paris" aims at continued innovation so as to play a crucial role in Europe.

The general plan for "The metropolis of Great Paris" is to build up an innovative and sustainable international metropolitan, an *intelligent* city with French characteristics. It is designed to motivate the economy of the whole France.

The plan for "The metropolis of Great Paris" in 2030, based on the sustainability of development, is to improve attractiveness of Paris and the impact of the region, so as to situate the whole area into a new development model.

2.1 The Place of Diversity in Lifestyles

In 2030, various facilities in the area will be more convenient for the residents in Paris. To promote efficiency in transportation is an ultimate hope for residents in"The metropolis of Great Paris" to improve their living quality. "The metropolis of Great Paris" is not a unified and highly-intense place; rather, it has various scenic spots, surroundings and urban facilities for different lifestyles.

2.2 The Place of Solidarity and Mutual-Assistance

Equality in societies and areas requires the attractiveness of cities, which is also one of crucial foundations for improving the city's international influence. Better conditions will be created for citizens including housing, employment, facilities and service. Opportunities for equal medical treatment and social service will be provided all over the area. Special attention and management will be given to those unequal events related to society, economy and environment in many parts of the area. More emphasis will be placed on integration within the society, complementary and balance among regions.

2.3 The Place of Attractiveness and Innovation

"The metropolis of Great Paris" has a strength in dynamism since it embraces the whole world. By 2030, "The metropolis of Great Paris" will have been a more attractive place with each part making efforts for that and enjoying the success. To keep its economic position and its international attractiveness relies not only on the diversity, stability and richness but also on the full-scale perspective of its economy. Pace of life in the future will be more comfortable; link between citizens will be closer; composition of economic activities will be more balanced.

2.4 The Place of Sustainability and Stability

The complementary between city and nature is necessary. The strengths and fortunes of different parts shall be shared. The rapid development of some regional economies will contribute to the whole area; meanwhile, the future development and attractiveness improvement of agriculture, forest resource, natural parks and villages shall not be ignored. Nature will be looked as "partner" of development and all human activities related to nature will be integrated into the diversity of the nature itself, which thus makes the urban area take on more pressure, adjust to the climate changes and keep a balanced relation with the nature.

3. Challenges Faced by the Metropolis of Great Paris in 2030

The plan for "The metropolis of Great Paris" is associated with the life of residents in terms of transportation, housing, employment, and environment. And it is also concerned with the future of "The metropolis of Great Paris" and France as a whole in aspects like scientific research, innovation, attractiveness and economy. The French government hopes that the contributions produced by this plan will be shared by all regions involved. However, in the process of carry out this plan, challenges remain in the following three aspects.

3.1 Solidarity in the Area

To improve solidarity in the region and to reduce risks as much as possible,"The metropolis of Great Paris" will be faced with several issues including retaining dynamism of population, improving education of a growing population, restoring tension between regions and societies, reducing inequalities among regions, increasing tenure housing and public infrastructure, establishing highly-efficient and equal medical and public service system, as well as promoting facilities and service in aspects of housing, working, economic and entertaining activities which are closely linked to life quality. All these issues are central to keep regional diversity, to adjust to changes and innovations as well as to make residents have a better life.

3.2 Climate Change

Like other international metropolitans,"The metropolis of Great Paris" is confronted with challenges in terms of energy, climate change, reduction of diversity in nature and also food. A highly intense population makes the region more vulnerable to pollutions and damages. Only a more flexible region can be able to resume from serious environmental, economic or social damages. Several problems are necessary to be dealt with including reducing greenhouse gas emission, facilitating energy transformation, protecting natural resources and ecological system, decreasing possibilities of being damaged and estimating influences of climate disasters, in order to provide resident with good urban life and to attract more residents and enterprises.

3.3 Attractiveness of the "The Metropolis of Great Paris": A More Ecological and Social Economy

Apart from the issues of social harmony and environmental protection, Paris, as the heart of France's economy, also needs to address the issues of keeping its economic position and attractiveness in the world. To keep the momentum of its sustainable development, the region shall reconsider the way of its economic growth, so as to intensify its role in the economy of France, Europe and the world as a whole.

Tokyo in 2030: Vision and Challenges

1. The Vision of Tokyo in 2030

From a small fishing village to a super metropolitan, the development of Tokyo has always been a model for other cities. In September 2013, Tokyo was elected to host the 2020 Summer Olympics. For the Games and a sustainable development of the city, the municipal government of Tokyo, in December of 2014, issued a new plan entitled "Creating the Future: The Long-term Plan for Tokyo", which contains a big aim for "the top one city in the world".

The general plan for Tokyo is to build up "first-class international metropolitan", in other words, a city which "is able to provide the most happiness for its residents". It aims to excess cities like London, New York and Paris in terms of social welfare, economic dynamism, urban infrastructure as well as arts and culture revitalization. The plan includes basic aims and related strategies, specific policies for the aims and a three-year plan. Five dimensions are the basis of all the policies: (1) to activate the economy and to improve life quality of residents; (2) to combine tangible and intangible strengths; (3) to reduce the limit of cooperation between government and social organizations; (4) to make full use of advanced technology; (5) to increase women's and aged people's participation in social activities.

"The Long-term Plan for Tokyo" puts forward with two general aims:

1.1 To Host the Best Olympics and Special Olympics in History

Taking the Olympics and the Special Olympics as an opportunity, the plan aims to improving the development and outlook of Tokyo as well as inheriting the heritage of the Olympics. Three strategies will be carried out: first, to realize the strengths of Tokyo as a mature city so as to host two Olympics Games successfully; second, to build a people-oriented metropolitan with excellent infrastructure; third, to present Japanese's hospitality and Tokyo's charming beauty.

1.2 To Tackle Major Issues for a Sustainable Development

In terms of the issues like low-birth rate, aging and decreasing of population, five strategies will be implemented as following: to build up a safe and comfortable city, to build up a city with good social welfare, to build up a top-level international city, to provide sound environment and facilities for the following generations through further development of the city, and to revitalize Tama and offshore islands.

2. Challenges Faced by Tokyo in Future Development

In the next twenty to twenty-four years from now, Tokyo will be confronted with the following challenges:

2.1 Safety and Security

Residents in Tokyo hope to tackle the problems like fraud on aged people and crimes caused by tracking women. In recent years, there are increasingly more aged victims as customers, accidents related to dangerous drugs, online-banking fraud and unauthorized access crimes, as well as crimes pertaining to violent groups, arms and drug smuggling.

2.2 Social Welfare

Demand for baby-caring is increasing due to more families with working parents. By April 2014, there are 8 672 kids being left home alone. Therefore, Tokyo municipal government has to face several challenges in terms of baby-caring service, facility, talents and children protection.

Aged population is estimated to grow to 3.27 million by 2025 and those with senile dementia will grow from 0.38 million in 2013 to 0.6 million in 2025. The increase of aged people requires the improvement of a comprehensive social system of medical treatment, nursing, precaution, daily assistance and housing for the aged. The municipal government shall also emphasize on the diagnosing and treatment of senile dementia at early stage. The recruiting and turnover rate in nursing faculty is relatively higher than that of other jobs, implying a lack of long-term talents. The large population in Tokyo and the limited land resources make the government get into the problems of how to ensure eligible lands by policy bonus and reconstruction projects in terms of building facilities and housing for baby-caring and aged people.

Given the fact the disabled people live a relatively isolated life, places for collaborative training and activities are in demand in order to help them live in a community. In 2004, the employment of disabled people in Tokyo is lower than the average in the country. Disabled's living and working remain a difficult issue to deal with.

2.3 Globalization

Economy: Due to the decrease of population in the whole Japan, economic activities is estimated to be less prosperous in the long-term with less working people and shrinking domestic demand. For a sustainable development, Tokyo is expected to outstand in the international competition so as to motivate the economy of Japan as a whole. Yet, in terms of activating the economy, challenges remain in various aspects for Tokyo, like incorporating foreign investment, attracting talents, participating exchanges with international enterprises and innovation.

Construction: Given the fact that Tokyo has a reputation of traffic block, a proper design of streets and blocks is in need to assist in its economy development.

Employment: There remain a lot of young men who have not been employed in formal positions in Tokyo, and this group of people occupies 35.7 percent (2.16 million) with a growing tendency. Formally-employed people have salaries with an age-oriented increase, yet informally-employed ones only have salaries without increase. And the latter do not have opportunities for further education either. The two groups have quite different payment and welfare. Among those who have been employed, about 25 percent high school graduates and 33 percent university graduates leave office within three years. Moreover, many aged people hope to get a job for money, health or contributions to the society. Nowadays, it is rather difficult for working people to balance between work and family, which gives rise to problems like working over-load, inequality in baby-caring duties between men and women as well as more demand for nursing service. In recent years, the employment rate for women is growing generally yet decreases during marriage and fertility and gets back to increase in nursing period, which demonstrates "M" line. Inadequate young people and more aged people have led to the decrease of working population. Thus the society is required to motivate more women to work and wipe out the "M" line.

Education for talents: With the 2020 Olympics as its aim, Tokyo needs more international talents. Currently, school children in this city are getting more education yet, compared with certain counties where students hold higher degrees, students in Tokyo have relatively lower degrees. Physical strength of primary school students is growing but getting polarized; in contrast with other places in the whole country, high-school students in Tokyo have lower levels of physical strength. Various activities in public schools improve students' sense of working, however, some students even have no design for their future.

2.4 Sustainable Urban Development

Energy reform: Tokyo has already reduced its energy consuming: 16 percent less in 2012 than that in 2010. However, families and organization shall make more efforts to save energy in use. And residents have higher expectations for new energy: hydrogen energy. For more usage of new energy in public, the government needs to cut down the price and take deregulation.

Green Tokyo: Up till now, Tokyo has undertaken many efforts in planting, but its green rate remains no change from 2003 to 2013. Grasslands including forests and farmlands are being reduced because of the city's development. Urbanization interferes animals' habitats, reduces their space for fertility and threatens the whole system by alien species invasion. Demand for sea water bathing is increasing; sewer system needs to be improved; atmosphere requires promotion as its air quality seldom meets the criteria for PM2.5 and photochemical oxidants.

Safety in city: Infrastructure requires much upgrading including the maintenance and extension of line pipes of sewer system. Expressway in Tokyo including Hata Line One has been used for more than 50 years; quite a few damages demand maintenance and innovation with new technology. Problems like low birth rate, aging and decrease of population give rise to a strategy of redesigning blocks and communities. The number of buildings exceeds that of families in Tokyo. We have to improve surroundings for housing due to a decrease of population and an increase of single families. Aging facilities and people undermines vitality, convenience and safety of this region

Regional development: Tama and offshore islands with rich natural resources are places for living in Tokyo. More efforts shall be made in earthquake prevention and disaster reducing because of its low birth rate and an aging society. In addition, the exploiting of natural resources should be situated in a sustainable development.

Singapore's Future 50 Years: Vision and Challenges

1. The Vision of Singapore in 2065

On the 9th of August 2015, Singapore will mark its 50th anniversary as an independent city-state.

Singapore has made economic miracle in the past 50 years though it barely have natural resources, making it the 1st highest per capital GDP region in the Asia. Faced by challenges like further globalization and increasingly networked citizens, Singapore will develop itself into a sustainable immigration city that is more public, vigorous, tolerant and liveable in the next 50 years, in order to ensure its role as a global financial and economic center in the Asia-Pacific region.

1.1 Maintaining Global Competitive Advantages

On one hand, Singapore should maintain its political advantage in long-term stability; on the other hand, it should keep its strength as a global logistics, financial and economic center. Singapore is a city-state, it has done a better job in ensuring social stability and equal representation in politics. Today, it prides itself for being a successful nation based on meritocracy, Singapore must preserve its unity and avoid "rocking the boat", creating environment for economic and social development. As the most mature regional centers in the world, Singapore must play a central role in future's regional and world development. The evolving complexity of the global and Asian, monetary and financial landscape, and the impact this will have on Singapore's domestic economy, underscores the need for Singapore to build stronger and more flexible ties with other financial centers and regional economic hubs, in order to keep economic in track and deal with the global economic shifts, capital flows and new financial centers.

1.2 Rebuilding the National Identity

For a relatively young nation with little or no natural resources, and whose greatest asset is its people, the character and development of Singaporeans will be crucial to the nation's future success. The need for an ethos of greater tolerance, inclusivity and respect applies to Singapore civil society. Singaporean should aspire to be kinder to all who share the spaces that we work, live and play in, regardless of age, gender and ethnicity. More effort must be made to create a sense of belonging, especially among those on the margins of society, maintaining and promoting its multiculturalism and diversity. Measures must be taken to change this culture of entitlement to a culture of opportunities, through educating younger generations on personal and social responsibilities. Encouraging a spirit of entrepreneurship that embodies traits like creativity and adaptability is essential for Singapore to evolve as a society and be resilient in this new globalised era.

1.3 Creating a Sustainable and Liveable City

Singapore's focus on sustainability has always been ahead of its time. Besides being ranked as one of the world's greenest cities, it has set an example on sustainable living across multiple areas, including eco-friendly buildings, development of green and blue spaces, promoting the use of public transport with high standards for vehicular emissions, energy-efficient technologies, promoting minimum water efficiency standards, waste recycling, improving air quality and public cleanliness. A nation that was not meant to be is today one of the most liveable cities in the world. In the 50 years future, Singapore will continue to be a garden city, finding the right balance in growing economy and maintaining competitive edge, while meeting the aspirations of society, preserving living spaces and sustaining the environment. As a regional hub for trade and finance, home to an educated and informed population, there is much that Singapore can and should do to encourage sustainability, both here and across the region.

2. Challenges Faced by Singapore in Future Development

Singapore has realized high-speed development in the history, and it can continue to thrive in the future if it addresses the potential risks from three fields. These challenges are:

2.1 Geopolitical Dynamics and Security Risks Around the World, Particularly in Asia

The world has entered an unprecedented era of multi-regional, multi-civilisational multipolarity. North America, Europe and the Asia Pacific are all world regions with global or superpower influence. Despite today's economic uncertainty, financial contractions, military drawdowns, demographic transitions, and social dislocation, the United States, European Union and China appear willing and able to retain their global power status into the coming decades, and will be joined by India and Brazil at that level.

In addition, the trend of robust regional integration appears to be accelerating on all continents as well, indicating that the further one looks into the future, the more likely it is that the main pillars of world order will be regional constellations. The world would thus move from geopolitical hierarchy, though not into simple bipolarity between the US and China, but a genuinely dispersed form of network multi-polarity.

As the world's most populous region, Asia will itself have an internal multi-polar dynamic. Northeast Asia is a potent zone of intense geopolitical and economic change. The coming decades should also witness ASEAN come into its own. Already the world's fourth largest economic area, its combined GDP is larger than India's, even though it has approximately half the population. Importantly, ASEAN's younger population and lower wages have made it a larger destination for FDI than China for 2013—2014. Assuming that the ASEAN Economic Community (AEC), Free Trade Area of the Asia Pacific (FTAAP) and Regional Comprehensive Economic Partnership (RCEP) all come to pass on current timelines, by 2030 or sooner ASEAN will have become the world's next factory floor with robust supply chain distribution across the region and global exports in all directions. However, ASEAN's internal disparities are stark, with a huge gap between the most developed countries, such as Singapore, and the least developed, such as Myanmar and Cambodia. These deepening economic ties must be leveraged to increase prosperity and diminish the region's severe income inequality. Rising FDI must be coupled with a main focus on infrastructure development and social policies such as healthcare and education.

Singapore can be a crucial player in regional institutional development. While there is no Brussels or Washington of Asia, Singapore plays a de facto role as a pan-Asian hub, trusted by China, America, India, Australia and Japan at the same time, and considered diplomatically savvy and competent. Diversity makes us a microcosm of Asia—but also a reminder that building unity across two dozen countries with such diverse cultures will be much more difficult in Asia than even in post-war Europe.

However, a more prominent regional role for Singapore should not mean a lesser role for ASEAN. ASEAN's economic integration must also be coupled with a push for the grouping to develop a meaningful diplomatic voice. This applies not only to the outstanding maritime disputes in contested waters, but also emerging challenges, such as the damming of the Mekong River, ethnic tensions and the outflow of refugees from Myanmar's borders, and other crises. To move from crisis management towards consistent efforts to build stability, ASEAN must consider steps to police its region more effectively—such as creating a common peacekeeping force, a proposal which has been supported by several ASEAN members including Indonesia and Malaysia.

2.2 Risks from Global Economic Shifts, New Financial Centers, and Capital Flows

In addition to its role in ensuring regional political and social stability, deeper Asian integration is also essential if the region is to weather future macro-economic volatility. Today's trends of quantitative easing, interest rate divergence and currency devaluations, combined with new regulatory requirements at the global and regional level, portend a world of financial insecurity, despite new macro-prudential measures aimed at preventing a repeat of the 2007—2008 financial crisis.

It is thus imperative that Asian countries deepen their efforts begun with the Chiang Mai Initiative in 2000, not only to expand each other's access to liquidity in the event of currency crises, but the far more important long-term priority of deepening regional capital markets through long maturity local currency bond markets and regional-scale financial institutions that channel stable funding to SMEs and other companies across the region. It is the crucial step in the coming decade and beyond to insulate Asia from the West's structural weaknesses.

As the most mature financial centre in Asia, Singapore must play a central role in these crucial economic transformations. Global liquidity needs a more permanent presence in Singapore with greater allocations to Asia's internal frontier markets, whether Papua New Guinea and Sumatra or Cambodia and Myanmar. The central banks of Southeast Asia should buttress regional bond markets to enable long-term investment horizons. Crucially, more public and private funding—whether through export promotion agencies (which Singapore itself lacks) or banks—should be allocated to trade finance to allow more Asian companies to reach global markets as China has so capably done over the past decades.

Indeed, another global structural economic trend on which Asian countries must continue to capitalize is the prevalence of cross-growth market regional trade as the main driver of globalization today—and likely in the future. It is worth pointing out, for example, that the TPP trade agreement currently being negotiated only represents a subset of Asia's rising trade with Central and South America. Already the so-called Pacific Alliance—which includes Mexico, Colombia, Chile and several other Latin countries—has a combined GDP larger than Brazil and faster growth as well. ASEAN should continue an open regional orientation focused on building as many mutually beneficial trade relationships as possible.

As in geopolitical matters, Singapore is a price-taker rather than price-setter in geo-economics as well. Navigating the global financial system's slow transition from US Dollar dominance towards a multi-currency landscape will therefore be integral to nation's economic health and to make the most of volatile capital flows. It is likely that even the US Dollar's current strengthening and Sing-Dollar's commensurate weakening will not substantially boost

Singapore's manufacturing exports, in the face of intensifying competition over supply chains in Asia. Competitiveness strategy must therefore be based on non-monetary factors, such as technology productivity and strengthening of our services sector, both within Singapore and as a hub for regional and global firms.

Further denominating trade in diverse currencies may become essential to Singapore's financial strategy. This would put pressure on the Monetary Authority of Singapore (MAS) to hold even larger capital reserves in RMB in addition to the US Dollar and other currencies. While Singapore is already a hub for RMB trading and "dim sum" bonds, China's capital account liberalization will require that Singapore be prepared for far larger-scale inflows and outflows simultaneously with China.

The evolving complexity of the global—and Asian—monetary and financial landscape, and the impact this will have on domestic economy, underscores the need for Singapore to build stronger and more flexible ties with other financial centers and regional economic hubs. Regulators in Asia will need a better handle on the stability of each other's financial markets and health of companies exposed to cross-border corporate debt. Being the de facto capital of Asia will be more than a diplomatic responsibility for Singapore; it will also be an economic one.

2.3 The Evolution of Social Compacts

Beyond observing political and economic trends at the regional and global level, Singapore also needs to consider its domestic challenges and the nation's social stability as it crosses the historic 50-year milestone.

The social compact or contract between a people and its government is among the most critical relationships in any society. Defined as an implicit agreement between the governed and the government, it shapes and sets limits for the rights and duties of each member of society.

However, the 21st century has seen the nature of society rapidly shift in many countries around the world, especially Southeast Asia. This has been attributed to a variety of factors, including the rise of a growing and increasingly vocal middle class in countries like Malaysia, Thailand, Indonesia and even Singapore, accompanied by surging levels of education and standards of living, as well as the pervasiveness of social and digital media.

The onus is now on Singapore's governments to meet the rising expectations of a vocal, informed, and increasingly networked citizenry. Any failure to engage with the public could irrevocably damage Singapore's social compact in the years to come.

Many citizens still believe in the need for strong and capable leadership. In the current political climate, strong leadership needs to come alongside greater citizen empowerment. Singapore's leaders must ensure that they listen to more diverse views and opinions, and continue to focus on policies that address long-term issues requiring sustainable solutions, not short-term quick fixes.

Even as the government adapts, Singaporeans will need to change as well. This does not simply entail the government catering to the demands of Singaporeans. It also means a sense of belonging and genuine civic awareness is needed, where citizens, as well as other residents, are willing and able to offer constructive views to be heard and considered.

In addition to hearing the voices of Singapore citizens, it is equally important that the voices of non-citizens be heard. This includes permanent residents and shorter-term residents studying or working here. In the years to come, Singapore will need to resolve the ongoing debate regarding how open the city-state should be towards foreign labour and immigration. But Singapore will always rely to some extent on foreign talent; non-citizens will always be a part of Singapore's society and care must be taken not to alienate foreigners, or discriminate against them, as this could have drastic implications for Singapore's economic growth and social stability.

2.4 Risk of Losing National Identity

As Singapore considers its future over the next 50 years, another critical element to consider is not just the shape of government in the years ahead, but also the character as a people. The public discourse over the fate of Singapore also needs to be directed inwards.

For a relatively young nation with little or no natural resources, and whose greatest asset is its people, the character and development of Singaporeans will be crucial to the nation's future success.

The city-state is seeing potential fractures, an alarming trend in a society that has long been known for its stability and business-friendly nature. Fault-lines are now visible, including income inequality, anti-foreigner sentiment and the political divide between ordinary Singaporeans and perceived economic or social elites. Singaporeans have become largely materialistic in nature, focused heavily on progressing careers and accumulating wealth to improve the standard of living. This focus has led to other aspects being neglected, such as social inclusiveness, consideration for others, and compassion for the less fortunate and an appreciation. Singapore has inadvertently bred an unhealthy mindset of performance and perceived success. A strong consumerist culture evidenced by the high density of shopping malls is motivating people to strive for higher education and professional skills, but also creating a narrower definition of success in the form of better jobs and salaries.

The need for an ethos of greater tolerance, inclusivity and respect applies to Singapore civil society. Singapore has a thriving community of non-government organizations representing a range of causes, but at present many default to an "appeal to higher authority" approach, appealing to the state to bring about social change, rather than being more self-driving.

Measures must be taken to change this culture of entitlement to a culture of opportunities, through educating younger generations on personal and social responsibilities. Encouraging a spirit of entrepreneurship that embodies traits like creativity and adaptability is essential for Singapore to evolve as a society and be resilient in this new globalised era.

While it is important to retain a strong sense of belonging to a country, it does not imply that Singapore's identity needs to be exclusionary. Singapore prides itself on its multiculturalism and diversity, and should continue to provide that sense of belonging not just to its citizens and Permanent Residents, but also to other groups within society.

2.5 Connected Problems among Ecology, Environment and Climate Change

The community in Singapore is mainly concerned with political, economic and social challenges, but there are other challenges to consider as the nation moves beyond its 50th anniversary.

For example, the haze is the most visible environmental problem. Besides, although the nation's water, food and energy security is stable for now, Singapore is far from self-sufficient. We cannot assume that this will continue, given uncertain regional and global conditions. There is also the question of how the island's future landscape will look like. Singapore has prided itself on being a garden city, but with the nation facing increasing demands to provide more or better housing and transportation infrastructure, the preservation of Singapore's green spaces is far from guaranteed.

In the future 50, there are six developmental challenges Singapore must face, including food security, water security, impact of climate change, energy security, sustainable growth without massively depleting "natural capital" and inclusive growth. Each of these issues has interlocked causes and Singaporean must start integrating how they are dealt with because they are closely linked together.

APPENDIX

附　录

2015 年上海国际智库峰会办会、参会方简介

1. 主办方

1.1 上海市人民政府发展研究中心

上海市人民政府发展研究中心（前身是上海经济研究中心）于 1980 年 12 月 26 日正式成立，于 1995 年 12 月 22 日根据市政府决定，更名为上海市人民政府发展研究中心。上海市人民政府发展研究中心是为市政府决策服务，承担本市决策咨询的研究、组织、协调、管理、服务的市政府决策咨询研究机构。

主要职责：

（1）研究上海市经济、社会发展和改革开放中具有全局性、综合性、战略性的问题。

（2）了解动态、分析矛盾、研究对策、预测前景，及时向市委、市政府提出决策建议和咨询意见。

（3）负责上海市两年一度的市决策咨询研究成果奖的评奖工作。

（4）组织、协调市政府系统的决策咨询研究工作。

（5）负责上海市决策咨询系统建议库信息管理和维护工作。

（6）受上海市政府委托，管理有关组织和事业机构。

（7）编辑出版《上海经济年鉴》和《科学发展》杂志。

（8）承办上海市领导交办的其他事项。

2. 承办方

2.1 上海国际智库交流中心

上海国际智库交流中心是上海市人民政府发展研究中心搭建的开放式决策咨询研究公共平台之一。2010 年，市政府发展研究中心按照时任市

长韩正的指示要求，为进一步拓展本市决策咨询研究工作，汇集国内外专家学者智慧服务市委、市政府的科学决策、民主决策，不断扩大市政府发展研究中心的国际影响力，由市政府发展研究中心牵头，联合埃森哲、凯捷、博斯、德勤、IBM 等 13 家在沪的国际知名智库于 2011 年 1 月成立并举办了主题为："创新、转型、发展"首届上海智慧论坛。时任市长韩正同志发来贺电，时任市政府秘书长姜平同志出席会议并致词。

上海国际智库交流中心的主要职责是：

（1）开展政府决策咨询研究。

（2）服务企业发展开展应用研究、企业规划、管理咨询。

（3）开展双边和多边国际合作研讨。

（4）承担国际合作课题研究。

（5）提供专业人才培养、培训与信息服务。

5 年来，上海国际智库交流中心发挥独特的人才、资源和信息优势，对接中心的特聘专家、工作室、社会调查、课题研究、高校论坛等决策咨询研究公共平台，围绕上海的经济社会发展开展了大量国际合作研究，举办了 16 次双边论坛，4 次"上海智慧论坛"，1 次上海国际智库峰会，有效地提升了市政府发展研究中心整合国家智库的功能和作用，为市委、市政府科学决策、民主决策提供了大量来自国外知名智库的意见和建议。

2.2 上海发展研究基金会

上海发展研究基金会成立于 1993 年，是利用自然人、法人或者其他组织捐赠的财产，以从事公益事业为目的，按照国家有关规定的公募基金会、非营利性法人。

近年来，基金会为实现其宗旨而积极探索。基金会每月举办一次"上海发展沙龙"，邀请国内外知名专家、学者就当前的热点或敏感问题作演讲，并与参会者进行互动讨论；每年举办两到三次高层次的研讨会，邀请多位海内外专家与政、商、学界人士共聚一堂，就全球经济和中国经济的形势进行讨论和交流；举办"中国经济未来"系列小型研讨会，针对中国经济发展中一些深层次问题，进行深入的讨论。

上海发展研究基金会现由原上海市副市长、原市人大常委会副主任胡延照先生任会长；原上海市政协副主席王荣华先生，以及上海社会科学院院长王战先生任副会长；由乔依德先生任副会长兼秘书长。

2013 年底，上海发展研究基金会接受了捐赠，成立了卓越·国购发展专项基金，用以成立了卓越发展研究院，下设的中国经济研究中心和国际经济研究中心已经启动，分别由复旦大学教授李维森以及上海社会科学院研究员徐明棋兼任主任。

2.3 麦肯锡公司

麦肯锡公司是一家全球领先的管理咨询公司，1926 年创立于美国，致力于为企业和公共机构提供有关战略、组织、运营和技术方面的咨询。麦肯锡在全球范围内咨询业务的客户包括了最知名的企业及机构，占据《财富》杂志全球 500 强公司排行榜的 80%。在大中华区，麦肯锡的客户遍及 15 个行业，还包括国家级、地区级及省市级的政府及机构。麦肯锡进入大中华区 30 余年来，一直致力于帮助本土领先企业改善管理技能和提升全球竞争力，并为寻求在本地区扩大业务的跨国企业提供咨询，同时也积极参与中国公共政策咨询和公共事业建设。目前麦肯锡在大中华地区开设了北京、上海、深圳、香港及台北五家分公司，共有 50 多位合伙人，300 多位咨询师，还有 100 多位研究员及 200 多位专业人员。

3. 参会智库

3.1 中国社会科学院

中国社会科学院是中国哲学社会科学研究的最高学术机构和综合研究中心。

中国社会科学院是在中国科学院哲学社会科学学部的基础上，于 1977 年 5 月建立的。第一任院长胡乔木，第二任院长马洪，第三任院长胡绳，第四任院长李铁映，第五任院长陈奎元，现任院长王伟光。

中国社会科学院现有研究所 31 个，研究中心 45 个，含二三级学科近 300 个，其中重点学科 120 个。全院总人数 4200 多人，有科研业务人员 3200 多人。他们中拥有一批在国内外学术界享有盛名、学术造诣高深的专家学者和在学术理论研究方面崭露头角的中青年科研骨干。

广泛地开展对外学术交流是中国社会科学院长期坚持的方针。近些年来对外学术交流不断发展。在交流规模上，从 1978 年 10 多批数十人次发展到 1995 年 1398 批、4100 多人次。在地区分布上，中国社会科学院对外交流已遍及世界 80 多个国家和地区，同国外约 200 多个社科研究机构、学术团体、高等院校、基金会和政府有关部门建立了交流关系，与 20 多个国家和地区签订了交流协议。

中国社会科学院以学科齐全，人才集中，资料丰富的优势，在中国改革开放和现代化建设的进程中，进行创造性地理论探索和政策研究，肩负着从整体上提高中国人文社会科学水平的使命。

3.2 普华永道

普华永道1849年创立于英国伦敦，经过百年发展，已经成为一家全球性运营的专业服务机构，通过在157个国家和地区中超过20.8万名的专业人才，致力于向客户提供基于行业的咨询、审计和税务服务，协助解决复杂的业务难题，提高客户运营效率、风险控制水平及提升自身价值。全球财富500强企业中的400多家是普华永道服务的客户。

2015年在雇主品牌咨询机构优信（Universum）全球最具吸引力雇主排名中，普华永道被评为"对商学院毕业生最具吸引力雇主"第二位。普华永道中天会计师事务所在2003年开始的中国注册会计师协会下属会计师事务所百强评选中，连续13年名列第一。

3.3 野村综研（上海）咨询有限公司

野村综合研究所（NRI）作为全球领先的咨询集团，是日本最早和规模最大的智库。NRI成立于1965年，2001年在东京证券交易所主板上市，拥有10000多名专业人员，年营业额超过35亿美元，是目前世界上集智库功能、咨询功能和系统集成功能为一体的最大级咨询集团。

NRI在上海、北京、大连、香港和台北设有独立的业务公司，拥有3000多名专业人员。其中野村综研(上海)咨询有限公司(NRI上海)是NRI在中国内地的智库及咨询业务总部，业务领域涵盖面向中国各级政府的公共发展战略咨询、面向全球企业及中国企业的管理咨询。

在公共发展战略咨询领域中，NRI上海已为包括上海、北京、天津、重庆在内的中国近50个主要城市的政府提供咨询服务，内容涉及城市中长期发展战略、城市核心功能及功能区域发展战略、产业规划及实施路径等方面。

3.4 高风咨询

高风咨询公司是一家顶尖的战略和管理咨询公司，植根于中国，同时拥有全球视野、能力以及广泛的资源网络。高风咨询公司为客户解决他们最棘手的问题——在当前快速变化、复杂且不确定性的经营环境之中所出现的问题。高风咨询公司不仅为客户"构建"问题解决方案，同时亦是协助方案的执行与落地，与客户携手合作。高风咨询公司的价值观引领着其工作行为——公司致力于将客户的利益放在最根本和最重要的位置；高风咨询公司是客观的，致力于与客户建立长期的合作关系，而不是单独的项目；高风咨询公司将人才视为战略资产，而非纯粹的"人头"；高风咨询公司，从最基层到最高级的顾问，都以帮助客户解决难题和并肩合作提升价值为信条。

3.5 中国欧盟商会上海分会

中国欧盟商会由 51 家会员企业于 2000 年成立，其目的是代表不同行业和在华欧盟企业的共同声音。中国欧盟商会是一个在会员指导下开展工作的、独立的非营利性机构，其核心结构是代表欧盟在华企业的 45 个工作组和论坛。

欧盟商会目前已拥有约 1800 家会员公司，并在 9 个城市设有 7 个分会，分别是：北京、南京、上海、沈阳、中国华南（广州和深圳）、中国西南（成都与重庆）及天津，每个分会都由当地董事会管理，并且直接向执行委员会汇报。

欧盟商会作为在华欧洲企业的独立官方代言机构得到了欧盟委员会和中国政府的一致认可。它也是民政部认可的外国商会。

欧盟商会是正在成长中的欧洲商业组织的成员之一。该组织将来自全球 20 个非欧盟国家的欧洲商业团体和商会联系在一起。

中国欧盟商会上海分会成立于 2002 年 4 月，如今已拥有近 600 家会员企业，是中国欧盟商会最大的分会。其会员企业构成了 26 个活跃的工作组和论坛，广泛覆盖了各行业和跨行业议题。每年，上海分会和北京及其他分会一起，共同起草年度《欧盟企业在中国建议书》和《商业信心调查》，为会员企业创造更好的在华营商环境提供参考意见。

3.6 埃森哲

埃森哲注册成立于爱尔兰，是一家全球领先的专业服务公司。作为《财富》全球 500 强企业之一，全球员工超过 30.5 万人，为遍布 120 多个国家的客户提供战略咨询、数字和信息技术以及运营服务。在截至 2014 年 8 月 31 日的财政年度，全球净收入达 300 亿美元。

埃森哲在大中华区开展业务已超过 25 年，拥有一支约 1 万人的员工队伍，分布于北京、上海、大连、成都、广州、深圳、香港和台北。作为绩效提升专家，埃森哲致力将世界领先的商业技术实践于中国市场，帮助中国企业和政府制定战略、优化流程、集成系统、促进创新、提升运营效率、形成整体竞争优势，从而实现基业常青。

埃森哲于 1993 年在上海设立办公室，目前在上海已有数千名员工。埃森哲大中华区主席李纲先生分别于 2009 年和 2012 年被上海市政府授予"白玉兰纪念奖"及"白玉兰荣誉奖"，以表彰他对当地经济建设和社会发展所作出的杰出贡献。

3.7 强生公司

强生是全球最具综合性、业务分布范围最广的医疗保健企业。强生始终遵循企业信条的价值观，致力于践行"关爱全世界，关注每个人"的企业使命。

强生于 1985 年在华创立了第一家合资企业。多年来，强生不断发挥行业领军作用，以创新、高质量的产品和服务，为中国亿万家庭带来健康。如今，强生在中国的业务涉及消费品及个人护理、制药、医疗器材三大领域，在北京、上海、广州、苏州、西安等 90 多个城市，拥有员工总数近 10 000 人。2013 年，强生宣布在西安高新技术产业开发区投资兴建先进的大型生产基地，以更好地服务中国和泛亚区其他国家。

强生是首家在中国成功实现"端到端"研发模式的跨国企业；并通过实现从早期研发到临床应用，致力于加速中国创新产品的研发，促进中国创新型经济的发展。强生的三大业务领域在中国均设有研发机构，并在上海建立了强生亚太创新中心，将源自中国和亚太区域的创新成果推向国际市场。

2015 年，强生连续第 31 年入选美国《财富》杂志发布的全球最受赞赏企业排行榜，排名从 2014 年第 19 位上升至第 11 位。在制药行业排名第一，保持了 2014 年以来的领先势头。

3.8 哈佛上海中心

哈佛上海中心成立于 2010 年 3 月，标志着哈佛与中国及整个亚洲地区的长期合作迈上新的台阶。在哈佛商学院和哈佛中国基金的带领下，哈佛上海中心为哈佛大学各个学院的师生、校友提供资源。在庆祝哈佛上海成立的媒体见面会上，哈佛大学校长德鲁·福斯特（Drew Faust）女士表示，哈佛上海中心的成立，旨在为商学院与中国合作伙伴提供研讨会和管理培训的机会，促进哈佛大学和中国高校、各种机构、政府等的合作，为哈佛校友提供新的机遇，同时，随着在中国学习和实习的哈佛学生的人数不断增多，也为他们提供帮助和支持。

3.9 德勤管理咨询

德勤管理咨询是德勤全球旗下，与审计、税务、风险管理、财务咨询并重的五大服务之一。德勤品牌 1917 年进入中国市场，德勤管理咨询于 1998 年在中国注册独立的法律实体，并于 2011 年成立德勤中国全球交付中心。在一个多世纪的中国本地化服务过程中，德勤一直秉承"融贯东西，成就卓越"的理念，为中国的客户提供管理与技术、咨询与实践并重的高质量专业服务。德勤在全球 150 多个国家拥有超过 20 万名专业服务人员；在中国已经拥有超过 1500 名的双语专业咨询专家与顾问。以北京、上海、深圳、哈尔滨、成都及香港为六大人才集聚地，通过德勤中国的丰富服务网络，为整个大中华区的大中型国有企业、在华跨国公司、高科技高成长的民营企业提供覆盖企业全价值链的高质量行业专精化的战略与运营管理咨询、人力资本咨询和信息技术服务。

3.10 北京大学

北京大学创办于 1898 年，初名京师大学堂，是中国第一所国立综合性大学，也是当时中国最高教育行政机关。辛亥革命后，于 1912 年改为现名。

作为新文化运动的中心和"五四"运动的策源地，作为中国最早传播马克思主义和民主科学思想的发祥地，作为中国共产党最早的活动基地，北京大学为民族的振兴和解放、国家的建设和发展、社会的文明和进步作出了不可替代的贡献，在中国走向现代化的进程中起到了重要的先锋作用。爱国、进步、民主、科学的传统精神和勤奋、严谨、求实、创新的学风在这里生生不息、代代相传。

近年来，在"211 工程"和"985 工程"的支持下，北京大学进入了一个新的历史发展阶段，在学科建设、人才培养、师资队伍建设、教学科研等各方面都取得了显著成绩，为将北大建设成为世界一流大学奠定了坚实的基础。今天的北京大学已经成为国家培养高素质、创造性人才的摇篮、科学研究的前沿和知识创新的重要基地和国际交流的重要桥梁和窗口。

3.11 日本贸易振兴机构

日本贸易振兴机构 (JETRO) 是由日本政府出资设立，致力于促进贸易和投资的政府机构。目前，拥有东京和大阪总部，亚洲经济研究所和43个国内事务所，在海外54个国家和地区拥有73个事务所，包括在中国北京、上海、广州、大连、青岛、武汉、成都、广州、香港等地分别设有代表处。近年积极致力于协助外国企业开展对日直接投资，为有意向到日本发展的外国企业提供包括信息及个别咨询等在内的各种支援。

3.12 美中贸易全国委员会

美中贸易全国委员会（USCBC）是非政府、无党派的，非营利的机构，拥有大约220家在华经营的美国会员公司。自1973年成立以来的40多年中，该委员会为会员公司提供了大量的信息以及咨询、倡导等服务，并举办了多项活动。通过设在华盛顿的总部以及北京和上海的办事处，美中贸易全国委员会以其独特的定位优势在美、中两地为会员提供服务。

美中贸易全国委员会的使命是扩大美中商务联系，使全体会员从中受益，进而在更广阔的层面上使美国经济获益。我们提倡与中国进行建设性的商务联系——共同致力于消除贸易投资壁垒，并为双方营造一个规范、可预测的、透明的商务环境。

在美中贸易全国委员会的会员公司中，既有诸多知名的大型企业，也有相当比例的小型企业和服务业公司。美中贸易全国委员会董事会是我委员会的管理机构，由杰出的企业领导人组成。本届董事会主席由杜邦公司董事长兼席执行官柯爱伦女士（Ellen J. Kullman）担任。自2004年以来，傅强恩先生（John Frisbie）任美中贸易全国委员会会长。

3.13 上海美国商会

上海美国商会成立于1915年，现今已有3800多个会员，被称为在华"美国商业之声"，是亚太地区规模最大且发展最快的美国商会。

上海美国商会作为一个非营利、无党派的商业联合组织，为持续营造积极健康的中美商务环境发挥着桥梁纽带作用。上海美国商会坚持以贸易自由、市场开放和信息流通为原则，致力于提供优质高效的商业信息和资源以助推会员企业的发展。

3.14 泰科电子

泰科电子（**TE Connectivity**）是全球技术领军企业，年销售额达 120 亿美元。在连接日益紧密的当今世界，TE 的连接和传感解决方案发挥着核心作用。TE 与工程师协作，帮助他们将概念转变为现实——通过经受严苛环境验证的智能化、高效、高性能 TE 产品和解决方案，实现各种可能。TE 在全球拥有 72000 名员工，其中 7000 名为设计工程师，合作的客户遍及全球 150 多个国家和众多领域。

3.15 IBM

IBM 是一家全球整合的信息技术与咨询服务公司，成立于 1911 年，总部设在纽约州阿尔蒙克。业务运营覆盖了全球 170 多个国家和地区，拥有全球最优秀的人才，为企业、政府和非营利机构解决问题、提供尖端的技术和服务。

无论所从事的事业还是做事的方式，**IBM** 都是一家以创新为核心且不断变革的公司。IBM 业务包括开发和销售软件、系统硬件产品，以及提供广泛的信息基础设施架构、云计算和商业管理咨询服务。

IBM 于 1985 年在北京设立代表处。7 年后于 1992 年成立 **IBM** 中国公司，是第一家在中国的全外资公司。**IBM** 在中国开展包括研发、销售、服务在内的全线业务，目前在中国拥有近 80 家分公司，设有研发中心、全球客户中心和全球服务执行中心等机构。

30 多年来，**IBM** 全力配合中国的改革开放和发展日程，凭借先进的创新科技、出色的管理和独树一帜的产品和服务，引领并推动中国信息产业的发展，支持包括金融、电信、能源、制造、零售等行业客户的成长与转型。

Introduction to Summit Organizers
and Think Tanks

1. Host

1.1 The Development Research Centre of Shanghai Municipal People's Government

The Development Research Centre of Shanghai Municipal People's Government (SDRC) was formerly known as Shanghai Center for Economic Research (SCER) which was founded on Dec. 26th, 1980, and was renamed by SDRC on Dec. 22nd, 1995. SDRC is a decision-making research institution led by Shanghai Municipal People's Government, providing comprehensive consulting services with the functions of organizing, coordinating and managing the government research projects.

Main functions:

(1) Study on the overall and strategic issues concerning Shanghai economy, social development, reform and opening-up.

(2) Trace the dynamic trends, analyze the inconsistency, study the countermeasures and forecast the prospects, submit decision-making proposals and consulting advices to the CPC Shanghai Committee and the Shanghai Municipal People Government in due course.

(3) Organize the assessment of the decision-making and consulting research results as well as the appraisal of the distinguished research achievements once every two years.

(4) Organize and coordinate the decision-making and consulting research work within the government system.

(5) Conduct the information maintenance work of the Shanghai Decision-making and Consulting Proposals System.

(6) Administrate the related organizations and institutions entrusted by the Shanghai Municipal People's Government.

(7) Compile and publish Shanghai Economy Almanac and Journal of Scientific Development.

(8) Undertake other missions assigned by the leaders of the Shanghai Municipality.

2. Organizers

2.1 Shanghai International Think Tank Exchange Center

Shanghai International Think Tank Exchange Center is one of the open and public decision-making and consulting research platforms, set up by the Development Research Center of Shanghai Municipal People's Government(SDRC). In 2010, SDRC, as required by the then Mayor Han Zheng proactively made contact with thirteen world-renowned think tanks in Shanghai like Accenture, Capgemini, Deloitte and IBM, aiming to further Shanghai's decision making and consulting research by drawing on the wisdom of experts and scholars form home and abroad to enable the CPC Shanghai Committee and Shanghai municipal government to do decision-making in a more democratic and scientific way and constantly expand the influence of SDRC in the world. In January, 2011, the center was established and the first "Smart Shanghai Forum" with the theme "Innovation, Transformation and Development" was also held. Mr. Han Zheng, the then Shanghai Mayor, sent his message of congratulation and Mr. Jiang Ping, the then secretary-general of Shanghai government, attended the forum and delivered an address.

The main responsibilities for the Shanghai International Think Tank Exchanges Center are as follows:

(1) To conduct decision-making research for the government.

(2) To provide application research, business planning, managerial consulting services for enterprises.

(3) To organize international bilateral and multilateral corporation seminar.

(4) To study international cooperation and exchanges subjects.

(5) To provide development, training and information services for

professionals.

For the past five years, the Shanghai International Think Tank Exchanges Center has conducted plenty of international cooperation researches with focus on the economic and social development of Shanghai by taking advantage in talents, resources and information, jointly with the public decision-making consulting research platforms of experts, workshops, social surveys, research projects and college forums. Until now, the Shanghai International Think Tank Exchanges Center has held bilateral forums for 16 times, "Shanghai Intelligent Forum" for 4 times and a "Shanghai International Think Tank Summit", which effectively improves the function and role of the Development Research Center of Shanghai Municipal People's Government in integrating the think tank resources at the national level, and provides lots of advices and suggestions to the CPC Shanghai Committee and the Shanghai Municipal People's Government from leading think tanks at home and abroad.

2.2 Shanghai Development Research Foundation

Shanghai Development Research Foundation (SDRF) was established in 1993. As a public-foundation and a non-profit legal person established in accordance with the relevant governmental regulations, SDRF is devoted to the public welfare undertakings by utilizing donations from individuals, legal persons and other organizations.

For the last several years, SDRF has been continuously endeavoring to fulfill its missions. We hold "Shanghai Development Salon" monthly, inviting distinguished experts and scholars home and abroad to make speeches on hot topics and sensitive questions, and make interactive discussion with the attendees. The high-level symposiums are held twice or thrice annually, gathering numbers of domestic and overseas experts, and the noble guests from political, business and academic circles together to discuss the important issues in the development of global economy and Chinese economy. In addition, SDRF holds a series of mini-seminars themed "The Future of Chinese Economy" for a thorough discussion on the depth-rooted problems in the development of Chinese economy.

Shanghai Research Development Fund (SDRF) is led by our chairman, Mr.

Hu Yanzhao, the former Deputy Mayor of Shanghai and also the former Deputy Director of the Standing Committee. Mr. Wang Ronghua the former Deputy Chairman of Shanghai CPPCC, and Mr. Wang Zhan the Deputy Chairman of Shanghai Academy of Social Sciences, are the Deputy Chairmen of SDRF. Mr. Qiao Yide has also been appointed as the Deputy Chairman and Secretary General of SDRF. The Development Research Center of the Shanghai Municipal People's Government is the supervisory authority of SDRF.

By the end of 2013, Shanghai Development Research Foundation accepts donations, set up Zhuoyue · Guogou, a special fund, to build Excellence Academy of Development Research(EADR). About EADR, China Economic Research Center and the International Economic Research Center has been launched. Professor Li Weisen of Fudan University and Research Xu Mingqi of Shanghai Academy of Social Sciences are the two center director.

2.3 McKinsey & Company

McKinsey & Company is the leading global management consulting firm and by far the largest global management consulting firm in Greater China. Globally, we are the trusted advisor and counselor to many of the most influential businesses and institutions in the world. We serve more than 80 percent of Fortune magazine's list of the Most Admired Companies. In Greater China, we advise clients in over 15 different industry sectors, and work with dozens of government agencies and institutions at the national, regional and municipal levels. Our primary mission is to help our clients achieve substantial and enduring impact by tackling their biggest issues concerning strategy, operations, organization, technology and finance. Today we have more than 350 consultants and over 50 Partners located across four locations in Greater China: Beijing, Shanghai, Hong Kong, and Taipei. They are supported by more than 100 research professionals, and over 200 professional support staff.

3. Think Tanks

3.1 Chinese Academy of Social Sciences

The Chinese Academy of Social Sciences (CASS) is the premier academic organization and comprehensive research center of the People's Republic of China in the fields of philosophy and social sciences.

CASS was established in May 1977, replacing the Department of Philosophy and Social Sciences of the Chinese Academy of Sciences. Professor Hu Qiaomu was the first president accredited to CASS, and he was followed by Professor Ma Hong, Professor Hu Sheng, Professor Li Tieying and Professor Chen Kuiyuan. Professor Wang Weiguang is the current president.

CASS is now made up of 31 research institutes and 45 research centers, which carry out research activities covering nearly 300 sub-disciplines. At present, CASS has more than 4 200 staff members in total, of which more than 3 200 are professional researchers.

Conducting broad international academic exchange remains one of CASS's guidelines, and this has gained pace in recent years. The quantity of scholars participating in academic exchanges has gone from dozens of people divided into 10 batches in 1979, to over 4 100 people divided into 1 398 batches in 1995. In the meanwhile, CASS has established a constructive relationship with over 200 research organizations, academic communities, institutions of higher learning, foundations and related government departments, covering more than 80 countries and regions.

3.2 PwC

PwC firms help organizations and individuals create the value they're looking for. PwC is a network of firms in 157 countries with more than 208 000 people who are committed to delivering quality in assurance, tax and advisory services.

Providing organizations with the advice they need, wherever they may be located, our highly qualified, experienced professionals listen to different points of view to help organizations solve their business issues and identify and maximize the opportunities they seek. PwC's industry specialization allows us to help co-create solutions with our clients for their sector of interest.

In 2015, PwC firms provided industry-focused Assurance, Consulting & Deals and Tax services for 418 of the companies in the Fortune Global 500 and 443 of the companies in the FT Global 500. PwC's many smaller listed, private and government clients benefit from the same depth of industry and technical expertise.

The Chinese Institute of Certified Public Accountants published its Top 100 Accounting Firms in China in 2015. PwC China ranked first in the list. This is the 13th consecutive year that PwC won this award.

3.3 Nomura Research Institute, Ltd., Shanghai

As a world leading consulting group,Nomura Research Institute, Ltd. (NRI) is Japan's oldest and largest think tank. NRI was established in 1965 and listed on the Tokyo Stock Exchange in 2001. With over 10 000 professional employees and an annual business turnover exceeding 3.5 billion USD, it is currently the largest consulting group in the world that integrates a think tank, consulting, and system services.

NRI has independent companies established in Shanghai, Beijing, Dalian, Hong Kong, and Taipei with over 3 000 professional employees. The Nomura Research Institute Shanghai, Ltd. (NRI Shanghai) is mainland China's think tank and consulting headquarters, covering public development strategy consulting services for all levels of Chinese governments and offering management consulting for global and Chinese enterprises.

In the field of public development strategy consulting, NRI Shanghai has already provided consulting services to the city governments of over 50 main cities in China, including Shanghai, Beijing, Tianjin, and Chongqing, which involves aspects such as municipal mid and long-term development strategies, core municipal function and function area development strategy, and industrial planning and execution.

3.4 Gao Feng Advisory Company

Gao Feng Advisory Company is a pre-eminent strategy and management consulting firm with roots in China coupled with global vision, capabilities, and a broad resources network. Gao Feng help their clients address and solve their toughest business and management issues—issues that arise in the current fast-changing, complicated and ambiguous operating environment. Gao Feng commit to putting their clients' interest first and foremost. Gao Feng are objective and view their client engagements as long-term relationships rather than one-off projects. They not only help their clients "formulate" the solutions but also assist in implementation, often hand-in-hand. They believe in teaming and working together to add value and contribute to problem solving for their clients, from the most junior to the most senior.

3.5 European Chamber, Shanghai Chapter

The European Union Chamber of Commerce in China (European Chamber) was founded in 2000 by 51 member companies that shared a goal of establishing a common voice for the various business sectors of the European Union and European businesses operating in China. It is a member-driven, non-profit, fee-based organization with a core structure of 45 working groups and for are presenting European business in China.

The European Chamber has nearly 1 800 members in seven chapters operating in nine cities: Beijing, Nanjing, Shanghai, Shenyang, South China (Guangzhou and Shenzhen), Southwest China (Chengdu and Chongqing)and Tianjin. Each chapter is managed at the local level by local boards reporting directly to the Executive Committee.

The European Chamber is recognized by the European Commission and the Chinese authorities as the official voice of European business in China. It is recognized as a foreign chamber of commerce by the Ministry of Civil Affairs.

The European Chamber is part of the growing network of European Business Organizations (EBO). This network connects European business associations and chambers of commerce from 20 non-EU countries around the world.

The Shanghai Chapter was established in April 2002 and currently has over 600 member companies, the largest of all Chamber chapters. It has grown substantially in terms of membership, the number of working groups and fora, as well as its events and lobby activities. The Shanghai Chapter currently has 26 active working groups, desks and fora covering a diverse range of industries and services. Shanghai-based working groups cooperate closely with working groups in Beijing and other chapters to provide in put into the annual European Business in China Position Paper, Business Confidence Survey and other advocacy initiatives in order to give recommendations to improve business environment in China.

3.6 Accenture

Accenture is a global management consulting, technology services and outsourcing company, with more than 305 000 people serving clients in more than 120 countries. Combining unparalleled experience, comprehensive capabilities across all industries and business functions, and extensive research on the world's most successful companies, Accenture collaborates with clients to help them become high-performance businesses and governments. The company generated net revenues of US$30.0 billion for the fiscal year ended Aug. 31, 2014.

Accenture has been operating in Greater China for more than 25 years. Today, the Greater China practice has approximately 10 000 people servicing clients across the region and has offices in Beijing, Shanghai, Dalian, Chengdu, Guangzhou, Shenzhen, Hong Kong and Taipei.

Accenture Shanghai Office was established in 1993. Now Accenture have thousands of employees in Shanghai. Gong Li, Chairman of Accenture Greater China, was honored with Magnolia Silver Award in 2009 and Magnolia Gold Award in 2012 by Shanghai Municipal Government to recognize his outstanding contributions to the local economic and social development.

3.7 Johnson & Johnson

Johnson & Johnson is the world's most comprehensive and broadly-based healthcare company. Guided by the values of its Credo, Johnson & Johnson is dedicated to the aspiration of "caring for the world, one person at a time."

Since the founding of its first joint venture in China in 1985, Johnson & Johnson has been an industry leader in the healthcare market. Through the company's advanced healthcare solutions, Johnson & Johnson helps to bring a positive impact to the health and life quality of Chinese families. Today, Johnson & Johnson's businesses span three sectors in China: consumer and personal care; pharmaceuticals and medical devices. The company currently employs approximately 10 000 people across more than 90 locations, including Beijing,

Shanghai, Guangzhou, Suzhou and Xi'an. In 2013, the company announced plans to build a large state-of-the-art manufacturing facility in Xi'an to serve China and the broader Asia-Pacific region.

Johnson & Johnson is the first multinational company in China to achieve the "end-to-end" R&D model, which nurtures the development of early-discoveries into clinical applications. The achievement exemplifies Johnson & Johnson's commitment to promoting innovation as a driving force of China's economic growth. Today, Johnson & Johnson has established three R&D organizations in China, and an Asia Pacific Innovation Center (APIC) recently opened in Shanghai to connect innovations from China and the region to the global market.

In 2015, J&J joined the U.S. Fortune magazine list of the World's Most Admired Companies for the 31st consecutive year. Most notable was its ascension to number 11 on the list, from 19 last year. Within the pharmaceutical industry, J & J ranked first, continuing its leadership from 2014.

3.8 Harvard Center Shanghai

The Harvard Center Shanghai, opened in March 2010, represents an important step in Harvard's long engagement with China and Asia. Spearheaded by the Harvard Business School and the Harvard China Fund, the Center is built as a resource for Harvard faculty, students, and alumni across all of Harvard's Schools. In her speech at the reception marking the opening of the Harvard Center Shanghai, President Drew Faust said the Center would play a vital role "as a hub for seminars and executive training with the Business School and Chinese partners; increasing collaboration between Harvard faculty and Chinese universities, organizations, and government; new opportunities for alumni; and expanded support for Harvard students, whose study and internship programs in China seem to be growing exponentially."

3.9 Deloitte Consulting

Deloitte Consulting is one of the five Deloitte Global's functions together with Audit, Tax, Enterprise Risk Services and Financial Advisory Services. Deloitte entered the China market in 1917 and started its consulting business as a separate legal entity since 1998 in China. Deloitte China Global Delivery Center was established in 2011. Within more than one-century's service history in the local market, Deloitte adhere to the idea of 'Integrating cultural diversity and contributing outstanding value to markets and clients', providing high-quality professional services with a focus on both management and technology, consulting and practice to Chinese clients. Deloitte has more than 200 000 professionals in more than 150 countries around the world. In China, Deloitte Consulting has over 1 500 professional experts and consultants with bilingual service capabilities. Deloitte's talents from the Beijing, Shanghai, Shenzhen, Harbin, Chengdu and Hong Kong offices provide industry-oriented and high-quality strategy, human capital and IT consulting services covering the whole value chain of corporates to clients all over the Greater China region through Deloitte China's extensive service network. Their clients include SOEs, MNCs and rapidly growing private enterprises.

3.10 Peking University

Peking University is a comprehensive and national key university. The campus, known as "Yan Yuan" (the garden of Yan), is situated at Haidian District in the western suburb of Beijing.

The university has effectively combined research on important scientific subjects with the training of personnel with a high level of specialized knowledge and professional skill as demanded by the country's socialist modernization. It strives not only for improvements in teaching and research work, but also for the promotion of interaction and mutual promotion among various disciplines.

Thus Peking University has become a center for teaching and research and a university of a new type, embracing diverse branches of learning such as basic and applied sciences, social sciences and the humanities, and sciences of medicine, management, and education. Its aim is to rank among the world's best universities in the future.

3.11 Japan External Trade Organization

The Japan External Trade Organization (JETRO) is a government-related organization that works to promote mutual trade and investment between Japan and the rest of the world. Originally established in 1958 to promote Japanese exports abroad, JETRO's core focus in the 21st century has shifted toward promoting foreign direct investment into Japan and helping small to medium size Japanese firms maximize their global export potential.

3.12 The US-China Business Council

The US-China Business Council, Inc. (USCBC) is a private, nonpartisan, nonprofit organization of roughly 220 American companies that do business with China. Founded in 1973, USCBC has provided unmatched information, advisory, advocacy, and program services to its membership for four decades. Through its offices in Washington, DC; Beijing; and Shanghai, USCBC is uniquely positioned to serve its members' interests in the United States and China.

USCBC's mission is to expand the US-China commercial relationship to the benefit of its membership and, more broadly, the US economy. It favors constructive engagement with China to eliminate trade and investment barriers and develop a rules-based commercial environment that is predictable and transparent to all parties.

Among USCBC's members are many large and well-known US corporations, but smaller companies and service firms make up a substantial portion of the overall membership. USCBC is governed by a board of directors composed of distinguished corporate leaders; the current chair is Ellen J. Kullman, chairman and chief executive officer of E.I. du Pont de Nemours & Company. John Frisbie has been USCBC's president since 2004.

3.13 The American Chamber of Commerce in Shanghai

The American Chamber of Commerce in Shanghai, known as the "Voice of American Business" in China, is one of the largest American Chambers in the Asia Pacific region. As a non-profit, non-partisan business organization, AmCham Shanghai is committed to the principles of free trade, open markets, private enterprise and the unrestricted flow of information. Founded in 1915, AmCham Shanghai was the third American Chamber established outside the

United States.

For 100 years, AmCham Shanghai has been at the forefront of American business success in China. Throughout 2015, AmCham's centennial year, AmCham has produced a series of events and publications that celebrated its storied history and the opportunities of the coming century. By reflecting on the past, present, and future of the U.S.—China commercial relationship, the centennial program communicated how American business and AmCham Shanghai have contributed to China's development in the past and will do so in the future. The program showcased examples of our impact on China's growth and raised the profile of American business in Shanghai.

3.14 TE Connectivity

TE Connectivity (NYSE: TEL) is a $12 billion global technology leader. Its connectivity and sensor solutions are essential in today's increasingly connected world. TE collaborate with engineers to transform their concepts into creations—redefining what's possible using intelligent, efficient and high-performing TE products and solutions proven in harsh environments. TE's 72 000 people, including over 7 000 engineers, partner with customers in close to 150 countries across a wide range of industries.

3.15 IBM

IBM is a globally integrated technology and consulting company headquartered in Armonk, New York. With operations in more than 170 countries, IBM attracts and retains some of the world's most talented people to help solve problems and provide an edge for businesses, governments and non-profits.

IBM is an innovation company. Both in what we do and in how we do it, we pursue continuous transformation. We develop and sell software, systems hardware, a broad range of infrastructure, cloud, and consulting services.

IBM set up its representative office in Beijing in 1985. Seven years later in 1992, IBM China, the first wholly owned foreign enterprise in China, was established. With operations in around 80 cities, IBM China is engaged in full portfolio of business including sales & distributions, research & development, and service delivery.

Over the past three decades, IBM has been a strong supporter of China's reform and opening up agenda. By leveraging its advanced technologies, outstanding management and unique products and services, IBM has been leading China's IT industry and supporting the growth and transformation of Chinese enterprises from various industries such as finance, telecommunication, energy, manufacturing, retail and many others.

POSTSCRIPT

后 记

为充分发挥上海市委、市政府首席智库的功能，组织好上海国际智库交流中心成员单位参与"面向未来 30 年的上海"发展战略研究，凝聚国内外专家学者的思想和智慧，上海市人民政府发展研究中心借助国际智库集聚上海智力资源的优势，于 2015 年 12 月 18 日，牵头召开第二届上海国际智库峰会。峰会以"2050 年的上海：发展愿景与挑战"为主题，通过积极搭建开放式、互动式的国际交流平台，深入探讨了城市未来发展的战略目标和城市提升过程中面临的瓶颈挑战，为上海未来 30 年经济社会发展提供了许多卓越的见解。为不使这些宝贵的观点和研究成果湮没，我们将其原汁原味地汇编成书，以飨读者。同时，书中还收录了上海市人民政府发展研究中心国合办翻译整理的会议参阅材料《其他全球城市未来发展愿景与挑战》。

本书的出版得到了各位与会国际智库和专家学者以及上海世纪出版集团格致出版社的大力支持，上海市人民政府发展研究中心国合办承担了大量译校和主要编辑工作，信息处和科研处的同仁也给予了积极协助，在此一并表示感谢。

To give full play to the role as the leading think tank of Shanghai Municipal People's Government and CPC Shanghai Committee, organize members units of Shanghai International Think Tanks Exchange Center for research project "Shanghai in the Next 30 Years" to pool the wisdom of domestic and foreign experts and scholars, the Development Research Center of Shanghai Municipal People's Government (SDRC) partners with Shanghai International Think Tanks Exchange Center to garner the intellectual strength and hold the 2nd Shanghai International Think Tank Summit on December 18, 2015. With the theme of "Shanghai 2050: Vision and Challenge", attendees have an in-depth exchange on strategic objectives and the bottlenecks in cities and urban development through building an open, interactive platform and offer many remarkable views on the economic and social development of Shanghai in the next 30 years. In order to make the most out of these valuable ideas and research achievements, we are compiling them into a book for your reading. Conference reference materials that translated and compiled by International Exchange and Cooperate Office of the SDRC are also included in the book.

The publication of the book is not possible without the strong support of International Think Tank and experts and scholars as well as Shanghai Century Publishing Group Truth & Wisdom Press. International Cooperation & Exchange Office of the Development Research Center of Shanghai Municipal People's Government undertakes the majority of translation and editorial work, with support from colleagues of Information Division and Scientific Research Management Division of the SDRC. We are truly grateful to all of them for their generous help.

图书在版编目(CIP)数据

2050年的上海:发展愿景与挑战:2015上海国际智库咨询研究报告/肖林主编.—上海:格致出版社:上海人民出版社,2016.11
(上海市人民政府发展研究中心系列报告)
ISBN 978-7-5432-2675-3

Ⅰ.①2… Ⅱ.①肖… Ⅲ.①区域经济发展-研究报告-上海 Ⅳ.①F127.51

中国版本图书馆CIP数据核字(2016)第251837号

责任编辑　忻雁翔
装帧设计　人马艺术设计·储平

2050年的上海:发展愿景与挑战──2015上海国际智库咨询研究报告
肖　林 主编

出　版	世纪出版股份有限公司　格致出版社 世纪出版集团　上海人民出版社 (200001　上海福建中路193号　www.ewen.co)	印　刷	上海中华商务联合印刷有限公司
		开　本	787×1092　1/16
		印　张	17.75
	编辑部热线　021-63914988 市场部热线　021-63914081 www.hibooks.cn	插　页	8
		字　数	298,000
		版　次	2016年11月第1版
发　行	上海世纪出版股份有限公司发行中心	印　次	2016年11月第1次印刷

ISBN 978-7-5432-2675-3/F·966　　　　　　　　　　　　　　　　　　定价:98.00元